AF323361

Before Santa Fe

ARCHAEOLOGY OF THE CITY DIFFERENT

Before Santa Fe

ARCHAEOLOGY OF THE CITY DIFFERENT

Jason S. Shapiro

MUSEUM OF NEW MEXICO PRESS

SANTA FE

Project director: Mary Wachs
Manuscript editing: Kay Hagan
Design: Bette Brodsky
Composition: Set in Adobe Garamond with Dearest display
Manufactured in U.S.A.
10 9 8 7 6 5 4 3 2 1

Library of Congress Cataloging-in-Publication Data
 Shapiro, Jason S.
Before Santa Fe : archaeology of the city different / by Jason S. Shapiro.
    p. cm.
Includes bibliographical references and index.
    ISBN 978-0-89013-521-1 (clothbound : alk. paper)
    1. Indians of North America–New Mexico–Santa Fe Region–Antiquities. 2. Paleo-Indians–New Mexico–Santa Fe Region. 3. Excavations (Archaeology)–New Mexico–Santa Fe Region. 4. Archaeologists–New Mexico–Santa Fe Region–History–20th century. 5. Santa Fe Region (N.M.)–Antiquities. I. Title.
E78.N65S49 2008
978.9'56–DC22
2008013199

MUSEUM OF NEW MEXICO PRESS
Post Office Box 2087
Santa Fe, New Mexico 87504
www.mnmpress.org

This book is dedicated to my mother, Mildred Shapiro,
who always gave me both love and confidence.

Table of Contents . . .

UNEXCAVATED
IID
PLACITA
UNEXCAVATED
UNEXCAVATED
UNEXC.
PLAZA
KIVA C
KIVA D
KIVA E
KIVA F
KIVA A
KIVA B
SANTA FE RIVER

Foreword

For nearly four hundred years the Palace of the Governors has marked the north side of the Santa Fe Plaza as witness to changes in governance, demographics, and styles.[1] A National Historic Landmark, the Palace is an emblem of the history of those four centuries. But even that venerable history is not the whole story of Santa Fe's past. Just a short distance in all directions from the Palace, and underlying the streets and buildings that comprise downtown Santa Fe as well as along the Santa Fe River basin, there is an even older history.[2] For more than 12,000 years Santa Fe has seen a succession of different cultures and different ways of making a living. It might have earned its title "the City Different" not by civic invention but by the ways in which people actually lived through this longer span of time. The archaeology of Santa Fe follows a similar trajectory as is found elsewhere in the Southwest from Big Game hunters to horticulturalists to pit house dwellers and then Pueblo settlements. At key points in time, however, the Santa Fe sequence is slightly different either in the length of time that a tradition persisted or in its local expression.

In 1912, city leaders and local archaeologists devised a plan to cultivate tourism by creating a unique architectural aesthetic known as "Santa Fe Style," in truth a selective appropriation of regional styles and references to the region's cultural antecedents. Seventy-five years later an ordinance was adopted by the city council that required developments that exceed 2,500 sq. ft. in specified historic districts downtown or more than 2 acres in other defined archaeological districts in the city be evaluated by professional archaeologists and thoroughly recorded before the area could be developed.[3] The county joined in this important preservation initiative by enacting a parallel ordinance in 1988. While this has been criticized by some people as a costly price imposed on new development, there is no doubt that the archaeological ordinance is responsible for saving irreplaceable archaeological resources and giving us the fuller view of Santa Fe history and archaeology presented here by Jay Shapiro.

Spanish settlers arrived in New Mexico in the late sixteenth century and established their first capital near the Tewa pueblo of Ohkay Owinge near the confluence of the Rio Grande and Rio Chama. Santa Fe was not settled by the Spanish until more than a decade later, although when they did arrive in Santa Fe there would clearly have been evidence of earlier archaeological settlements. When Juan Martinez de Montoya visited the site that would become Santa Fe in 1608, he must have seen the remains of the Pueblo villages on the hills just north of the town site, on the bluffs south of the Santa Fe River in the area that we now call the Barrio de Analco, and on the site where later settlers would build the Guadalupe Church. But neither he nor Pedro de Peralta, arriving here in late 1609 or 1610, described what they saw on the land.

Tewa Pueblo people who live north of Santa Fe in the area of Pojoaque and Tesuque have ancestral ties to Santa Fe still strongly felt, as were articulated in 2006 and 2007 when archaeologists exposed numerous burials and a kiva on the proposed site of the convention center near ancestral Ogapoge Pueblo on Federal Place. The city has been praised both for its adherence to the spirit of the archaeological ordinance for this project and its willingness to negotiate with Tesuque Pueblo over the *in-situ* preservation of a portion of the site to avoid disturbing the human remains and the ceremonial structure.

The siting of the Palace of the Governors is a curious one. Perhaps this site was selected because it was not cluttered by the architectural remains of the earlier Pueblo sites that were built by Tewa and Keresan people in the 14th and 15th centuries. While we may not ever really know the answer to this question of why the Spanish built the Palace where they did, it is a valuable lesson in the application of archaeology even when we have historic documentation.

Archaeology acts as a beneficial companion to history. It speaks through direct physical evidence about what happened in the past. It provides an important source of information about how people lived on the land and adjusted to changing climatic and social conditions. In this volume, Jay Shapiro has used the 12,000-year record of people living in the 1200 square miles that constitute the Santa Fe district of the Northern Rio Grande Archaeological Province. He examines the interplay of cultural adaptability and environmental possibilities and the cycles of want and plenty that underlay people's decisions about how to live on the land and interact with their neighbors. Archaeology is a record of a past beyond the history of an individual and often beyond even the oral traditions of indigenous peoples. There are lessons in this body of evidence about how people responded to drought and how they expanded in times of plentiful rainfall. Shapiro's study reminds us to look to the past as one source of information as we plan our future in the environmentally marginal paradise that has been Santa Fe for 12,000 years.

— Frances Levine, Director,
Palace of the Governors/New Mexico History Museum

Acknowledgments

This book represents a synthesis of the work of many dedicated people. I do not consider myself an expert in many facets of local archaeology, but I have had the incredible good fortune to know and work with people who really are experts. Each of them has given freely of their knowledge, and for that I am grateful. Special thanks are accorded to Stephen Post, Deputy Director, Office of Archaeological Studies, and Cherie Scheick, Southwest Archaeological Consultants, both of whom were always willing to share their extensive knowledge of local archaeology and who helped me immeasurably by pointing me in so many right directions where, if left to my own devices, I may have stumbled around indefinitely.

Other individuals who contributed to this book include:

Linda Cordell, friend and colleague whose sound advice, probing queries, and valuable recommendations made this a much better book than it otherwise would have been.

Doug Schwartz for our many lunchtime conversations in which we shared information and challenged each other in our interpretations of what really went on in Santa Fe so very long ago.

Librarian Mara Yarborough and assistant Minnie Murray at the Laboratory of Anthropology, Museum of New Mexico, who, if a book or article was not already present in the library, knew exactly where and how to find it.

David Hurst Thomas, Kristen Mable, and Barry Landua at the American Museum of Natural History, who helped immeasurably with access to and copies of the photographs and notes in the Nels Nelson Collection.

In addition to the foregoing individuals, Nancy Akins, Eric Blinman, Jeff Boyer, Mike Bremer, Leslie Cohen, Kurt Kemptner, Stephen Lakatos, Steven Lentz, Frances Levine, Janet McVickar, David McNeece, James Moore, Ann Palkovich, Melissa Powell, Christella Sisqueiros, James Snead, Christopher Turnbow, Carla Van West, Richard Wilshusen, Ron Winters, and Reggie Wiseman all gave freely of their research, knowledge, and perspectives.

My editors, Mary Wachs and Kay Hagan, did their best to ensure that the jargon was limited and the writing was clear. In other words, they took my manuscript and turned it into this wonderful book.

And of course there are my kids, Adam and Rachel Shapiro and Connor Jorgensen, who never let me forget the "big picture" about what is truly important in life and never let me get so deeply immersed in this project that I forgot to come up for air.

Finally, Celia, my wife, partner, and best friend who encouraged and supported the writing of this book.

For any and all mistakes, miscues, and misinterpretations in this book, I alone am responsible.

Introduction

The moment I saw the brilliant proud morning shine high up over deserts of Santa Fe, something stood still in my soul.   D. H. LAWRENCE

In 2010, the City of Santa Fe, New Mexico, will celebrate its 400th anniversary as a Euro-American city, but its record of occupation is actually more than thirty times longer. A simple definition for "archaeology" is *the study of ancient human behavior and past cultures based on their material remains.* The richness of the archaeological record in and around Santa Fe is a unique part of the city's cultural heritage that also should be celebrated.

In a sense, archaeologists are storytellers. We take the bits and pieces of what people have left behind and weave them into narratives that try to explain the "once upon a times" of those who lived before us. The ultimate goal of this book is to tell a real story — the story of those people who lived, worked, prospered, and died in the area of Santa Fe over the course of 12,000 years. I have tried to provide some understanding for Santa Fe's contemporary residents and visitors about the people who came before, and how their struggles and achievements relate to our lives today.

The impetus for this book came from two sources. For several years I have taught a course at Santa Fe Community College entitled "Prehistoric Peoples of the Southwest." This general archaeology course covers approximately 15,000 years of Southwest culture history, beginning with the First Americans and the Paleoindian big game hunters and ending with the Spanish *Entrada* of the 16th century. The class tends to attract a broad spectrum of students from ages eighteen to eighty, few of whom aspire to careers in archaeology. My challenge has been to produce an informative and accessible introduction to the subject matter without getting bogged down in the technical and theoretical minutiae on which graduate students and professional archaeologists thrive. In striving for accessibility, I found that despite the numerous fine volumes covering the archaeology of the Southwest in general, there was no book-length treatment focusing on the archaeology of Santa Fe geared specifically for the interested layperson. The second source of motivation for this project developed from my tenure on the City of Santa Fe's Archaeological Review Committee, created when Santa Fe's Archaeological Ordinance[1] passed in 1988. Consisting of five individuals — three archaeologists, one historian, and one member from the development/real estate community — the committee reviews proposed building projects within the City of Santa Fe in order to determine their impact upon cultural resources. This committee reviews literally dozens of reports every year describing a wide variety of prehistoric and historic cultural resources — from 5,000-year-old Archaic Period campsites to the remains of Santa Fe's once vigorous railroad complex dating to the first half of the 20th century. With the exception of a few "high-profile" sites, such as the Palace of the Governor's excavations in 2003–2004 and the Pueblo de Santa Fe excavations in 2005–2006, or the 1995 symposium "Archaeology in Your Backyard," virtually none of the information from these reports is presented to the general public. The result is that few people who visit or live in this city are aware of the pervasiveness, extent, and time depth of cultural remains in and around Santa Fe. One of the intentions of this book is to synthesize and present some of what is called "gray literature" produced by the community of contract archaeologists,[2] who conduct these culture impact studies.

In writing this book, I was guided by two overriding questions: "What's going on here?" and "So what?" The study of archaeology is ultimately the study of human behavior, and the "What's going on here?" question refers to the "who, what, when, where, and how" of what occurred. What is the evidence of cultural behavior that we are looking at? What happened in the past and why did it happen at a particular place and time? Given the limitations of the archaeological record, it may not always be possible to answer those questions completely, but it is often surprising just how much information archaeology can provide.[3] The second question — "So what?" — is deceptively simple. I want to show why the places and events that I include in this book are so important. The second question conveys what archaeology can tell us about the earliest people who lived here, and presents their lives as vivid and germane parts of the big picture of Santa Fe's cultural heritage.

In 1937 Edgar L. Hewett summarized what was known about the archaeology of Santa Fe as follows:

The city of Santa Fe is built upon the ruins of ancient Indian buildings. Under the breastworks on the summit of Fort Marcy are the walls of old Kwapoge. The Palace of the Governors was built on the ruin of an Indian pueblo, the name of which has disappeared even from tradition, but its massive walls of puddle adobe, laid down before the art of making bricks was introduced by the Spaniards, may be seen under glass in some of the rooms of the Palace at the present time. Other towns of the ancient Tano land are scattered along the Rio Santa Fe from the capital city to La Bajada, and along all the waterways between the Rio Santa Fe and the mountains to the south. North of the crest above Santa Fe are the surviving villages of the Pueblos and in every direction indications of considerable population in antiquity.[4]

At the time, Hewett's comments were accurate enough, but over the course of the following seventy years our understanding of Santa Fe's archaeological past has deepened significantly. For example, earlier generations of archaeologists concluded "the evidence for intensive occupation of [the Santa Fe area] prior to the 12th century is very scarce."[5] Within the last two decades, numerous studies have revealed an abundance of previously undiscovered sites in and around Santa Fe that are more than 1,000 and possibly even 2,000 years old. These studies suggest that perhaps the "conventional wisdom" needs reassessment. Similarly, the northern Rio Grande region surrounding Santa Fe has often been viewed as peripheral to other parts of the Ancestral Pueblo world, such as the Four Corners area or the San Juan Basin, in terms of significant cultural developments. A closer analysis reveals that while the Santa Fe area has long been part of the Pueblo world, it has repeatedly followed its own unique cultural trajectories. To dismiss it as merely "peripheral" to other regions is a mistake.

The chapter sequence is as follows: Chapter 1 sets the stage and provides an environmental context for the study of the archaeology of Santa Fe and how it relates to the archaeology of the greater Southwest. Chapter 2 describes the early history of archaeology in Santa Fe, provides a brief introduction to the practice of archaeology, and describes some of the questions that archaeologists try to answer. Chapters 3 through 7 portray the five chronological periods that archaeologists use to define the cultural sequences that occurred in and around Santa Fe prior to the historic period that began in the late 16th century. The names, the time frames, and distinctions among these cultural periods—Paleoindian, Archaic, Developmental, Coalition, and Classic—are explained in much greater detail in each subsequent chapter. Chapter 8 is a brief review of events in the 16th century when Europeans, as well as a variety of non-Puebloan Indian groups, first entered this region and changed ongoing cultural processes in unpredictable ways. The Epilogue offers a brief summary and a few conclusions.

Every author has biases and it seems to me that one should be as explicit about them as possible. This book is written from the perspective of contemporary anthropological archaeology. I have included the most up-to-date information but archaeology is not static and our understanding of the past is always increasing. As any scientific endeavor, archaeology is a never-ending story. There is always the possibility that someone may discover something new or approach an old problem in an innovative way that will change our views. No self-respecting archaeologist will ever claim that he or she knows everything about a particular period or that one particular approach to understanding the past is the only correct approach. Archaeological terminology can appear unnecessarily complex, and I have tried wherever possible to explain technical concepts using everyday language. For specialized terms I have included a glossary.

Because I am not an historian, I have limited the scope of this book to the period before European contact had a measurable effect on societies living in the Southwest. One frequent query is whether the archaeological record supports the existence of continuities between prehispanic groups and groups living today in the vicinity of Santa Fe? I think the answer is "absolutely." Obviously, all of the societies that existed in the Southwest at the time of European contact have undergone massive social, political, and economic changes over the past several hundred years. Although some things have been retained and others lost, there are numerous descendent populations still living in the Southwest, most of whom have their own rich oral traditions that describe their histories. Due to the limitations of time, space, and my own expertise, I have elected not to include traditional Puebloan accounts of their culture histories here, but to refer interested readers to the many excellent sources available.[6]

Archaeology takes the long view of human affairs, and archaeologists spend a lot of time attempting to arrange sequences of events in the proper chronological order. Time is important, so I want to insert a brief word about how dates are notated in this book. Many archaeology books, reports, and monographs continue to place events in linear time using the traditional notations of "B.C." (Before Christ) and "A.D." (*Anno Domini*, In the Year of Our Lord). I believe that B.C. and A.D. are too narrowly Eurocentric and need not be used if there are reasonable alternatives. A number of newer publications have begun to recognize and use the terms "B.C.E." (Before Common Era) instead of B.C., and "C.E." (Common Era) instead of A.D. and I have adopted those conventions here. I also use the term "B.P." (Before Present) in connection with very old dates. For example when discussing a Clovis site that is 11,000 years old I may refer to that site as being dated 11,000 B.P. However, I would not normally refer to a 600-year-old Classic Pueblo site as being dated to 600 B.P. but would instead give its date as 1400 C.E.

In addition to taking the long view, archaeology also takes a broad view, and many archaeologists focus their research on comparative analyses of past human behavior. Most of my comparisons are between what people were doing in Santa Fe relative to people in other parts of the Southwest, but Figure 1 provides a broader perspective for the events I discuss.

I also want to clarify the designation of one of the cultural groups featured in this book. The people who occupied the northern Southwest and the Colorado Plateau beginning as early as 1500 B.C.E. represent the initial manifestations of the Anasazi, the same people whose descendants later inhabited such well-known sites as Chaco Canyon, Mesa Verde, Canyon de Chelly, and the Hopi Mesas. The inhabitants of the Rio Grande Valley after around 600 C.E. represent a cultural subdivision referred to by many archaeologists as the "Rio Grande Anasazi." The term "Anasazi" has become controversial among contemporary Pueblo people and some archaeologists because it is a Navajo word variously translated as "Ancient Enemies" or "Ancient Ones." Although "Anasazi" and "Ancestral Puebloans" are often used interchangeably and although there exists a substantial corpus of historical and contemporary literature that specifically refers to "the Anasazi," I believe "Ancestral Puebloans" is a more respectful, accurate, and inclusive term, and I will use it throughout the remainder of this book.[7]

TIME SCALE	SANTA FE
12,000–8500 B.C.E.	* Paleoindian Period * Clovis, Folsom, and Cody cultures * Small, mobile bands hunting large herd animals
8500 B.C.E.–400/600 C.E.	* Archaic Period * Hunting, gathering, and foraging lifeways continue long after other areas begin to rely upon agriculture * First appearance of pottery by very end of period
400/600–1175/1200 C.E.	* Developmental Period * Initial development of small farmsteads and hamlets growing maize, beans, and squash * Expansion of villages * Construction of small surface pueblos
1175/1200–1325 C.E.	* Coalition Period * Period of population growth and construction of larger pueblos * Expansion of settlements into new areas * Extensive use of water control technology
1325–1600 C.E.	* Classic Period * Growth of largest aggregated pueblos * Development of alliance systems

Figure 1. The Archaeology of Santa Fe in a larger context.

THE SOUTHWEST	THE WORLD
* Paleoindian Period * Clovis, Folsom, and Cody cultures * Small, mobile bands hunting large herd animals	* Late Paleolithic in Europe * Cave paintings in France, Spain, and Portugal * Beginnings of agriculture along Tigris and Euphrates rivers, Indus River, Yellow River, Valley of Mexico, and Andean Highlands * First pottery (Japan, 10,000 B.P.)
* Archaic Period * Agriculture enters the Southwest (1500 B.C.E.) * Beginnings of Basketmaker, Pioneer Hohokam, and early Mogollon cultures * Adoption of bow and arrow and pottery	* First cities in Mesopotamia * Sumerian, Babylonian, Assyrian, and Hittite empires * Rise of Old and New Kingdoms in Egypt * Period of Greek city-states * Rise of Rome * Teotihuacán city-state in Valley of Mexico * Chavin, Moche, and Tiwanaku cultures in Andes
* Beginnings of Puebloan and Fremont cultures * Developments in Chaco Canyon (900–1150) * Classic Mimbres (1000–1150) * Colonial and Sedentary Hohokam expansion in Phoenix and Tucson Basins (800–1100)	* Fall of Rome * Middle Ages in Europe * Mongol Empire * Vikings in Greenland (1000) * Crusades begin * Toltecs (Central Mexico) * Chichen Itza (Yucatán) * Chimu Empire (South America) * Great Zimbabwe (Africa) * Mississippian chiefdoms in eastern North America
* Developments around Mesa Verde in southwest Colorado * Classic Hohokam, Sinagua, and Salado cultures in Arizona * Settlement shifting out of Four Corners, Gallina, and Mogollon Highlands	* Crusades conclude * Magna Carta (1215) * Inquisition established (1233) * Kublai Khan founds Beijing (1266)
* Decline of Classic Hohokam and Paquimé (Casas Grandes) * Rise of katsina system * Coronado expedition (1540–1541)	• Ottoman Empire established • Black Death in Europe • Aztec Empire • Inca Empire • Columbus (1492) • Renaissance in Europe • Spanish Armada (1588)

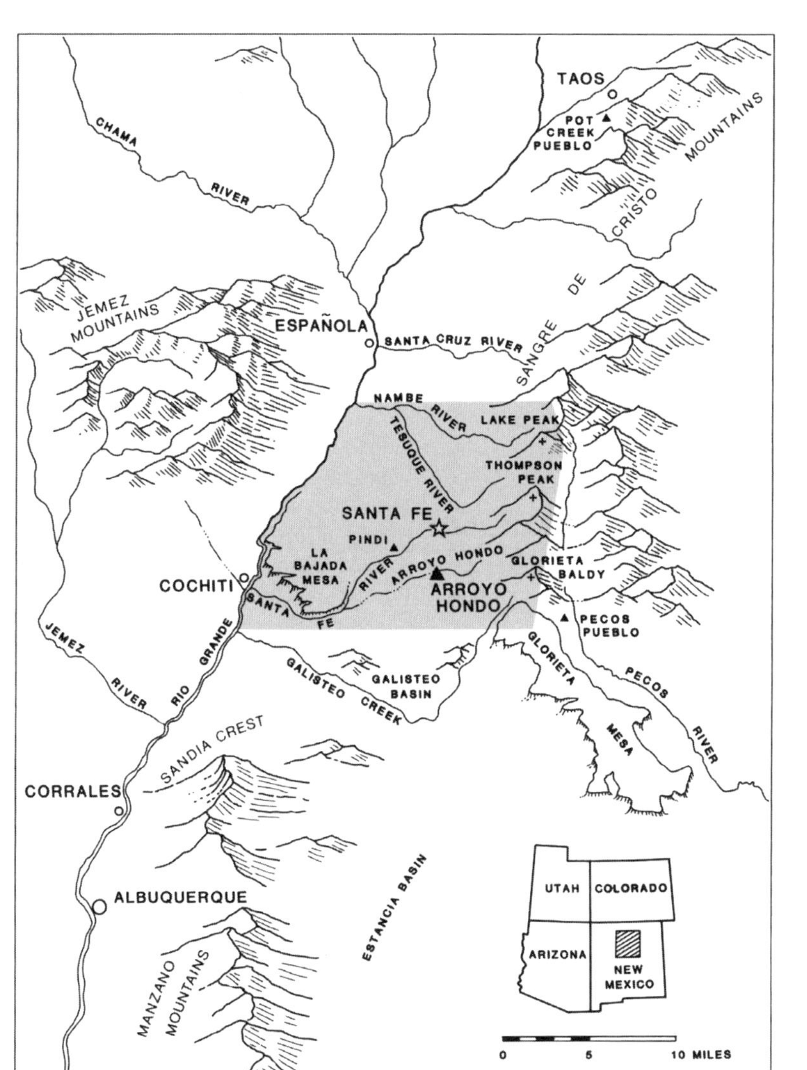

Fig. 2. Map showing Santa Fe and various sites mentioned in middle Northern Rio Grande region. Habicht-Mauche (1993). Courtesy of School for Advanced Research.

Chapter 1

❧

Setting the Stage

12,000 YEARS OF OCCUPATION IN AND AROUND SANTA FE

PEOPLE TRAVEL FROM ALL OVER THE WORLD IN ORDER TO ATTEND SUMMER performances of the Santa Fe Opera, located in the Tesuque Basin a few miles north of the city. Built in 1998 with spectacular views of the Sangre de Cristo Mountains to the east and the Jemez Mountains to the west, the award-winning opera house provides the perfect location for melodramatic, larger-than-life tales of pathos and joy. In a larger, deeper sense, the Santa Fe region has been the setting for a series of live performances far more dramatic than those portrayed in *La Traviata* and *Carmen*. People have lived in this place for 12,000 years. Some have moved on quickly, others have stayed for generations, but all have left their own indelible imprints on the archaeological landscape.

As archaeologists, we have the luxury of standing back from distances of hundreds or thousands of years and, armed with our knowledge about how things turned out, we can make weighty pronouncements about what could or should have been done to ensure the "success" of now-extinct societies. Easier said than done here, because the Southwest does not give up its bounty easily. Despite the region's natural beauty and ecological diversity, people have always had to work hard to survive. The first part of this chapter explores aspects of the natural environment that sustained the people who lived here for all those centuries.

Before we can set the stage, we need to build or, in this case, define it. Anyone with a passing interest and an Internet connection can learn that contemporary

I

Santa Fe is a city of approximately 70,000 people, comprising approximately 37.3 square miles, located approximately 7,000 feet above sea level, and receiving approximately 14 inches of annual precipitation.[1] Unfortunately, those "approximations" tell us little about the settings encompassed by this book. In a 1988 report summarizing the archaeology of Santa Fe, Michael Elliott worked with what he called "the greater Santa Fe area, technically known as the *Joint City County Planning and Platting Jurisdiction,*"[2] but even that larger area of roughly 250 square miles is too small to tell the full story. For the purposes of this book I have focused on an area "bordered on the east by the Sangre de Cristo Mountains and on the south by a point midway between the Santa Fe and Galisteo Rivers"[3] within what R. Bruce Dickson calls the *middle northern Rio Grande,* a region encompassing approximately 1,200 square miles (fig. 2).

One of the reasons that events sometimes played out differently in Santa Fe than in other areas was because of its geographical context and special ecology. Consider the landscape near the Santa Fe River, close to the foothills of the Sangre de Cristo Mountains and with relatively easy access across the broad, gently sloping piedmont to the Rio Grande. In the opinion of one writer, "Few places in Western North America rival the enormous plant and animal diversity found along the Middle Rio Grande, adjacent mesas, and the mountains within ten miles or so of the river."[4]

This may sound like a bit of hyperbole, but it is an apt observation to which I will return because, in fact, the local ecological conditions gave people many choices about where they could live, what they could eat, and how they could provide for their families. One critical distinction to keep in mind is between resource *diversity* and resource *abundance*; that is, even though there have always been a tremendous variety of local resources, the availability of any particular item could be quite limited. The point is that prior to the widespread adoption of maize, the local environment could always support *some* people, but the actual number of people was often relatively small.[5]

As an example of unique local conditions, consider how the beautiful Sangre de Cristo Mountains also play an important role in modifying the local climate. The mountains form a barrier to moving air masses that rise up and over the mountains in a process called *orographic lifting* that results in both summer and winter precipitation. This same blocking effect moderates the winter climate because it prevents winter Arctic air masses moving in from the Great Plains.[6] The Jemez Mountains to the west perform much the same function in blocking severe winter storms coming across the Colorado Plateau. The "So what?" response is that without these mountains, Santa Fe's winter climate would be far more severe.

An ongoing theme in this book is the dance between two seemingly incongruous but equally valid observations: "the archaeology of Santa Fe is unique" and "the archaeology of Santa Fe is a microcosm of the archaeology of the Southwest." Over more than a century of research, archaeologists have developed a kind of all-purpose sequence of cultural development in which the first people in the Southwest were small bands of nomadic hunters who were supplanted over time by slightly larger bands of seminomadic foragers, who were in turn supplanted by still larger and more complex societies that practiced agriculture, used pottery, and lived in bigger and more permanent villages. This "broad brush" sequence also applies in most respects to Santa Fe and its environs, but the actual progression of local developments sometimes lagged behind what was going on in other parts of the Southwest. Those differences have sometimes been the subject of value judgments, such as "the Santa Fe region was a cultural backwater," but to me the differences merely highlight the complexities of Southwest archaeology. There are many excellent texts that cover this field in great detail,[7] but I want to provide a bit of general background information here in order to put "the archaeology of Santa Fe" in a specific context.

The geographical region that archaeologist Linda Cordell calls "the cultural Southwest"[8] covers New Mexico, Arizona, parts of Utah, Colorado, California, and the Mexican states of Sonora and Chihuahua. Within this region are four distinctive physiographic provinces: Colorado Plateau, Southern Rocky Mountains, Basin and Range province, and Great Plains (fig. 3). Santa Fe is situated in the northern Rio Grande Valley, within the Southern Rocky Mountain province where it meets the Basin and Range country, and not far from both the Colorado Plateau and the Great Plains. The significance of Santa Fe's location is that it is at a contact point for people moving between different physiographic provinces, each one of which provides alternative choices for subsistence, settlement, and building materials. All four provinces were settled and exploited with varying degrees of intensity by ancient indigenous peoples, but few places were as well positioned as Santa Fe to take advantage of the individual characteristics of each province.

Any examination of the environmental settings in the Southwest will eventually consider relationships between soils, rainfall, vegetation, and the extent to which biological adaptations enabled both animals and people to take advantage of natural conditions. In 1913 Edgar Lee Hewett could assert "Physiographic conditions are es-

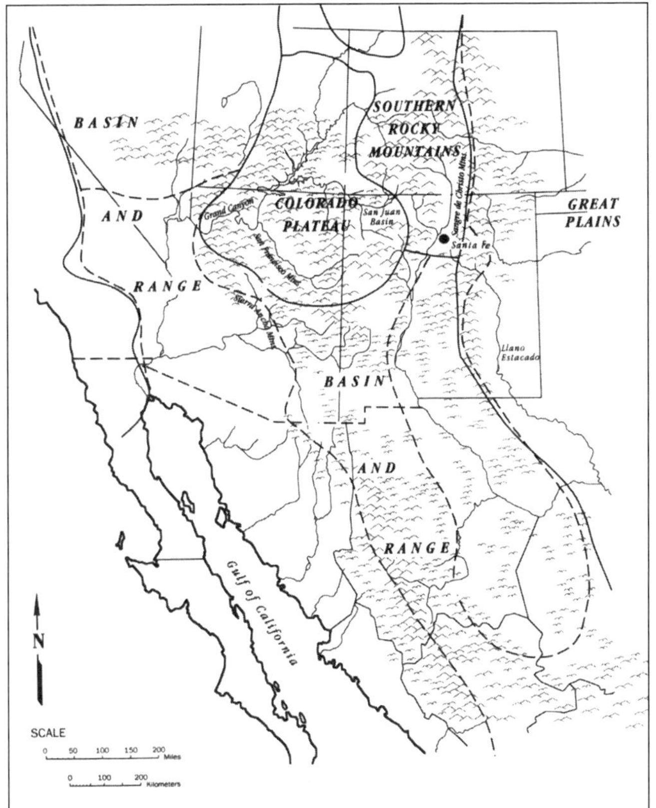

Fig. 3. Map of Southwest showing physiographic provinces. Map by David Underwood (Cordell 1997), courtesy of Elsevier Press.

sentially correlative with facts of culture,"[9] but geography is not destiny. The idea of environmental determinism, a belief that the physical environment controls one's fate, is no longer viewed as a complete explanation for cultural change. On the other hand, there is some soundness in the saying "nature provides but man decides." This is the idea of geographical or environmental "possibilism," an approach that recognizes how geography presents both opportunities and limitations that are unevenly distributed across the landscape. The groups that occupied the Southwest satisfied their basic needs for food, shelter, clothing, companionship, and personal recognition in diverse ways. In doing so, they irrevocably transformed the landscape. Over time this process, called anthropogenic modification, played an increasingly important role.[10] When one looks at the ongoing interplay between natural environmental conditions and human-induced impacts from mundane, day-to-day activities like hunting and gathering, cutting trees, clearing land for growing crops, and building houses, sorting out the specific details associated with cultural evolution is not so cut-and-dried.

Every archaeological site report includes a section that describes local geology and soil structure.[11] These descriptions are vital for understanding the ecological relationships between plant and animal communities but will not tell the readers of this book about their connections to human behavior. Let's begin with the geologic composition of the Sangre de Cristo Mountains near Santa Fe, which are mostly granite with high concentrations of the mineral silica. "So what?" Eroded silica does not create rich organic soils or retain soil moisture very well. The closer one gets to the mountains, the larger the volume of broken boulders and cobbles contained within the soil, making farming difficult. As one moves further to the west, southwest, and south, away from the city along the Santa Fe River and gently sloping piedmont, one finds soils more amenable for plant growth. In other words, it is harder to grow things closer to the Sangre de Cristo foothills than further to the west and south. The area along the Santa Fe River several miles south of the city near La Cienega is one place where old volcanic deposits have undoubtedly contributed to more productive soils as minerals such as iron, magnesium, sodium, and potassium have weathered out. This area shows evidence of cultural activity dating from the Archaic through the Classic Periods.

The flip side of Santa Fe's relatively limited deposits of excellent soils for farming is that its location close to the Sangre de Cristo and Jemez mountains means that there are numerous deposits of high-quality lithic material (stone) useful for the production of flaked stone tools.[12] Many people are familiar with the obsidian (volcanic glass) that can be found at a variety of sites throughout the Jemez Mountains. In some places, such as the Valles Caldera near Los Alamos, this material is so fine-grained that many archaeologists have referred to it as "weapons grade obsidian" — the prehistoric gold standard for the production of projectiles, knives, scrapers, and a variety of other cutting tools. Across the Rio Grande and closer to the city are geologic accumulations of fine-grained cherts, which, while not quite as desirable as obsidian, were perfectly adequate for the production of piercing, cutting, and scraping tools. In the foothills around Santa Fe, numerous quarries have been identified, some of which were used for thousands of years and into historic times.[13] In addition to lithic resources, the soils within the Tesuque Formation of the Espanola Basin (the large geological unit where Santa Fe is located) contain numerous deposits of silty, sedimentary clays.[14] These clay soils, when mixed with water, provide the raw material for both adobe construction[15] and pottery. As soon as the indigenous residents understood the nature and value of ceramic technology, there were abundant clay sources from which they could choose. Local pottery manufacture is a phenomena dating to perhaps 1,500 years ago.

A perennial object of jokes among Santa Fe visitors — as well as some locals — is the often-dry streambed of the Santa Fe River, particularly where it passes through downtown. Prior to its initial damming in 1881, however, this perennial river was the single most dependable source of water for the area around Santa Fe. Originating in the Sangre de Cristo Mountains and flowing southwest for approximately 20 miles to the Rio Grande near Cochiti, the river provided a linear focus of settlement for ancient people and was undoubtedly one of the primary reasons that Santa Fe attracted Spanish colonists.

Environmental conditions in the Southwest are extremely variable in terms of both place and time. By this I mean that there are not only marked seasonal changes but also long-term changes that play out over decades, centuries, and millennia. Readers should keep in mind that irrespective of similarities in temperatures and rainfall patterns, the environment that we experience today is not the same environment that pre-Hispanic people experienced. Over the past millennia many water sources have dried up, arroyos have been cut, and much of the naturally occurring flora and fauna have disappeared. The last few thousand years have been subject to general and consistent climatic patterns, but we need to be sensitive to the existence of some highly erratic and severe periods that acutely affected the choices available to indigenous people.

Climate is a function of altitude, temperature, and rainfall. While much of the Southwest, including Santa Fe, can be described as arid or semiarid, the conditions that define those broad categories can differ. Average precipitation across the Southwest varies from 1 to 2 inches in some portions of the Sonoran Desert to 40 inches across parts of the San Juan and Rocky Mountains. Because precipitation is often unpredictable, however, the very concept of an "average" precipitation year is not particularly useful. The Southwest also exhibits markedly seasonal rainfall patterns (fig. 4). Santa Fe, for example, experiences a pattern of heavy summer monsoons that deliver the majority of the year's precipitation. Other areas, such as central Arizona, experience a bimodal regime in which moisture-laden winter storms balance the summer monsoons. "So what?" While seed germination in the spring relies upon groundwater, continued growth depends upon the summer monsoons. The failure of those summer storms to appear on schedule can be devastating for maize-dependent farming communities.

Temperature controls the length of the growing season and may be the "stealth agent" behind a number of large-scale population movements that archaeologists have charted from the 11th through the 15th centuries. Topography complicates the length of a growing season. Even though sufficient precipitation may fall, people living at higher altitudes face cooler temperatures with the implication of both earlier and later frosts, and the potential for shortened growing seasons. As one ascends in

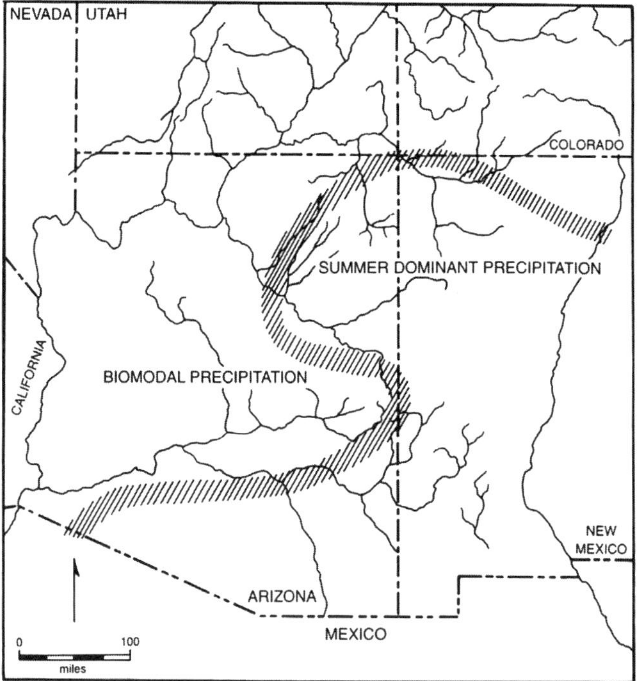

*Fig. 4. Seasonal precipitation in the Southwest. Illustration
by Marjorie Leggitt, Legitt Design (Cordell 1997), courtesy of
Elsevier Press.*

elevation, the number of frost-free days decreases and the amount of precipitation increases. Under most conditions, maize needs an average of between 110–120 frost-free days in order to ripen. Even though this "magic number" has been modified through the development of different maize varieties at some point, regardless of the amount of precipitation, maintaining an agricultural lifestyle in mountainous areas becomes very difficult. The same holds true in colder areas. One of the climatic explanations for the well-known and highly debated 13th century depopulation of the Colorado Plateau has less to do with diminished rainfall than the fact that the climate became notably cooler during the prelude to the Little Ice Age.[16] The growing seasons in more northerly areas became too short to maintain the maize-based agriculture that had sustained the Ancestral Puebloans for several hundred years. Santa Fe has an average growing season of 165 days,[17] well within the zone for successful maize growing, but there have been historically recorded periods of shorter growing seasons.[18] In an extraordinary response, Ancestral Puebloan farmers devel-

SOURCE	ANNUAL PRECIPITATION	TEMPERATURE (° FARENHEIT)	AVERAGE FROST & FREEZE DATE
Folks 1975	11–14″ below 8,000′ elevation	Average max. 61–66	Last frost May 3
	70% precipitation falls between May-October	Average min. 32–37	First frost October 15
Kelley 1980	14.4″	Highest average max. 84.3 (July)	Average frost-free period of 165 days
		Lowest average min. 19.3 (Jan.)	Last frost May 7
			First frost October 15
Western Regional Climate Center 2006	9.77–13.84″	Highest average max. 81.9–86.0 (July)	90% chance of frost-free period of 133–147 days
	Most precipitation falls between May and October	Lowest average min. 18.4–18.8 (Jan.)	50% chance of frost-free period of 158–168 days

Fig. 5. *A comparative summary of temperature, precipitation, and average frost dates for Santa Fe County. Table by Jason S. Shapiro, adapted from Procter (2006).*

oped many unique varieties of corn: drought-tolerant varieties, frost-tolerant varieties, and several varieties that could ripen much more quickly than the conventional 120-day growing season recounted in so many archaeology books.[19]

Many archaeologists have spoken (and argued) about drought, but few people have bothered to define it. Most probably view drought as some indeterminate period with substantially less rainfall than average. Aside from the problem of what "substantially less" means is the statistical fact that rarely does any individual year coincide with the mythical "average precipitation year."[20] Speaking at the New Mexico 2004 Drought Summit, State Engineer John D'Antonio offered a succinct and operational definition of drought, namely "drought occurs whenever there is not enough water to meet human needs."[21] D'Antonio's definition may sound anthropocentric, but from a cultural standpoint not all decreases in precipitation are equal. Small, mobile hunting and gathering populations have distinctly different needs as well as environmental perceptions when compared with those of large, immobile agricultural communities. In other words, when dealing with arid areas, archaeologists need to think beyond climatic statistics to include culturally defined impacts and ideas about decreases in rainfall. This does not mean I will not use the term "drought" or that no objective measures exist. When fields of corn, beans, and squash continue to die because of a lack of rain for several seasons, it's a drought!

Anyone who has spent much time in Santa Fe knows that rainfall can be highly erratic, particularly during the summer monsoon season when one part of a neighborhood may be thankfully deluged while another part remains bone dry. Based on about fifty years of records, the average Santa Fe rainfall is approximately 14 inches,[22] but other measurements compiled from different records and different times and places reflect the area's rainfall variability (fig. 5). The breakpoint for successful agriculture teeters around 12 inches — anything less and farmers run the risk of crop failure. To say that droughts had and continue to have enormous impact on this region's residents is an understatement, but I cannot overemphasize the importance that water played in the economic life of both pre-agricultural and agricultural cultures. For instance, to adapt to arid environments, many plant species go through a dormant period and do not reproduce via fruits, nuts, or seeds until they receive the right amount of moisture. Consequently, the most edible and nutritious parts of plants are often available only during particular times of the year. People who depend on those plants have to know not only where they grow but when they grow as well.

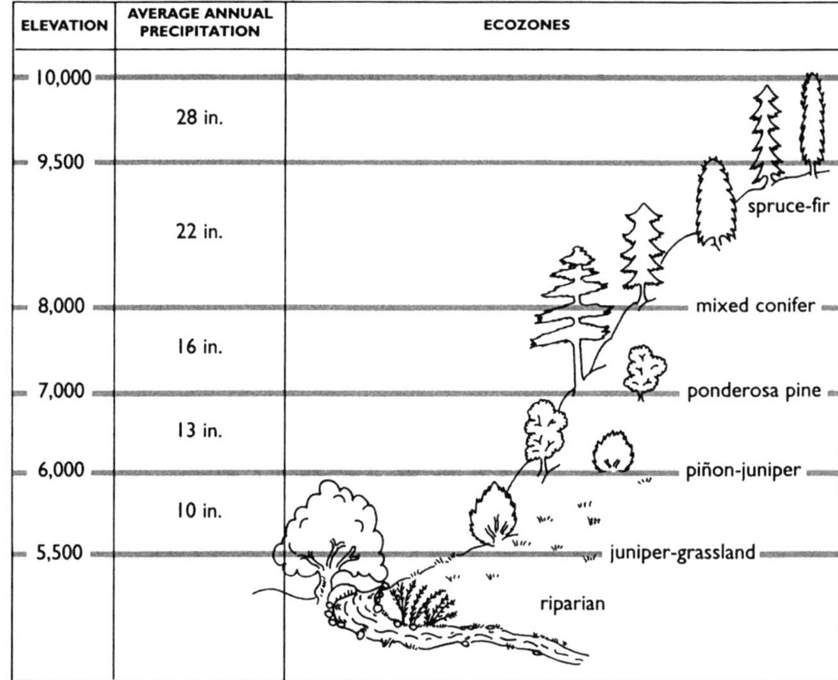

Fig. 6. Ecozones, or vegetative communities, found broadly across the Rio Grande Valley. Illustration by Gail D. Tierney (1995), courtesy Museum of New Mexico Press.

Ecozones are plant and animal communities that are defined by a particular combination of landforms, elevation, rainfall, and temperature. The middle Rio Grande Valley includes six ecozones, with the lower elevations tending to be both warmer and drier, and higher elevations cooler and wetter (fig. 6). I have often mentioned to my students that if they really want to understand how these ecozones look and change with altitude, they should take a ride on the Sandia Peak Tram in Albuquerque and keep looking down as the tram covers approximately 6,000 vertical feet. Nothing that I can present in a classroom or book is more illustrative of the ways in which ecozones shade into one another, from high desert grasslands across piñon-juniper woodlands, through Ponderosa pine forest into spruce-fir forest, and finally into the alpine zone almost 12,000 feet above sea level.

The significance of these life zones for human occupation is that they contain mixtures of plant and animal species that change from zone to zone and from season to season, presenting people with different raw materials for food, medicines, and tools. Plants define the zones because vegetation does not move very much, but even though the zones appear stable, the boundaries are always in flux. Changes in soil conditions, exposure to sunlight, and weather conditions that vary over time cause vegetation zones to expand or contract. Santa Fe is within the piñon-juniper ecozone, and one might wonder why, considering its elevation, Santa Fe has been such a magnet for people for thousands of years. Part of the answer is found in the following description:

> The piñon-juniper plant community, or ecozone, especially where it overlaps the ponderosa pine ecozone at an elevation above 6,000 feet, provides a habitat for more species of edible plants than any other major biological community in the region and in all New Mexico. With the skillful development of hunting, gathering, and agriculture, the piñon-juniper ecozone eventually came to comprise the core area for human habitation in the region.[23]

In addition to a wide variety of edible plants, the foothills, piedmont, and mountain areas around Santa Fe were home to numerous animal species, including mule deer, pronghorn antelope, rabbits, squirrels, turkey, quail, and grouse.[24] In other words, the area around Santa Fe was an excellent place to live if you happened to be dependent upon wild foods for your subsistence, but it was also pretty good if you decided to become a farmer. Although this environmental backdrop is important for understanding how Santa Fe fits into the physical setting of the Southwest, what this book is really about is human behavior — the kinds of decisions that people have made over the course of thousands of years that enabled them to occupy an extremely challenging landscape. During the past century, archaeologists have devoted a lot of time to focusing upon the most recent 2,000 years of Southwest culture history. We have learned a great deal about how Puebloan farmers lived, developed their unique forms of social organization, and built truly impressive structures using only mud, stone, and the simplest tools. Yet that is only a small part of the 12,000-year story of the occupied Southwest. Until about 3,500 years ago, all of the people who occupied the Southwest lived as small bands of mobile hunters, gatherers, and foragers. With the initial introduction of maize in the Sonoran and Chihuahuan desert basins, people then shifted their behavior to become hunters and gatherers who grew some crops, or "foraging horticulturalists." It was not until much later, well after the introduction of beans, squash, and other domesticated plants, that people could be described as mostly sedentary agriculturalists with a diminished reliance on wild foods. This wave of sedentism crested at different times, from as early as 1500 B.C.E. in southern Arizona and northern Sonora to as late as 500 or 600 C.E. in the Rio Grande Valley, but hunting and gathering never completely disappeared. Contemporary Puebloans still use a wide variety of local wild plant foods in concert with domesticated crops.

Early in the 20th century, anthropologist Clark Wissler examined what was known about indigenous groups in North America and noticed a correspondence between environmental conditions, prehistoric cultures, and historic groups. He developed the concept of *culture areas*, large geographical areas within which the ecological conditions related to cultural adaptations. In other words, among people living within each of these areas there were broad similarities concerning how they got their food, built their houses, and organized themselves. Wissler understood that "culture areas" were artificial constructs, but he used the concept as a tool to help understand the relationship between people and their environments. Among the cultural traits that Wissler found distinctive to the Puebloans were textile weaving, masonry construction, color-decorated pottery, turkey domestication, and a reliance on maize and cultivated foods.[25] To the north and west, people in the Great Basin and Rocky Mountains lived primarily in small hunting and gathering bands. To the east, people on the Great Plains organized themselves into larger groups of more mobile hunters and gatherers living in tribal societies. To the south, larger societies developed in Mesoamerica (portions of Mexico and Central America) that sometimes encompassed hundreds of thousands of people within unified political systems. These state societies relied upon intensive agricultural productivity and were characterized by the evolution of state religions, class structures, and occupational specialization. Archaeologists have not discovered evidence of such complexity in the Southwest but still wrestle with some basic questions: How did these people organize themselves into large groups and how were those groups managed? How were leaders chosen? How were disputes resolved? When, where, and why did people use warfare to impose their views or simply survive? Archaeologists have offered answers that I consider provisional because, although they are based on the best information available, they are still subject to debate.

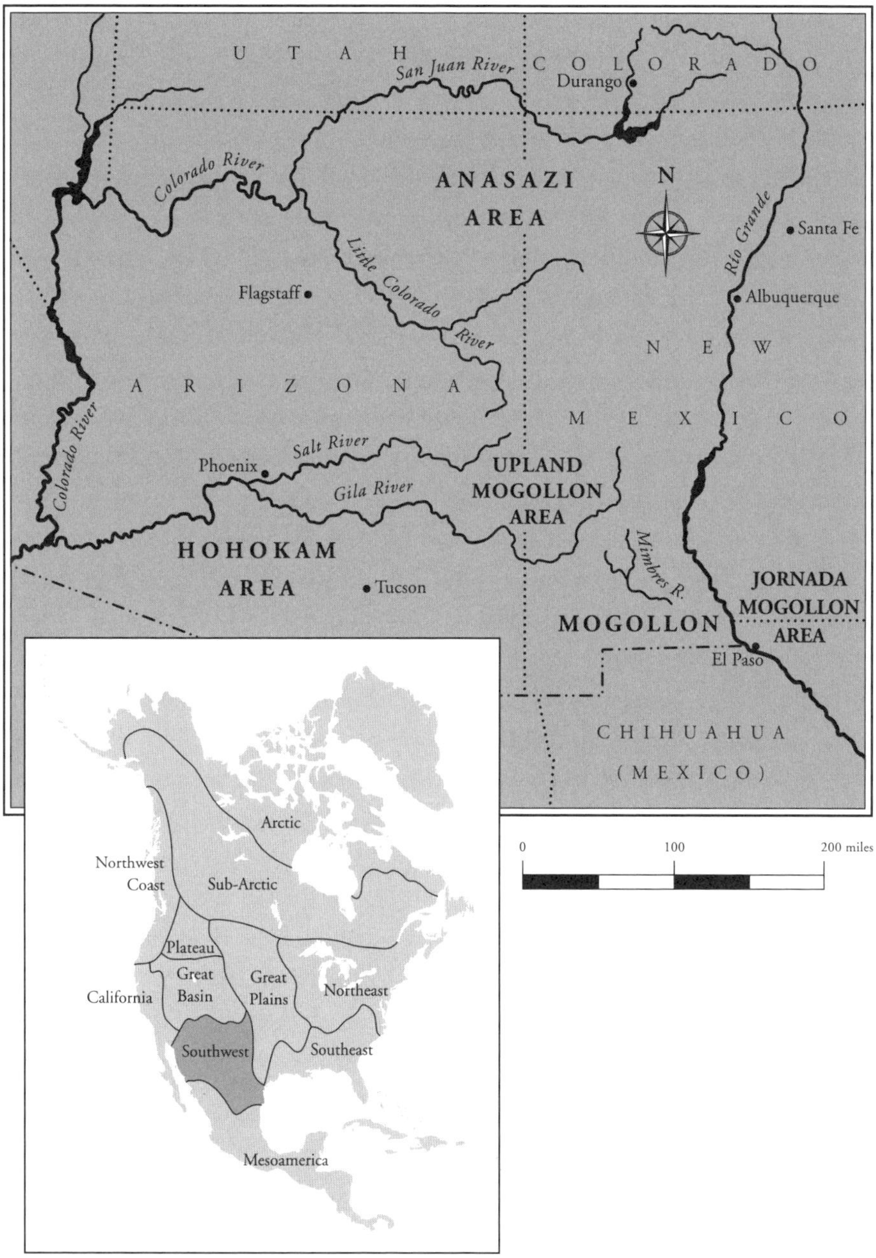

Fig. 7. The culture areas of North America, after Wissler (1914). Map by Deborah Reade

The three main cultural divisions in the Southwest—the Ancestral Puebloans (formerly "Anasazi"), the Hohokam, and the Mogollon (fig. 7)—did not coalesce into recognizable cultural traditions until sometime around 1 C.E., give or take a couple of hundred years. These groupings should not be confused with modern ideas about "tribes" but represent classifications created by archaeologists. Obviously we do not know how indigenous people may have categorized themselves, but this does not mean that the archaeological classifications are capricious. Archaeologists based the categories upon what they learned about the artifactual remains, subsistence practices, and settlement patterns of indigenous cultures. Some archaeologists do not like these big cultural labels because of the details they obscure concerning behavioral heterogeneity among the three groups, but judicious use of classification schemes can help us understand the broad sweep of Southwest prehistory in general, and of Santa Fe archaeology in particular.

Visitors to Chaco Canyon, Mesa Verde, Canyon de Chelly, and the Hopi Mesas may feel that they have a real understanding of the Ancestral Puebloans, but the nature and scope of that culture reached far beyond the Four Corners region.[26] Much of the early history of Southwest archaeology is connected with the excavation and description of Ancestral Puebloan sites built by people whose cultural beginnings may be traced to as early as 1500 B.C.E. When we think of Ancestral Puebloan culture we think of pottery-making, corn growing people living in adobe or masonry pueblos, a not inaccurate conception except that all groups within the Southwest could be characterized in the same way. What distinguishes the Ancestral Puebloans from these other groups are the areas in which they lived, as well as the specific nature of their pottery, subsistence practices, architecture, and settlement systems. During various periods, Ancestral Puebloans occupied areas from the Grand Canyon in Arizona to eastern New Mexico and from southwestern Colorado to central Arizona and New Mexico. They are central to the most recent 1,500 years of Santa Fe archaeology.

The second major group, the Hohokam,[27] was multilingual, multiethnic Sonoran Desert dwellers who may be the ancestors of historic and present-day O'odham groups. The Hohokam occupied areas in southern Arizona and particularly clustered along the Salt and Gila Rivers. The Hohokam cultural area included a tremendous diversity of settlement types and locations. There may have been between 40,000 to 80,000 Hohokam people in the 14th century, although by the time of Spanish contact this number was possibly as small as 5,000. The Hohokam developed the widest range of water control and agricultural strategies and used them quite productively for 1,000 years. In some areas, such as the Phoenix Basin, they created a series of larger and more sophisticated systems involving hundreds of miles of irrigation canals, floodgates, and dams. This strategy would require a relatively high degree of centralized, or at least cooperative, management intimately related to the control and distribution of water.

Of all the major cultural groups in the Southwest, the Hohokam appears to have had the most persistent relations with the large and sophisticated societies of Mesoamerica. A number of cultural and stylistic traits associated with the Hohokam, such as small ceramic figurines, iron pyrite mirrors, small copper bells, and ball courts, probably came from Mesoamerica. Finally, to the extent that there is any type of complicated hierarchy in the prehistoric Southwest, such societies probably developed among the Hohokam. People will continue to argue about the complexity of Chaco Canyon and Casas Grandes, but there is much evidence to suggest that during the 13th and 14th centuries the Late Classic Hohokam developed some kind of highly complex, if unstable, social and political system in which a small number of "elites" seemingly controlled a much larger number of "commoners."[28]

Archaeologists identified the last of the three major Puebloan groups, the Mogollon, about fifty years after they classified the Ancestral Puebloans. This group was named for the mountains in southwestern New Mexico, which were in turn named for an early Spanish governor of this portion of New Spain from 1712 to 1715. The cultural definition of the Mogollon is based primarily upon architecture and pottery, both of which are standard classification criteria used in the Southwest.

In terms of natural geography and physiography, the Mogollon region was probably more variable than the other two major cultural regions, and the groups that have been called "Mogollon" ranged from areas in Arizona, southern New Mexico, and even into Texas. In historic times the Western Apache adapted to some of these same mountain environments. Given the variability of the areas the Mongollon occupied, particularly the mountain transition zone, they were probably among the most adaptable occupants of the Southwest.

People who know almost nothing else about the Mogollon are often familiar with the exquisite pottery made during the Mimbres Phase of the 11th and early 12th centuries. Although most Mimbres pottery is decorated with geometric designs people tend to remember those pieces exhibiting motifs of animals and humans. The decorated pottery is only the most visible part of an overall cultural manifestation that included social, economic, and architectural developments, but the zoomorphic and anthropomorphic figures associated with Classic Mimbres pottery represent some of the most creative and evocative pottery designs ever produced in the Southwest. By the mid-13th century the distinctive Mogollon traditions disappeared and became subsumed within western Puebloan traditions in eastern Arizona or within other traditions in northern Mexico.[29]

At the risk of generalizing, I will summarize some fundamental similarities in the economic, social, and technological stages of the Ancestral Puebloans, Hohokam, and Mogollon.

1. All of the groups experienced a pre-ceramic stage, covering most of the period that the Southwest has been occupied. During this stage, it is difficult to tease out the cultural identities of the three major groups, all of which could be described as "seasonally mobile hunters, gatherers, and foragers."

2. All of the groups eventually began creating pottery that could best be described as "plainware"— undecorated, rather course ceramic material that was usually brown or gray. This development coincided with the period when people began living in small pit house settlements for large portions of the year, a practice called *sedentism*.

3. All three groups became reliant upon agriculture to a greater or lesser degree.

4. All three groups eventually built small surface structures using a combination of stone (masonry) and/or mud (adobe). Initially these structures were rather simple affairs used for storage, but they evolved into much more elaborate multi-unit structures, many of which contained hundreds or, in the case of the Ancestral Puebloans, thousands of rooms.

5. All three groups eventually built larger towns, or pueblos. The post-Mimbres Mogollon and the Ancestral Puebloan towns were the largest in terms of numbers of rooms, but the Hohokam towns covered the widest areas. These "town periods" were marked by a relatively higher degree of social, political, and ideological elaboration.

In this first chapter I have painted the ecological backdrop for thousands of years of cultural evolution, but I do not wish to minimize the role of human agency. One of the problems that archaeologists must face is that most of our data sets make it difficult if not impossible to isolate individual actors. The more carefully we examine the archaeological record, the more variation we encounter in the decisions of individual actors within the broad boundaries of their natural and cultural constraints. Certainly, people have always been more than automatons responding to environmental stimuli in standard and predictable ways, and understanding the actions of these unnamed and unknown actors is part of the ongoing challenge of archaeology.

Fig. 8. Adolph Bandelier and father at the Bandelier House at 325 East De Vargas Street in Santa Fe. Courtesy Museum of New Mexico Photo Archives (9171).

Chapter 2

Archaeology and Archaeologists

HOW DO WE KNOW WHAT WE THINK WE KNOW?

Walking tours of "historic Santa Fe" often pause at a 19th-century house located at 325 East De Vargas Street where former Swiss businessman Adolph Bandelier once lived (fig. 8). As I stood in front of that house, it occurred to me that formal study of the archaeology of Santa Fe began on August 23, 1880, the day Bandelier arrived from St. Louis, Missouri, to begin a career in archaeology that would span the next thirty-four years.[1] During the subsequent decades, scores of archaeologists studied and wrote about the archaeology of Santa Fe and its environs in scholarly articles, conference papers, and archaeological survey reports.[2] I have drawn much of the basic information for this book from recent studies, but I have also relied on the accumulated knowledge that provided the field's foundation. In order to explore the question "How do we know what we think we know?" I do two things in this chapter. The first is to elucidate a few of the most important sources of information that have contributed to our understanding of "the archaeology of Santa Fe." The second is to briefly explain some of the practicalities about archaeology in the Southwest.

When Adolph Bandelier began his work, the practice of archaeology in America was in its infancy. In their *History of American Archaeology*, Gordon Willey and Jeremy Sabloff refer to the interval between 1840 and 1914 as the "Classificatory-Descriptive" Period because during those seven decades "the principal focus [of archaeology]…was on the description of archaeological materials, especially architecture and monuments, and rudimentary classification of these materials."[3] In other words, archaeologists were still trying to answer the "What's going on here?" question. Consistent with that portrayal, Bandelier was responsible for some of the earliest descriptions of archaeological remains in the vicinity of Santa Fe. As a result of conversations with local Tewa Indians, Bandelier became convinced, correctly it now appears, that an Ancestral Puebloan ruin called by the Tewa name *O'gha po'oghe* was located somewhere under downtown Santa Fe. Even though Bandelier did not excavate many sites, he made numerous observations about Ancestral Puebloan origins, as well as the use of pottery types as cultural identifiers and time markers. He also developed a new methodology for studying the Ancestral Puebloans. Bandelier felt that only with the systematic integration of archaeology, ethnographic interviews with living Puebloans, and the analysis of historical and archival materials could we understand the ancient indigenous cultures.[4] This comprehensive approach established a model that most "modern" archaeologists who succeeded Bandelier have endeavored to follow.

No book about Santa Fe archaeology could be complete without discussing the impact of Edgar Lee Hewett, but, as with Bandelier, it is almost impossible to summarize a monumental career in a few paragraphs.[5] Referred to (behind his back) as "El Toro," for his stubborn personality and manner,[6] Hewett came to New Mexico in 1897 in order to head the institution that eventually became New Mexico Highlands University. Like his mentor Bandelier, Hewett was a self-taught archaeologist. In contrast to Bandelier, Hewett created an institutional empire and was instrumental in the establishment of the School for American Archaeology,[7] the Museum of New Mexico, the San Diego Museum of Man, and the anthropology departments at the University of New Mexico and San Diego State University.[8] At one time or another, Hewett directed all of these institutions. For many years, Hewett conducted archaeological summer field schools, particularly on the Pajarito Plateau not far from Santa Fe.[9] Hewett's critics argued that the field schools were not "research driven" and provided no real scientific training, and in fact these field schools were primarily an avenue for Hewett's main interest, promoting education and knowledge for its own sake.[10]

Long before Hewett's death in 1944, American archaeology was no longer the province of self-taught "scholar-entrepreneurs" like Bandelier and Hewett.[11] Decades of university-trained professionals, concerned not only with describing how people lived in the past but also with explaining the processes of cultural change over time, had transformed the discipline. During the second half of the twentieth century, numerous survey and excavation projects were conducted in and around Santa Fe, all of which contributed to a more complete picture of local culture history.[12] One of the most ambitious local archaeological projects was the excavation of Arroyo Hondo Pueblo, a 14th-century settlement located a few miles south of Santa Fe.[13] The project began in 1970 and proceeded over several years under the direction of Douglas Schwartz and the School of American Research. The field team systematically excavated approximately 150 rooms representing almost all of the pueblo's 24 roomblocks and recovered hundreds of thousands of artifacts.[14] They analyzed the excavated materials from a variety of perspectives that yielded information concerning local ecology, climatic changes, architectural features, settlement growth, pottery, diet, and demography. All of this information was collected in the nine-volume Arroyo Hondo monograph series published by SAR Press.

I have already alluded to a unique source of local archaeological information in the Introduction, namely the Santa Fe City and County Archaeological Ordinances. These ordinances grew out of the concept of "salvage archaeology" that developed in the 1950s and 1960s when archaeologists often worked just ahead of bulldozers on construction sites in order to recover as much information as possible.[15] The significance of both the city and county ordinances is that they apply to *private* rather than public projects. To receive construction permits, proposed developments subject to the ordinances are required to conduct an archaeological assessment that involves site surveys, testing for potential cultural deposits, and, in some cases, the mitigation of negative impacts upon significant cultural resources. Mitigation can take many forms and may entail the avoidance of selected portions of a site, the protective use of archaeological easements, or actual archaeological excavation. These assessments result in reports that detail the nature of the cultural resources encountered and treatment recommendations. In my opinion, the impact of these two ordinances has been nothing short of revolutionary. By making the evaluation of archaeological sites an integral part of the development process, the ordinances have contributed immeasurably to our understanding of the earliest occupations of Santa Fe.

The ordinances are not without controversy, and some members of the local community regard them as onerous impositions upon their freedom to develop their land. On the other hand, I am not aware of a single project that has been unable to proceed because of archaeological considerations. By and large, archaeologists are realistic people, and no archaeologist expects or necessarily even desires complete and total preservation of all things in a "never-to-be-disturbed" landscape. We would never learn anything new, nor would we have much to do. Non-archaeologists are often shocked to learn that the process of archaeology is *destructive* in the sense that a full and complete excavation of archaeological deposits will result in a large hole. That is why archaeologists place such a premium upon accurately recording their findings in excruciating detail since without that data — the basic information from the archaeological record — we have achieved nothing. Certainly archaeologists put a tremendous amount of effort into the preservation of artifacts, but what is really important to preserve is the *knowledge* gained from these excavations. Without the requirements of the city and county ordinances, much of Santa Fe's unique knowledge would not be collected.

In order to make sense out of the patterns of cultural materials, archaeologists create organizational frameworks that define cultural sequences and put them in chronological order. The two most common classification schemes that are used in the northern Southwest and the Rio Grande Valley are the Pecos Classification and the Rio Grande Classification (fig. 9). Archaeologist Alfred Kidder created the Pecos Classification of 1927 based on a series of diagnostic traits that he used to define cultural sequences in the Four Corners region.[16] The traits included subsistence activities and artifacts, but Kidder concentrated on ceramics and architecture because they are distinctive, relatively easy to observe, well preserved in the Southwest, and they reflect a process of change over time. The idea behind the Pecos Classification was to create a logical sequence that connected existing and historic Pueblo cultures with the indigenous cultures that had occupied the same areas long before the arrival of the Spaniards. Although some archaeologists have faulted the Pecos scheme for obscuring unique local cultural details, it is still widely used today, a remarkable achievement for something that is eighty years old. The Pecos Classification offered the first meaningful way to organize culture history in the northern Southwest, but as more of the archaeological record was revealed it became clear that the Pecos system could not be stretched to encompass every observed cultural pattern found by archaeologists — some things just did not fit easily into the scheme. This observation certainly applied to the Rio Grande Valley. Five decades ago, archaeologist

TIME SCALE	PECOS CLASSIFICATION	RIO GRANDE CLASSIFICATION
1600 C.E.	Pueblo V	Historical
1300	Pueblo IV	Classic (Begins around 1325 C.E.)
1100	Pueblo III	Coalition (Begins around 1175 C.E.)
900	Pueblo II	Developmental (Begins around 400/600 C.E.)
700	Pueblo I	
500	Basketmaker III	
1 C.E.	Basketmaker II	Archaic (Begins around 6000 B.C.E.)
	Preagricultural (Basketmaker I has been subsumed within the Archaic Period)	

Fig. 9. *A comparison of the Pecos and Rio Grande cultural classification schemes.*
Table by Jason S. Shapiro.

Fred Wendorf formulated an alternative cultural framework, the Rio Grande Classification (fig. 9). Wendorf's scheme relied on the same material traits of subsistence practices, ceramics, and architecture, but it identified explicitly local developmental sequences.[17] While it has been subject to some modification, the Rio Grande sequence provides a chronological outline that is favored by most archaeologists working in this area and is the one I chose for this book. Readers should keep in mind that classification schemes are not immutable but rather flexible tools that archaeologists use to organize their findings. The goal is not to force data into rigid frameworks but to create supple schemes capable of accommodating new concepts and findings.

One of the difficulties with chronological schemes is that each period encompasses hundreds or even thousands of years. Trying to unravel culture history in such large chunks of time, one is bound to miss or understate some elements. Because the archaeological record does not — indeed, cannot — preserve a 100 percent-complete record of any culture; there are *always* some missing pieces. Another part of the problem involves archaeological tools. Consider how much more of the microbial world was understood through the fine-grained observations of microscopes after they supplanted the much more generalized observations made through magnifying glasses. Beginning with the use of *radiocarbon dating* techniques in the 1940s and continuing to the present day, the development of more sophisticated analytical tools has allowed archaeologists to make finer and finer temporal distinctions, always with the idea that the knowledge of "when" is an important part of the overall goal of understanding "who," "what," "where," and "why."

There are many ways to mark the passage of time, from the minute fractions of seconds measured by physicists to the billions of years measured by geologists and astronomers. Archaeologists are concerned with the processes of human cultural history that span the period from yesterday back about 2.5 million years when the first evidence of "cultural activity" appeared, that is, stone tools in East Africa. They approach the problem of how to measure and organize time using two types of dating methods identified as *relative* and *absolute* dating. Geologists first developed relative dating in the 18th century and it involves arranging a series of objects or events along a time line from earlier to later without a precise idea as to the actual amount of time that has passed. Relative age often relies on a concept called *superposition,* an assumption that, in general, when we dig into the earth we find older objects located underneath younger objects. The problem with relative dating is that there is no way to know precisely how long cultural occupations lasted. One may construct a sequence of succeeding cultural periods from earliest to most recent, but there is no way to tie that sequence to any known dates. This was one of the early conundrums in determining how long people had been in the Americas. Scientists had an idea that people had been here a very long time, but no one could assign any verifiable dates to the sequences. The question was not finally resolved until the advent of the second category of dating.

The second kind of dating techniques is called *absolute* because the nature of the dates that one obtains from these methods is a specific number, and not just "older" or "younger." Before William Libby, a chemist at the University of Chicago, published the fundamental tenets of radiocarbon (C14) dating in 1949, there was no accurate way to date prehistoric remains. Probably the most well-known archaeological technique, radiocarbon dating is based on the principle that carbon exists in different forms (stable and unstable) and that living things continuously incorporate the unstable form of carbon (C14) into their tissues until they die. At that point no new carbon atoms are absorbed, and the proportions of the stable and unstable forms of carbon change at a specific rate.[18] Measuring that *proportion* allows things to be dated usually as a midpoint in a range, such as "1000 B.P. +/- 50 years." Radiocarbon dating is applicable to organic materials, that is, those containing carbon atoms that are between 100 and 80,000 years old. The procedures are most sensitive to the dating of objects between 500 and 50,000 years old, which makes them perfectly applicable to the time frames of interest to archaeologists in the Southwest.

Another type of absolute dating is *tree-ring dating*, technically known as *dendrochronology*. It was developed in the 1920s by A. E. Douglas, an astronomer who was studying the relationship between changes in sunspot activity and climatic changes on earth. Many tree species deposit annual growth rings whose width is dependent upon the amount of available moisture. Douglas was interested in correlating these variably sized growth rings with changing periods of moisture and sunspot periodicity, but he developed one of the most accurate ways to date prehistoric remains. The best tree species for this technique are Douglas fir, piñon, and Ponderosa pine because they are moisture-sensitive, produce two growth rings per year, and are pretty common in the northern Southwest. Under the best circumstances a sequence of tree-rings can indicate an actual calendar year during which the outermost ring on a piece of wood grew, but getting to that date requires matching a particular tree-ring sequence with established regional patterns (fig. 10). The next step involves taking the tree-ring date and applying it to cultural events. In other words, an observable biological event (a growth ring on a tree) becomes a proxy measure for human activities such as building construction or settlement growth.

In one sense, archaeologists study cultures that have failed, given our subjects are extinct societies that can no longer be directly observed. Ancient indigenous societies valued stability because their ability to deal with change was limited. On the other hand, when things did change, people adapted as best they could. As archaeologists, we have the privilege of going back and seeing the process of change

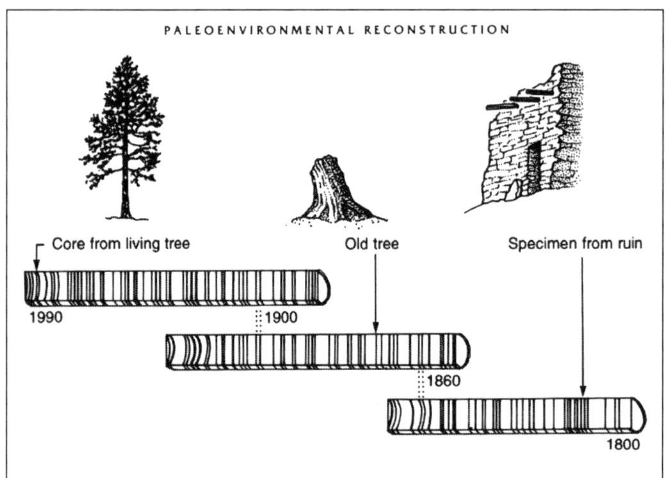

Fig. 10. A graphic portrayal of dendrochronology, or tree-ring dating. Illustration by Marjorie Leggitt, Legitt Design (Cordell 1997), courtesy of Elsevier Press.

unfold. Archaeology lets us see how all the pieces fit, because we are the ones who unearth the pieces and try to put them back together in some meaningful way. And what are those pieces? Those things that we call "artifacts" are the remnants of cultural behavior. By culture, I am referring to the *process of human adaptation based on experience, learning, communication, and the use of tools.* In other words, culture involves things that we are not born with but which we learn and can teach to others.

Artifacts and features are the material remains of the societies we study, and although digging is what most people associate with archaeology, it is only a very small part of what we do. Archaeologists are primarily interested in understanding past behavior. We want to comprehend the cultural systems that produced the material remains that we uncover. We want to know why things changed over time, and why past societies did not survive into the present. Sometimes we deal with concepts that are fairly abstract—no one has ever dug up a social system, or a political system, or a religious system. We know that such things existed, and archaeologists have discovered artifactual evidence from which they can infer things about these systems, but unlike ethnographers, who study living populations, archaeologists cannot actually talk to participants or observe their behavior. Because our "informants" are long deceased, we work with tangible remains such as artifacts, bones, architectural features, and rock art. Even though the cultures we study are extinct, I believe that by striving to understand these past societies, we are giving voice to those who can no longer speak. We are giving these ancient people the highest form of dignity—we are asking them to tell us who they were and how they lived.

I am fortunate to work in the Southwest, where the archaeological record is so rich, extensive, and accessible that archaeologists have successfully exposed and untangled thousands of years of culture history. Three reasons for that success are the presence of natural preservation processes, the exploration of the Southwest at the "right" time, and the time depth of occupation by indigenous people.

The arid climate that presented enormous challenges for people trying to make a living also created wonderful conditions for the preservation of organic remains. Stone tools and pottery fragments are exceedingly durable,[19] but items made of wood, bone, animal skins, or plant materials subjected to repeated freezing and thawing, or wetting and drying, are rarely preserved. This is not to say that all organic materials in the Southwest are always preserved, but compared to regions such as the Northwest or the Northeast, the degree of artifact preservation is stunning. As a general rule, the more recent the cultures being studied, the greater the numbers of artifacts and features that are preserved. With more things to study, a more accurate picture of past lifeways can be elucidated, and archaeologists can be more confident in their inferences.

The second factor relating to the preservation of archaeological remains is that with the exception of a few major cities, population densities and "development" remained relatively sparse in the Southwest until after World War II so that most cultural remains were not disturbed. During the 19th century many Americans believed that the entire region beyond the 100th meridian was worthless desert. This "Great American Desert" was a region to be avoided as best one could when getting to California and Oregon. Beginning in the 1860s, geologists, geographers, anthropologists, and archaeologists began to discover the archaeology of the Southwest, but it was not until the 1940s that large-scale disturbances occurred. Population influxes caused by the combination of new military facilities, water control and road building projects, air conditioning, tourism, and a growing cadre of GI Bill-trained archaeologists, resulted in more discoveries and consequently more impact upon previously unknown cultural resources. More archaeology was done in the Southwest because of the hundreds of thousands of sites waiting to be discovered, surveyed, and excavated. Sometimes the practice of archaeology in the Southwest reminds me of the old joke about the drunk who was walking around a streetlight in the middle of the night.

When questioned by a police officer as to what he was doing, the drunk replied, "I'm looking for my car keys." "Well, where did you lose them?" asked the officer. "Over there in that parking lot." "Then why are you looking for them over here?" Clearly exasperated, the drunk says, "Because the light's better." There has been a lot of archaeology done in the Southwest simply because the "light" is better.

What do I mean by the phrase, the exploration of the Southwest at the "right time"? The late 19th and early 20th centuries were a dynamic period in American history. In 1893 Frederick Jackson Turner published his famous essay "The Significance of the Frontier in American History,"[20] in which he described the closing of the American frontier. If the frontier was closed, then presumably it was safe to investigate those wonderful places that had been noted, and in many cases photographed, but never systematically studied. In addition, Congress wanted to know exactly what "the West" encompassed, and beginning in the 1860s a series of exploration and mapping surveys collected information about natural and cultural resources throughout the West.[21] This was also the time when scholars had begun to systematically analyze human cultures, and anthropology and archaeology emerged as academic disciplines. These developments were coupled with a burgeoning public curiosity about human cultures past and present that included a surging interest in museum displays. By the turn of the 20th century, the Southwest, with its innumerable archaeological sites, became open for study at the same time that universities were beginning to train people with the necessary research skills.

Not all archaeological investigations were necessarily driven by pure scholarship. In the 1880s, the end of active hostilities between the United States and western Indians initiated a period of unchecked commercial exploitation of archaeological sites. Museums as well as private collectors became fascinated with prehistoric "stuff," and the depredations eventually became serious enough to result in the passage of the Antiquities Act of 1906.[22] Despite its shortcomings, the Antiquities Act was the first clear effort at federal regulation of cultural resources. Noteworthy for the archaeology of the Santa Fe area, one of the earliest archaeological sites to achieve federal protection was Bandelier National Monument, established in 1906, under section 2 of the Antiquities Act.[23]

Insofar as the time depth of Indian communities is concerned, there has always been an assumption among both Euro-American colonizers and the Indians themselves that these communities have been in existence for a very long time. It was not until the mid-20th century when absolute dating methods were refined that archae-ologists could begin to assemble an accurate chronology of the Indian occupations of the Americas. Within the Southwest, the residents of Taos, Acoma, and the Hopi Mesas will each assert that *theirs* is the oldest continuously occupied community in America. Rather than attempt to sort out these claims it is sufficient to note that all three of those communities probably have been occupied for somewhere approaching 800 years, a testament to both economic and cultural survival. Additional pueblos formed and reformed over the course of several hundred years. The sixteen present-day pueblos in the Rio Grande Valley together with Acoma, Laguna, Zuni, and Hopi, were all in existence at the time of the 16th-century Spanish *Entrada* into New Mexico, and were still in existence at the time of the 19th- and 20th-century anthropological *entrada*. Although some of the pueblos had moved from their original ancestral locations, the time depth represented by these communities was evident to the early generations of anthropologists and archaeologists. It was natural for scholars to attempt to work backwards from lifeways that they could observe towards a pre-Hispanic past that could be reconstructed using the same systematic approach developed by Bandelier.

Archaeologists work hard to retrieve the past and present it in such a way as to have some meaningful impact for people today, but sometimes "impacts" can be unpredictable. When Adolph Bandelier died in 1914, he was conducting research in Seville, Spain, on behalf of the School of American Archaeology. He was also sufficiently destitute so that the School paid for his funeral and burial vault thereby retaining "ownership" rights to his remains. It was not until decades later, after Douglas Schwartz had become president of the School, that efforts were made to return Bandelier's remains to the place on the Pajarito Plateau where he had begun his work and which now bears his name. After some fifteen years of letters, meetings, and negotiations, Schwartz, accompanied by several dignitaries, climbed the talus slope above Frijoles Canyon in Bandelier National Monument. When he threw open the bag containing Bandelier's ashes, the prevailing wind literally blew old Adolph right back at and all over Schwartz![24]

Fig. 11. Drawings of Pleistocene animals. Illustration courtesy of Kent Tankersley.

The First Santa Feans

NOMADIC PALEOINDIANS OF THE LATE PLEISTOCENE

When Pedro de Peralta founded the City of Santa Fe in 1610, the Spanish colonists who came with him were well aware that they were not the first people to occupy this spot.[1] For one thing, this place in the landscape that was to become Santa Fe already had a name, *Ogapoge,* meaning "down at the Olivella shell-bead water," that was given by local Tewa-speaking Indians.[2] Even the Tewa people were relative latecomers, probably moving into the northern Rio Grande Valley in the late 12th or early 13th centuries.[3] The first Santa Fe visitors may have arrived as early as 12,000 years ago, leaving ephemeral traces represented by the presence of unique types of flaked stone projectile points at a mere handful of sites. These people are referred to by the aggregate term "Paleoindians," which denotes both a time period and a lifestyle, and are usually associated with the hunting of large animals, collectively called "megafauna."[4]

Archaeologist Brian Fagan has highlighted the qualities of "opportunism, flexibility, and mobility" as being essential for late stone age hunting societies,[5] and we have no reason to doubt that the Paleoindians who passed through Santa Fe possessed those qualities in abundance. The Santa Fe landscape of 12,000 years ago was so dissimilar from what we experience today that it might be called a different world. During the several thousand years that the last Ice Age, the *Wisconsinin,* was ending and the glaciers in the Rocky Mountains in northern New Mexico were receding, the entire Southwest was substantially cooler and wetter than it is today.

The area around Santa Fe would have been heavily forested with varieties of spruce, pines, and conifers, interspersed with grasslands, with a climate much like that in British Columbia or other parts of the Northwest today except that these Late Pleistocene environments were more complex with a mixture of both existing and extinct species.[6] Plentiful surface water in the form of streams, shallow lakes, and marshes would have provided excellent habitats for the varieties of animals on which continuously mobile Paleoindian bands depended for food. These animals included elephant-like mammoths[7] and mastodons, an extinct form of bison as much as 1,500 pounds heavier than the present forms, and extant species such as caribou, elk, and pronghorn antelope. Other species included giant ground sloths, horses, one-humped camels, and strange beasts such as pampatheres and glyptodonts that are unlike anything alive today.[8] In addition to these herbivores, carnivorous predators such as now-extinct saber-toothed cats, dire wolves, and short-faced bears together with grizzly bears and mountain lions, probably competed for food with the Paleoindians.[9]

As archaeologists we can be analytic or scientific or even quite glib about the vagaries of Paleoindian hunting behavior and the clever and sophisticated ways in which they fashioned their tools. To be honest, I cannot conceive of what it must have been like to try and kill an animal weighing several tons using even the best stone spear points, even if I brought along all my friends. The largest mammoths were twelve feet tall, weighed ten tons, and had tusks as long as sixteen feet. The earliest Paleoindians primarily used thrusting spears rather than throwing spears — the successful hunter had to be close! The thrusting spear system had separate parts — a projectile point, foreshaft, and mainshaft — all of which were designed to allow the valuable mainshaft to be reused. Even with sick, old, or injured animals, surely Paleoindian hunting was a physically demanding, bloody, and dangerous undertaking.

One of the ways that archaeologists learn about past human behavior is by studying skeletal remains for clues as to how those individuals lived and died. Although a limited number of Paleoindian skeletons have been recovered in North America, their study is problematic because provisions contained in the Native American Graves Protection and Repatriation Act of 1990 (NAGPRA)[10] require federal agencies and museums to return human remains to Indian tribes that can demonstrate their cultural affiliation. By way of contrast, numerous skeletons of Paleolithic hunters have been recovered throughout Europe and parts of the Near East. Scientists who have studied these skeletons have come away impressed with the levels of trauma these people endured, noting evidence of numerous breaks, fractures, and disloca-

tions, some healed and others not. The only contemporary group with which we might compare these early hunters is modern-day rodeo bull riders.[11] Think of Paleoindian
hunting bands as the toughest people you have ever met
spending every day "roughing it" on the hardest camping
trip that you can imagine.

The identity and origins of the Paleoindians is ines-
capably connected to the ongoing debate about the peopling of the Americas. After all, people did not evolve here
in Santa Fe (many would argue they still do not once they
move here) so the question remains "Where did these Paleoindians originate?" The *Pleistocene* was the geologic epoch that lasted from approximately 1.6 million years ago
until perhaps 12,000 years ago. It was during the Pleistocene that modern humans evolved in Africa and eventually colonized every continent with the exception of Ant-
arctica. We know the peopling of the Americas was the
final chapter in this late Pleistocene expansion, but one
of the fundamental issues in Paleoindian studies has remained unresolved for more than a century: "Did people
make an early or late entry into the New World?" Having said
that, the meaning of "early" versus "late" has changed a great deal
in the last hundred years.

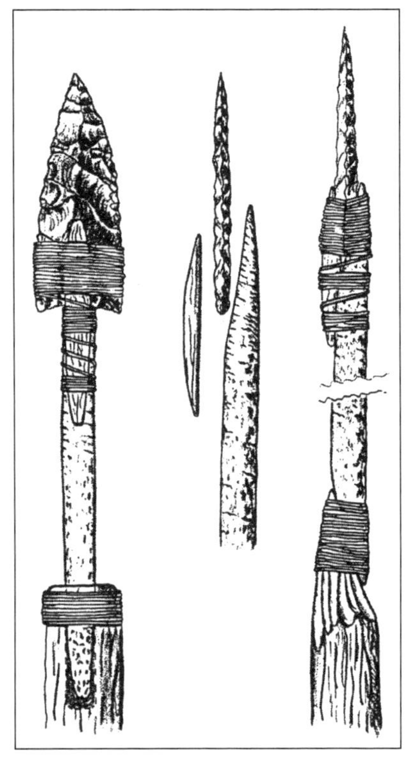

*Fig. 12. Reconstructed view of
Paleoindian thrusting spear system.
Illustration by Boldurian and
Cotter (1999).*

Prior to the 20th century, the antiquity of people in the
Americas was a big question mark. Even the most reputable scientists could only offer guesses that ranged from several thousands up to possibly hundreds of thousands
of years. In the absence of any indisputable way to date either bones or artifacts, the
question remained subject to speculation. A number of archaeological discoveries
gradually focused the competing arguments, and the longer archaeologists looked
at the question, the earlier the initial entry appeared to have occurred. The earliest association of Paleoindian artifacts and extinct animals discovered in North
America may be a report about which few people are even aware. In 1895 a team of
paleontologists working in Logan County, Kansas, discovered an unidentified but
probable late Paleoindian fluted lanceolate projectile point[12] in association with the
remains of an extinct species of bison.[13] The discovery in a stream-cut bank was

Fig. 13. Photograph of Folsom site, Folsom, New Mexico. Photograph by Jason S. Shapiro.

encased in a fossil bone bed overlaid by approximately twenty feet of sedimentary material, an early illustration of the difficulty associated with finding Paleoindian sites. For reasons that may never be known, what should have been an earth-shaking report concerning the antiquity of humans in North America was apparently ignored.

In contrast to the Logan County, Kansas, material, all beginning archaeology students learn the story of cowboy George McJunkin. While riding the range in northern New Mexico one day in 1908, McJunkin saw an enormous bison bone eroding out of an arroyo bank near the town of Folsom. He had seen lots of cattle and bison bones, but this was unlike anything he had ever encountered. Despite the apparent significance of the discovery, no one else even looked at the site until 1922, and it was not until 1927 and 1928 that the site was scientifically excavated. The remains of approximately 30 *Bison antiquus*, another extinct species that predated *B. occidentalis*, in association with 24 fluted projectiles,[14] a flake knife, and a flake scraper were recovered from what has been determined to be an ancient bison-butchering site. The Folsom discoveries made it clear that people had indeed been living in North America for thousands of years, but these Folsom finds were hardly the end of the story.

Place names can evoke different meanings for different people. Some people know that Clovis, New Mexico, was named after the king of the Franks, who converted to Christianity in 486 C.E., and other people know that Clovis was the location of Norman Petty's recording studio, where in 1957 Buddy Holly and the Crickets recorded "That'll Be the Day" and several other early rock and roll hits. Archaeologists know that Clovis gave its name to the cultural manifestation that finally demonstrated the enormous antiquity of humans in the New World. In 1936 at Blackwater Draw, a gravel-mining site between Clovis and Portales, New Mexico (fig. 14), archaeologists discovered a different type of stone projectile in sedimentary deposits at a level below the Folsom type artifacts, suggesting the existence of an older occupation than had been assumed. More than a decade later, the radiocarbon techniques securely dated the Folsom material to 10,000–11,000 B.P., and the Clovis material to 12,700–13,500 B.P.

If I were writing this book only a few decades ago and wanted to summarize the peopling of the Americas, I would simply have noted that sometime around 12,000 years ago a group of northern Asian hunters who had developed a particular type of stone tool technology that we call "Clovis" migrated across the Bering land bridge,[15] entered North America, and kept moving until they reached Tierra del Fuego, Chile, in a little more than a thousand years. It was a good story and was consistent with what archaeologists knew and understood about the handful of early sites in the Americas. Today the question of "who were the First Americans?" is more in dispute than it has been for three generations of archaeologists and has led to some highly contentious debates within the field. In the 1970s, 1980s, and 1990s, a number of newly identified sites, including Monte Verde, Chile; Pedra Furada, Brazil; Tlacoplaya, Mexico; Cactus Hill, Virginia; Topper, South Carolina; and Meadowcroft Rockshelter in Pennsylvania produced cultural materials and deposits that have been radiocarbon dated to being older than 14,000 B.P. with some dates assertedly as old as or even older than 30,000 B.P. In a comprehensive review of early sites in South America, Tom Dillehay lists approximately fifty sites containing cultural materials or evidence of cultural activity that have been dated to being older than 15,000 years.[16] A number of sites in both North and South America remain controversial in terms of their suggested dates, but it is impossible to ignore this growing body of archaeological data. I think that a majority of anthropologists and archaeologists today would agree that the initial human entry into the Americas occurred sometime prior to 15,000 years ago by people who preceded the Clovis culture.

Fig. 14. Photograph of Blackwater Draw site, Clovis, New Mexico. Photograph by Jason S. Shapiro.

The same two points of view first expressed in the 19th century, namely early versus late entry of people into the Americas, are still jousting, but the parameters have changed. The small but persistent group of scientists who supports a "late entry" scenario believes that the cultural groups labeled "Clovis people" were the first Americans and did not arrive until slightly before 13,000 years ago.[17] The growing number of "early entry" supporters are not sure what group actually constituted the first Americans but have been convinced that the initial entry into the Americas occurred in the vicinity of 15,000–20,000 years ago, and possibly as early as 30,000–40,000 years ago. What is perhaps more controversial today than dates, is the origin (or origins) of the first American inhabitants. Candidate groups range from northern Asians and Mongolians to southern Asians, Ainu from Japan, and even Paleolithic Europeans, represented by the Solutrean Culture,[18] who supposedly coasted the ice fields of the North Atlantic in skin boats until they presumably reached Canada. The discovery, analysis, and legal "tug of war" surrounding the 9,300-year-old skeletal remains of Kennewick Man has only deepened the conundrum.[19] The purpose of this book is not to resolve the questions associated with the initial peopling of the Americas but only to make readers aware that the issue remains unresolved. There is less controversy regarding Paleoindian sites in the Southwest because so few of them have been identified as being more than 13,000 years old.[20]

One of the challenges of studying the Paleoindian Period is that it is the most incomplete database of all prehispanic periods, and there is only a limited amount of information from which archaeologists can draw their inferences. The first problem is that the number of actual Paleoindian sites is relatively small, in part because of the destruction caused by natural processes such as deposition and erosion, freezing and thawing, floods, fires, and the sometimes underappreciated actions of plants and animals. A handful of Paleoindian sites have been found in coastal locations in the Northwest, and along the East Coast and Florida, but a working assumption among many archaeologists is that the majority of coastal sites have been "drowned" by rising sea levels caused by the great glacial meltdown that began around 15,000 years ago. On the other hand, many inland sites with Paleoindian artifacts have been discovered by chance because so much sediment had covered them that they were invisible from the land surface. This was the problem I alluded to in connection with the 1895 discovery in Logan County, Kansas.

Another reason for our limited knowledge about Paleoindians is that there were relatively few of them. If we make the reasonable assumption that contemporary

Fig. 15. Typical Paleoindian encampment. Illustration courtesy of Mike Gromly.

and historically identified hunting and gathering societies are acceptable models for Paleoindians, we are talking about small, mobile bands of somewhere between fifteen and forty people. Population estimates are notoriously difficult for this period, but a population of between several thousand up to a few tens of thousands of people for all of North America is probably within the ballpark.[21] Not only were there relatively few Paleoindians, but their mobile hunting and gathering lifestyle was not conducive to permanent camps or structures, and it encouraged the development of portable "tool kits" that were lightweight, multifunctional, and durable. These are the same kinds of tool kits associated with Upper Paleolithic groups living in Europe between 15,000 and 30,000 years ago, as well as with historical Inuit groups living in the Arctic during the 19th and early 20th centuries (fig. 16). The upshot of all of these considerations for archaeologists is that there were not very many Paleoindians, they left relatively small amounts of stuff in the archaeological record, and much of the material that they created and used has not been preserved.

Despite the disagreements surrounding the peopling of the Americas, archaeologists generally concur that for a period of between 200 and 800 years beginning a bit more than 13,000 years ago, most of North America and parts of Mexico were occupied by groups of people using a particular form of technology. These people have been collectively labeled as "Clovis," a culture to which readers have already

Fig. 16. Collection of historical Inuit stone tools. Photograph courtesy of Pete Bostrum.

been introduced. Literally thousands of Clovis artifacts made of stone, ivory, or bone have been recovered from sites all over North America and Mexico, including locations near Santa Fe, but those artifacts represent only small portions of the things these people used. Clovis items made from wood, plant materials, animal skins, or natural fibers did not survive the rigors of time.[22] Most people usually think of Clovis technology only in terms of their distinctively crafted projectile points, but Clovis people produced a range of stone tools, including scrapers, knives, gravers, perforators, awls, hide punchers, and spear-shaft straighteners (fig. 17).[23] The geographic extent of people using Clovis technology is encompassed by the following quote:

> The assembled Clovis tool kit was broadly distributed and used in procuring mammoths in the rolling prairies of New Mexico north to Wyoming, caribou in the apron of tundra from Michigan to Nova Scotia, and undoubtedly, extinct megafauna and deer in the Southeast with its vast forests and coastal plains.[24]

Fig. 17. Examples of Clovis tools. Photograph courtesy of Pete Bostrum.

Although it is some distance from Santa Fe, the previously mentioned site at Blackwater Draw provides important insights into Paleoindian culture. Blackwater Draw itself was a fortuitous discovery that was only detected because a federally funded road project between Clovis and Portales during the 1930s needed sand and gravel. The construction material was dredged from a location just off the road that had once been a pond fed by the Brazos River. Twelve thousand years ago, the pond would have been a good watering hole for large animals and an excellent place for Paleoindian hunters to trap and butcher these animals as they became mired in mud. The lacustrine setting also provided smaller, collectable aquatic foodstuffs such as fish, turtles, and water plants. Although the pond dried up about 7,000 years ago, the area did not immediately become as arid as it is today, and local people continued to hunt bison for a few thousand years. Eventually, when the conditions changed enough, first the bison left and then the people.

Some archaeologists still refer to Clovis people as the "Big Game hunters," but as a recent article by Donald Grayson and David Meltzer makes obvious, this label is probably a misnomer. In actuality scientists have discovered very few sites where Clovis tools were found in association with megafuanal remains,[25] but Blackwater Draw is one of them. Two Clovis points and a scraper (for hide processing)

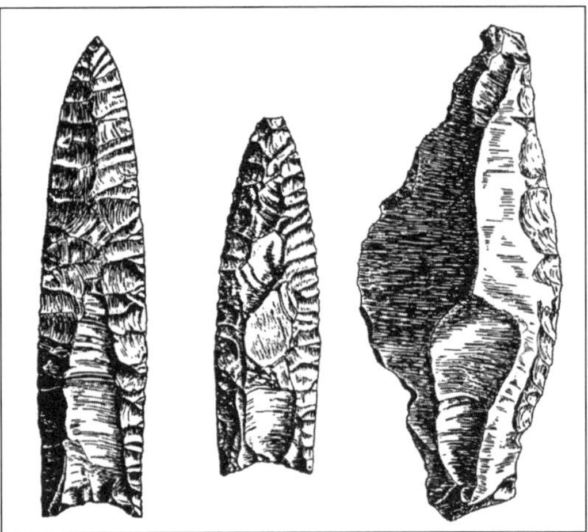

Fig. 18. Illustration of two Clovis points and a scraper found in association with mammoth bones. Illustration by Boldurian and Cotter (1999).

were found there in association with mammoth bones (fig. 18). Generalized big game hunting probably provided more calories per unit of effort than plant collecting,[26] but it is probably more accurate to describe the Clovis people as opportunistic plant collectors and foragers who also relied upon their exquisitely made flaked stone projectiles for hunting a variety of large and small animals. Boldurian and Cotter have noted that "Clovis tools were useful in many other aspects of food–getting, which included trapping small mammals, fowl, and slow-moving game such as land tortoises; foraging for turtles, fish, and eggs; and processing myriad plant foods."[27] As an example of their broadly based food choices, the discovery of manos (grinding stones) at the Blackwater Draw site supports the view that Clovis people were also grinding seeds and processing wild plants. The presence of what has been interpreted as a hand-dug Clovis period well at Blackwater Draw also suggests that these people took an active role in manipulating their environment in order to meet their needs.

Located north of Blackwater Draw in the Estancia Basin south of Albuquerque is the Lucy site.[28] Although the area is fairly arid today, towards the end of the Pleistocene the Estancia Basin would have been covered with small ponds and large shallow lakes or *playas*. The Lucy site is of interest because its lakeshore location is similar to that of Blackwater Draw, suggesting that some Paleoindians preferred settling near these bodies of water. This same conclusion is supported by archaeologist James Judge's massive survey of the area around Albuquerque, New Mexico, in which the densest concentration of Paleoindian sites occurred in the vicinities of shallow lakes.[29]

Following the disappearance of Clovis culture a number of subsequent Paleoindian groups appeared, beginning with the Folsom culture about 11,000 years ago and ending with several related groups in what has been called the Plano complex around 8,000 years ago. I have already noted the discovery of the Folsom culture in connection with a bison kill site at Folsom, New Mexico, and for the most part

Folsom projectiles are associated almost exclusively with extinct forms of bison. The fact that at least one Folsom artifact has been found in non-bison habitat, namely an upland forest zone on the Pajarito Plateau across the Rio Grande from the piedmont west of Santa Fe, suggests that Folsom people were more wide-ranging in their hunting behavior than has been assumed.[30]

As far as the question of Paleoindians living in or visiting Santa Fe and its environs, the answer is that they were certainly present, although relatively few Paleoindian artifacts have been found. Whether this shortage of evidence automatically implies minimal Paleoindian occupation is an open question because of those previously mentioned factors of visibility and preservation that limit our knowledge. Inasmuch as at least fifty-nine Paleoindian sites have been identified in the Albuquerque Basin, a mere 50 miles south of Santa Fe, there is a strong possibility that there was a more substantial local Paleoindian presence than has been discovered.[31]

The best-known Paleoindian site in the Santa Fe area is located on a small mesa several miles west of the city and within about a mile of the Rio Grande. The Caja del Rio site is set dramatically against the backdrop of the Pajarito Plateau with broad views in several directions. Aesthetics aside, the archaeological evidence suggests that small hunting bands used it periodically over virtually the entire Paleoindian cultural sequence. The variety of projectile types and other tools, including Clovis, Folsom, Plano, Midland, Angostura, and Cody/Scottsbluff points, testifies to the site's desirability as a camping place for a period in excess of four thousand years (fig. 19).[32] It must have been an excellent spot from which to observe and plan ambushes of migrating herds or to serve as a base camp for logistical collecting trips. Archaeologists are used to dealing in long periods of time ("a thousand years here, a thousand years there . . ."), but to put the Paleoindian use of the Caja del Rio site into some perspective, there was as much time distance between the earliest Clovis hunters and the last Plano/Cody/Scottsbluff hunters who used this camping spot as there is between us and the Sumerian city states that developed along the Tigris and Euphrates Rivers between 3,000–2,000 B.C.E.[33]

In addition to classifying the wide range of tool styles recovered from the Caja del Rio site, people have recognized that the tools were made from an equally wide assortment of materials, not all of which were locally available (fig. 20). Several tools, including a Clovis point, an Angostura point, and several unidentifiable knife blades, were fashioned from obsidian, presumably obtained from sources in the Jemez

CULTURAL PERIODS	APPROXIMATE TIME PERIODS
Clovis	13,000 – 11,500 B.P.
Folsom	11,500 – 10,500 B.P.
Agate Basin	10,500 – 9,500 B.P.
Scottsbluff	9,000 – 8,000 B.P.
Cody/Eden	9,000 – 8,000 B.P.

Fig. 19. A general time line for the Paleoindian materials recovered at the Caja del Rio Paleoindian site near Santa Fe. Table by Jason S. Shapiro.

Mountains. One Folsom point was made out of local white agate. A Clovis point, a Plainview point, and a Cody/Scottsbluff point were made from what the report describes as "different types of non-local flint." Finally, a Midland point was made from non-local alibates chert, possibly from west Texas.[34] The significance of these findings is twofold: on one hand, the Paleoindian hunters who used the Caja del Rio campsite were obviously aware of high-quality, locally available materials such as Jemez obsidian. On the other hand, some of these hunters also used decidedly non-local but equally high-quality materials, suggesting the possibility of extensive trading connections with people from other areas. More likely, the large territories these hunters covered over the course of their annual rounds likely included camping at high-quality stone procurement sites.[35]

The Caja del Rio site does not stand alone. Across the Rio Grande and up into the Jemez Mountains is another Clovis site that may also have two later Cody Complex components (ca. 8,500 B.P.).[36] Given the location of this site, we can infer that Paleoindians hunted game in a variety of settings at different elevations. Another local Clovis discovery was a small tool cache found in the Tesuque Basin, just a few miles to the north of Santa Fe. Three large biface blades[37] and a flake tool made from high-quality flint and obsidian obtained at least thirty-five or forty miles away from where the cache was found reinforce our perception of Clovis people as seekers of premium lithic resources.[38]

In addition to identified campsites there have been a number of what archeologists call *isolated occurrences* (IOs) discovered in the vicinity of Santa Fe, which typically, but not always, consist of a complete or identifiable portion of a Paleoindian projectile point.[39] Isolated occurrences are often of only limited value to archaeologists, but considering the number and distribution of Paleoindian tools and projectile points found in the environs of Santa Fe, I think there is a case to be made that at a minimum this area was a regular stopping place and productive hunting area for mobile Paleoindian bands. Paleoindian artifacts have been found north of the city at the confluence of the Chama and Rio Grande Rivers[40] as well as in the Abiquiu and Tesuque Basin areas, east of the city in the Sangre de Cristo Mountains and in the Galisteo Basin,[41] west of the city in the area of Las Campanas[42] as well as in the Jemez Mountains, southwest of the city in the vicinity of the community of Agua Fria,[43] and a bit further south on the Caja del Rio.[44] Most of these sites represent one or at best a few recognizable projectile styles made at different times and from a variety of local and non-local materials. The only thing that ties them all together is that they are indisputably Paleoindian. People are, without a doubt, social animals, and it is possible that the local availability of important resources such as game, water, wood, and high-quality stone made Santa Fe a place where small bands of people could rendezvous at certain times of the year in order to hunt, conduct group ceremonies, find suitable mates, and share information. I noted in Chapter 1 how the Sangre de Cristo Mountains shield Santa Fe from the frigid winter air coming down the Great Plains, and these mountains would have performed the same function during the harsh climate regimes of the terminal Pleistocene. This suggestion that Santa Fe was a relatively gentler place for people to

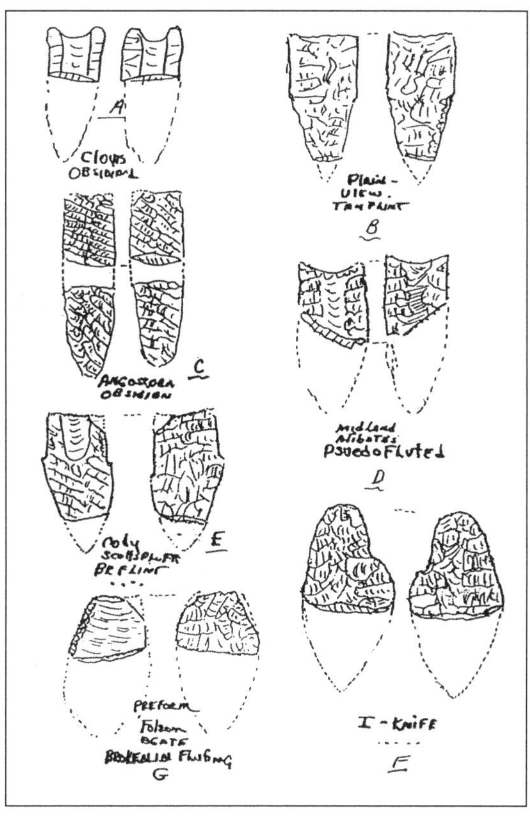

Fig. 20. Field sketches of selected Paleoindian points recovered from the Caja del Rio site. Sketches by Ed Hyde from a report by Williams, Roney, and Schoeneberg (1996).

gentler place for people to congregate during harsher times of the year is an extension of an idea developed in connection with Paleoindian life on the Great Plains. During the winter, "areas of the Central and Northern Plains were abandoned for better-watered and ecologically-richer refugia in the foothills and Front Range of the Rocky Mountains."[45] For nomadic Paleoindians with broad territorial ranges, the walk from the Plains east of Las Vegas, New Mexico, to winter refugia camps in Santa Fe would not have been very demanding, particularly if migrating herds of animals had the same idea.

At this point, an enterprising reader might wonder if Santa Fe were such a popular Paleoindian destination, why have archaeologists not found more remnants of Paleoindian life? A well-worn axiom among archaeologists is that "absence of evidence is not necessarily evidence of absence." As I noted, Paleoindian sites have been subject to as many as 12,000 years of intense weathering, erosion, and deposition. It is likely that a number of local Paleoindian sites either lie undiscovered under several feet of alluvial deposits, such as the Clovis site near Tesuque, or, for any sites in close proximity to the Rio Grande or Santa Fe rivers, periodic floods may have scoured them away. On the other hand, the number and array of identifiable projectile points discovered around Santa Fe makes it obvious that Paleoindians were familiar with this area. Even though no Paleoindian residential structures or burials have been discovered, we know Santa Fe offered a rich mixture of environmental settings, raw materials, and animals. Santa Fe *must* have been an advantageous place for Paleoindians because there were so few of them and they had such a huge number of habitats from which to choose that unless the area had a lot to offer they would not have returned here again and again for thousands of years.

The Paleoindian Period lasted approximately 4,500 years in the Southwest, from roughly 12,000 to between 8,000 and 7,500 years ago. The first people to stop living the Paleoindian lifestyle were in the far west, where long-term warming and drying trends first began to affect and change existing plant and animal communities. Readers should also keep in mind that Paleoindian life was not static. Over the course of 4,500 years, people learned to exploit particular environments more proficiently even as the environments themselves were changing. Archaeologists describe these changes reflected in the increasing specialization of Paleoindian stone tool technologies. We recognize the beauty and superb craftsmanship of Clovis projectiles, but these were generalized implements designed to kill and process a variety of large animals. People did not stop producing and using Clovis technology because

APPROXIMATE TIME PERIOD	DESCRIPTIONS OF SOUTHWESTERN CLIMATE (RELATIVE TO TODAY'S CLIMATE)
<10,000 B.C.E.	Cooler and moister
10,000 – 9,500 B.C.E.	Warmer and drier
9,500 – 9,000 B.C.E.	Warmer and moister
8,500 – 5,000 B.C.E.	Warmer and drier, beginning of the Holocene Period
6,500 – 5,000 B.C.E.	Decreased moisture and more local fluctuations and variability, which created more local patchiness (essentially same climate as today)

Fig. 21. Shifting climate during the Paleoindian Period. Table by Jason S. Shapiro.

they got bored with it but because the ecological conditions, including the presence of certain types of animals that made that technology so effective and rewarding, were no longer the same. By the end of the Paleoindian Period, people were producing an assortment of more specialized kinds of tools that reflected new and different ways of exploring plant and animal communities. The end of the Pleistocene was not "climatically smooth" and cyclical patterns of severe interspersed with more moderate weather placed new demands upon these late Paleoindian in terms of how they could make a living.

For example, after a few thousand warm, dry years, a freezing period called the Younger Dryas began about 12,700 years ago and lasted perhaps 1,000 years, after which global temperatures warmed again (fig. 21).[46] Beginning around 8,500 B.C.E. large-scale climatic oscillations resulted in the *Altithermal*, a period of almost four thousand years that was characterized by warmer and/or drier conditions. The warming up and drying out of the Pleistocene landscapes proceeded from west to east across the Southwest and heralded the beginning of the geologic epoch labeled the *Holocene*, the same period in which we are living today. Over the course of a few thousand years, these conditions caused the large Pleistocene lakes to dry up and the arid zones to expand throughout the Southwest. Even the Altithermal conditions were not constant as another global cooling event occurred about 8,200 years ago. Although less intense than the Younger Dryas, it still had an impact. Large-scale temperature fluctuations made seasonality more pronounced, with summers becoming hotter and drier and winters becoming colder and moister, substantially altering the plant and animal communities upon which the Paleoindians had learned to depend. Remember, we are talking about events that played out over thousands of years. People whose lifespans rarely exceeded forty years may not have perceived the prolonged climatic changes. As archaeologists looking at the accumulated changes in artifact styles and settlement locations, we can see how over many generations people adapted to new conditions by adjusting where they lived, what they ate, and how often they moved.

In my opinion, people are inherently conservative. Whenever possible they lived and foraged within familiar landscapes and kept the economic systems that worked. When environmental changes fostered the development of new plant and animal communities, people altered their lifestyles in ways that archaeologists find reflected in changes in tool technology and subsistence practices. We will never know who the first stone tool innovator was or why he or she convinced their band members to begin making a different kind of projectile, but we have learned how the forms of stone tools changed over time and how associated food procurement and organizational strategies changed as well. Where early Paleoindians procured high-quality stone from quarries hundreds of miles away, later groups began to rely on more localized stone sources that, while not as high quality, were plentiful and more accessible.

Several decades ago archaeologist H. M. Wormington described the manner in which Paleoindian subsistence strategies diverged following the disappearance of the Clovis culture.[47] She drew a distinction between western Paleoindian groups whose subsistence practices became more dependent upon plant collecting and the hunting of smaller, nonmigratory animals, and eastern Paleoindian groups whose subsistence practices became focused on bison hunting. More recently, Linda Cordell expanded this distinction to include a third, foothills-focused strategy.[48] Although neither the western nor eastern post-Clovis adaptations seem to apply to Santa Fe, Cordell's third, "foothills adaptation" seems to reflect what occurred. Santa Fe is located in close proximity to the physiographic provinces of the southern Rocky Mountains, Great Plains, and Colorado Plateau. The juxtaposition of these ecologically diverse areas would have made up for the relative lack of abundance of any particular food source and presented people with more options. In this case, the ecological setting may help to explain the wide diversity of both types and time periods of Paleoindian artifacts that have been found in the vicinity of Santa Fe. Unlike the post-Clovis foragers in the Great Basin or the bison hunters on the Great Plains, the Paleoindian visitors to Santa Fe were not faced with an "either/or" situation but could continue to choose from an assortment of subsistence alternatives and technologies that exploited both animals and plants.

All across the Southwest, the Pleistocene megafaunal populations became more and more reduced until they virtually disappeared around 10,000 years ago. Not surprisingly, as this was occurring Paleoindian reliance upon larger herd animals gave way to new styles of foraging that relied upon seasonally available plants as well as animal species that did not migrate. The process of modifying longstanding patterns of food collecting certainly affected people in Santa Fe and its environs, where the archaeological evidence suggests that mobile bands began exploiting smaller and more localized territories. Eventually the persistent warming trends associated with the Altithermal caused even more noticeable changes throughout the Southwest. The new opportunities associated with different plant and animal foods, as well as the techniques needed to collect, process, and store them, became integral to the next cultural period that we will examine, the Archaic.

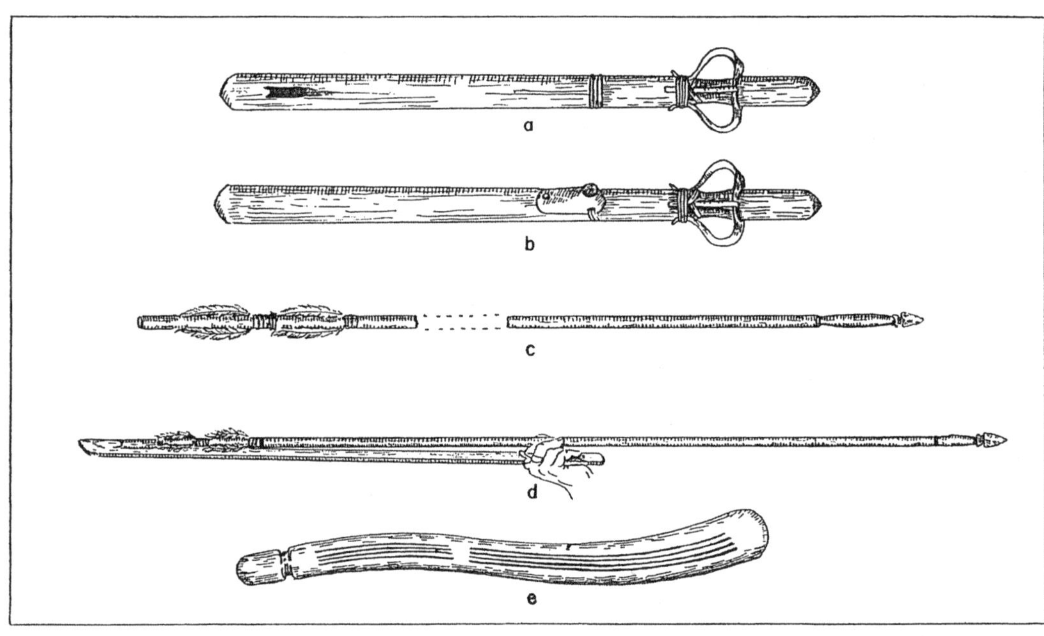

Fig. 22. Spear thrower, or atlatl, system. Illustration by H. M. Wormington (1957).

Chapter 4

Seasonal Visitors

ARCHAIC HUNTERS, GATHERERS, AND FORAGERS

Santa Fe is one of those places that seem to collect people from somewhere else — people show up and fall in love with the light, the space, and the "cute vernacular people living in their cute vernacular houses." Upon their arrival these newcomers often set out to redefine "the meaning of Santa Fe" to conform to their own vision, but usually all that happens is that the idea of Santa Fe gets reinvented again and again.[1] From Pedro de Peralta in 1610, to General Stephen Kearny in 1846, to the entrepreneurial wagon masters on the Santa Fe Trail, to the eccentric artists of the early 20th century, to the hippies and the "rich and beautiful" jetsetters later in the 20th century — many different kinds of people have found this town a satisfying and rewarding place to spend some time. Recently it was estimated that as many as 16 percent of the houses in Santa Fe are second or even third homes and are occupied only a few weeks or months in the course of a year. This contemporary phenomenon is not the first instance of transient, seasonal, and part-time residency in Santa Fe, but the belongings of the early seasonal residents were pretty minimal — yucca fiber sandals, spear throwers and stone-tipped darts (fig. 22), a few stone or bone tools, some baskets, cordage-woven nets, and maybe a rabbit fur blanket or two. Several thousand years ago, these few things were enough to make it in Santa Fe.

I explained in Chapter 3 how beginning with the Holocene Period around eight thousand years ago, noticeable changes began to occur in Paleoindian cultural patterns. As the last Ice Age ended and the earth became progressively warmer and drier, large areas of wetlands favorable to rich concentrations of plants and animals began to dry up, and the coniferous forests that characterized the end of the Pleistocene Period became much less extensive. Those climatic changes also resulted in strongly seasonal rainfall patterns that encouraged the profusion of certain varieties of annual seed-bearing plants. These new climatic patterns remained relatively stable over thousands of years and created ecological communities with more kinds of plants that could be collected, dried, and stored for later use. There was a corollary that many of the useful plants grew in widely dispersed areas and were only seasonally available. With the advent of ecological changes across the entire Southwest, people embarked upon different paths of cultural evolution, but all of them adopted subsistence strategies that emphasized small, mobile bands whose members became very familiar with selected locales. At this point, I want to introduce the Archaic Period. Unlike the Paleoindians who hunted a variety of megafauna because those animals were generally available, Archaic people adopted more generalized approaches to subsistence because long-term climatic changes had altered the availability of selected foods. People hadn't grown tired of mammoth rump roasts, but such items were no longer on the menu. The numbers of artifacts recovered from Archaic sites are not only greater than the numbers from Paleoindian sites, but they tend to be more variable in their appearance. Archaeologists attribute these differences to the fact that as groups of people began living in more geographically limited areas than their Paleoindian forebears, they developed more localized artifact styles.

Archaeologists assign thousands of years of prehistory to the Paleoindian and Archaic periods, and it is sometimes hard to convey to non-archaeologists both the time depth and the point of separation of these periods. Readers should consider that contemporary Santa Feans are much closer in time to the last pre-agricultural Archaic people who lived here a mere 1,500 or 1,600 years ago than those same Archaic people were to the last Paleoindian hunters, who disappeared 6,000 years earlier. The transition from Paleoindian to Archaic was a gradual process. As one study concluded, "The cultural package recognized by archaeologists as Archaic did not develop as a synchronous set in a linear fashion, *rather individual embedded strategies within Paleoindian societies developed at different rates*" (emphasis added).[2] Translation: the lifestyles and technologies that we associate with Archaic people did not all happen at the same time, in the same place, or in the same manner.

During the Archaic Period, people shifted the primary focus of their food selection away from reliance on larger herd animals, such as mammoth and bison, to smaller animals, such as antelope and deer. Eventually people adopted more generalized strategies that combined exploiting smaller, non-migratory game animals with more intensive collecting of a wide assortment of wild plants. Ultimately, the kinds of adaptations that archaeologists associate with the Archaic Period provided the cultural conditions for the adoption of agriculture, but that is really a story for the next chapter. Archaeologists often note how Archaic populations seemingly took advantage of a much wider gamut of food sources than did the Paleoindians, implying greater ecological awareness, but in fact many of these foodstuffs, particularly certain varieties of seed plants, were not yet available in sufficient quantities to have been worthwhile options for earlier groups trying to make a living in the cooler and wetter conditions at the end of the Pleistocene. Five or six thousand years ago local temperatures were similar to those we experience today, but there would have been more precipitation and consequently more woodlands and grasslands than are currently present, especially in the piedmont areas west of Santa Fe. These conditions would have created excellent habitat for mule deer and antelope, evidenced by the recovery of their bones from Archaic Period sites.[3] In addition to these medium-sized animals, abundant populations of rabbits, ground squirrels, turkey, quail, and grouse would have been available for hunting and trapping.[4] Despite or perhaps because of long-term climatic shifts, the mountains, meadows, fields, and streams around Santa Fe continued to provide many food options for hunters and gatherers.

In the middle northern Rio Grande, Archaic sites are distinguished from Paleoindian sites by the presence of smaller projectile points used on spear thrower darts (fig. 22), hearths or the presence of fire-cracked rock,[5] storage and roasting pits, grinding stones, and the occasional remnants of semi-permanent structures, such as pole-and-thatch shelters and small pit structures. I mentioned in the preceding chapter how Paleoindians at Blackwater Draw used grinding stones, but for the most part these particular tools have not been found in connection with local Paleoindian sites. The upshot is that in many respects Early Archaic behavior looks very different from late Paleoindian behavior (fig. 23).[6]

The idea of the Archaic as merely a "linkage period" between the earlier Paleoindians and the later Puebloans, when coupled with the ephemeral nature of Archaic sites, has resulted in this period being given somewhat less attention by archaeologists than more recent periods. Indeed, more than one archaeologist has noted how the Archaic has been "treated as if it constituted an extremely long prelude on the way to sedentary and more complex societies."[7] On the other hand, it was

PALEOINDIAN ADAPTATIONS	ARCHAIC ADAPTATIONS
Very high mobility and nonpermanent habitations and camps	High mobility retained but within a context of seasonal camping for longer periods in areas with predictable resources; some use of semi-permanent habitations
Very little midden (waste dump) accumulation	Somewhat greater midden accumulation because of longer occupations in resource-rich areas
Relatively more generalized technology, although it became increasingly specialized over time	More specialized technology, including more varieties of smaller projectile points, use of ground stone tools for more extensive plant processing, use of rabbit sticks, decoys, snares, and nets designed for specific resource capture
More limited resource base of large and medium-sized animals and some plants	More resource diversification in terms of types and varieties of plants and animals
Very low population densities on the land-scape and a focus on the most productive areas	Relatively greater population densities and expansion into more marginal areas
Exchange of high-grade lithics, including long-distance travel or trade for obsidian, chert, calcedony, and flint. Very careful and skillful production of stone tools	More use of local lithic resources and more expedient production of stone tools
Relatively large band ranges	Somewhat reduced band ranges
Relatively little use of or emphasis on food storage technology	Increased importance of food storage; construction of large, communal pits for seeds and nuts

Fig. 23. A comparison of Paleoindian and Archaic lifeways. Table by Jason S. Shapiro.

ARCHAIC PERIOD	PHASE NAME	ASSOCIATED DATES
	En Medio	800 B.C.E.−600 C.E.
	Armijo	1800−800 B.C.E.
	San Jose	3200−1800 B.C.E.
	Bajada	480−3200 B.C.E.
	Jay	6000−4800 B.C.E.
PALEOINDIAN PERIOD		Pre-6000 B.C.E.

Fig. 24. Archaic Period phases associated with the middle Northern Rio Grande Valley and their approximate time frames. Table by Jason S. Shapiro.

during the Archaic Period that groups throughout the Southwest began to express unique regional differences in how they lived that would eventually develop into the well-known manifestations associated with the Hohokam, Mogollon, and Ancestral Puebloans. It is also during the Archaic Period that people learned to understand and exploit the variable environments of the Southwest during climatic regimes that in many cases were not so different from the regimes that the Ancestral Puebloans experienced a few thousand years later or, for that matter, that we experience today.

Like the earlier Paleoindian Period, the Archaic Period is separated into phases according to observed changes in stone tool forms. One sequence of cultural stages applicable to the northern Rio Grande Valley is based upon the research of Cynthia Irwin-Williams and her concept of the *Oshara tradition* (fig. 24).[8] The stages represent different responses to environmental conditions over several thousand years, but there is a certain "hunter-gatherer-forager" continuity that carries through the Archaic Period. Despite the persistence of the Irwin-Williams classification system, which researchers have used for three decades, the phases are no longer considered inviolate. A recent exhaustive study of the Archaic Period in northern New Mexico boldly concludes, "The five phases of the Oshara tradition are largely based on a typology that is poorly defined and poorly dated."[9] This is not to say that cultural evolution did not occur over the course of 6,000 years, only that the details distinguishing one Archaic phase from another are not as clearly separated as Irwin-

Williams initially may have implied and that many aspects of Archaic life did not fundamentally vary for thousands of years.[10]

As with the Paleoindians, one ongoing query is "Who were these people and where did they come from?" There is a difference of opinion among archaeologists concerning whether Archaic groups represent local in-place cultural evolution as Paleoindians continued to adapt to locally changing conditions or whether the different nature of Archaic assemblages represent immigrant populations moving in from somewhere else. Some archaeologists take the position that much of what has been defined as "Archaic" can be explained by local developments without the necessity of finding migrant groups bringing "new" technologies. This perfectly reasonable explanation assumes that either the ecological changes were gradual enough or that local populations were sufficiently innovative to adjust to environmental changes. Given the length of the Archaic Period, it is not unreasonable to conceive of generations becoming accustomed over very long periods of time to alterations in the distribution of plants and animals, all the while attempting to maintain their familiar lifeways. Supporters of this view can point to a number of locations such as the Wilson-Leonard site in Central Texas, where thousands of years of occupational continuity has been documented.[11]

Other archaeologists, notably Cynthia Irwin-Williams, have concluded that there were so many differences between Archaic and Paleoindian assemblages in terms of their stone-working technologies, types of tools, and functional classes of artifacts that there could not have been any discernable connection between Paleoindian and Archaic groups. Irwin-Williams proposed that Archaic cultural deposits must have been created by new groups who moved into the Southwest, probably from areas to the west or south. One of the problems with this approach is that during the 1960s when Irwin-Williams was working, information about Archaic people was limited. Even today the full extent and nature of how people were living during the Archaic is still very much a work in progress. I do not wish to belabor the point, but the tension between local indigenous developments versus imported cultural innovations is a theme that flows through the archaeological literature and is the source of many unresolved conflicts in the interpretation of archaeological remains. Given the size and complexity of cultural evolution in the Southwest there may not be a "one size fits all answer" to the question. It may be necessary to consider the unique contexts of smaller and more localized areas in order to answer questions about the origins of particular manifestations of Archaic culture.

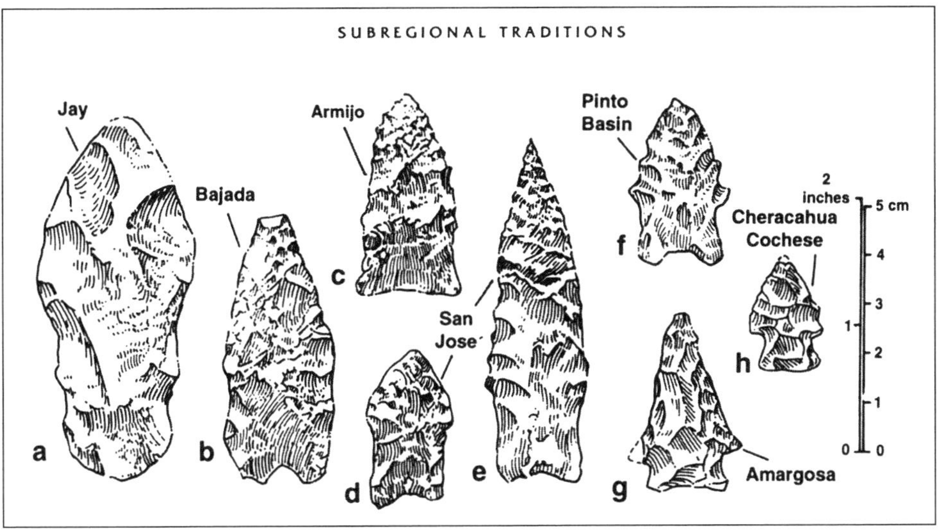

Fig. 25. Examples of some typical Archaic points. Illustration by Marjorie Leggitt, Legitt Design (Cordell 1997), courtesy of Elsevier Press.

The rationale behind technological innovation and change in the archaeological record is not always apparent. When presented with a series of what appear to be different projectile point types, archaeologists must wrestle with the question of whether different types automatically mean different cultures or whether they represent a single culture that produced a variety of points.[12] The range of Archaic point types typically found in the northern middle Rio Grande Valley represent differences in time, place, and hafting technology (fig. 25). Their diverse forms may also reflect that people were hunting different animals, no longer had easy access to superior sources of easily flaked stone, or had changed their ideas about what a "proper projectile" should look like. This last point is often the most difficult to demonstrate archaeologically. Artifacts embody social information. Stylistic distinctions can sometimes be used to develop and test models of more abstract behavior such as social organization ("We are the people who only make these kinds of points, or baskets, or sandals . . .") but this is a very demanding and often controversial method of analysis.[13]

Jay and Bajada points are the earliest Archaic projectile types that scientists have discovered in the vicinity of Santa Fe, both of which are characterized by fairly prominent stems and shoulders. Later Archaic projectiles such as San José and

Fig. 26. Archaic metate, recovered from Tierra Contenta subdivision, Santa Fe County, LA 54751.

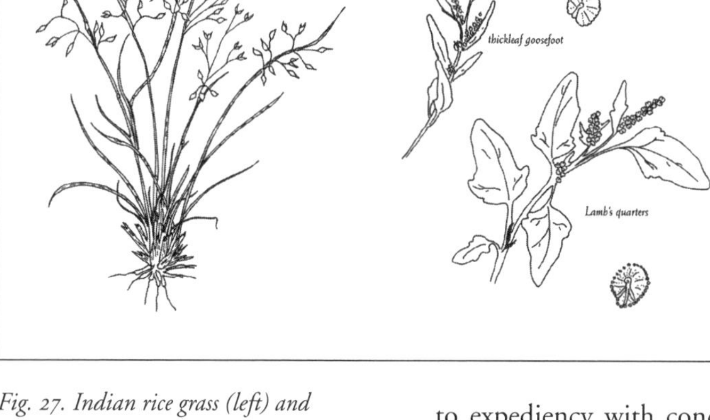

Fig. 27. Indian rice grass (left) and goosefoot. Illustrations by Gail D. Tierney (1995). Courtesy Museum of New Mexico Press.

Armijo points are typified in part by the presence of side notches which, along with stems, indicate different ways of fastening a point onto a spear, dart, or eventually, an arrow. Archaic projectiles not only look different from the preceding Clovis, Folsom, and other Paleoindian points, but they were made differently. The points themselves are smaller, and the processes of raw material selection and flake removal appear less careful and less precise. One no longer sees the beautiful fluting characteristic of the earlier points. These changes did not arise because these people were any less capable or sophisticated than their Paleoindian predecessors but in light of the more seasonal nature and more intensive exploitation of local plant resources, it no longer made economic sense for people to spend an inordinate amount of time traveling to the finest stone locations and creating the most finely crafted projectile points. Over time, superlative craftsmanship in tool production gave way to expediency with concomitantly less effort assigned to tool maintenance.[15] Irrespective of the reasons, archaeologist and expert flint knapper Bruce Bradley has observed, " . . . the complex [stone working] sequences seen in Folsom and Cody [Paleoindian] technology have never been seen again."[14] This is not to say that Archaic points were not effective or sturdy—some projectile styles persisted for 1,000 years or more, and locally-available basalt from which many points were made is extremely durable. In comparison with Paleoindian points, one can say of Archaic points that "good enough was good enough."

Another hallmark of the Archaic involves more pervasive use of what archaeologists call "ground stone technology." The presence of tools such as manos and metates[16] indicates that people were making more extensive use of wild foods such as seeds and nuts. The underlying granite geology of the Sangre de Cristo Mountains provided excellent raw materials for ground stone tools. The one-hand cobble manos and shallow basin metates developed by Archaic people represent precursors to a very significant economic shift that would eventually occur, the transition to agriculture (fig. 26). I'm not saying that the advent of ground stone implements equates with agriculture, especially since I discussed essentially the same technology in connection with the Clovis culture at Blackwater Draw. Rather, it was the ability of Late Archaic populations to use grinding stones to process a variety of wild seeds such as Indian rice grass (*Oryzopsis hymenoides*) and goosefoot (*Chenopodium* spp.) (fig. 27) that, in a sense, prepared people to make use of cultigens such as maize when they became available. In other words, people learned to become grain processors long before they became grain producers.

Although the geomorphology of Santa Fe does not provide a profuse landscape of caves and rock shelters,[17] in other parts of the Southwest those kinds of protected environments have preserved remnants of otherwise perishable artifacts that include sandals, baskets, cordage, and netting. These attest to the fact that plants were much more integral to daily life than merely as food sources. As the Archaic progressed, people moved around less because they were no longer following migratory herds of large animals for their basic needs. Less movement implies relatively more sedentism, a behavior generally associated with population increases. It also meant that people had fewer long-range social contacts, at least in comparison to the earlier Paleoindian Period. Fewer long-range contacts ultimately means less interchange of tools, foods, potential mates, and ideas, along with a much more intense exploitation of local areas. As groups of generalized foragers became increasingly more focused on the immediate areas in which they lived, they began to differentiate from one another, a development formalized by Irwin-Williams in her descriptive *Picosa* idea (fig. 28).

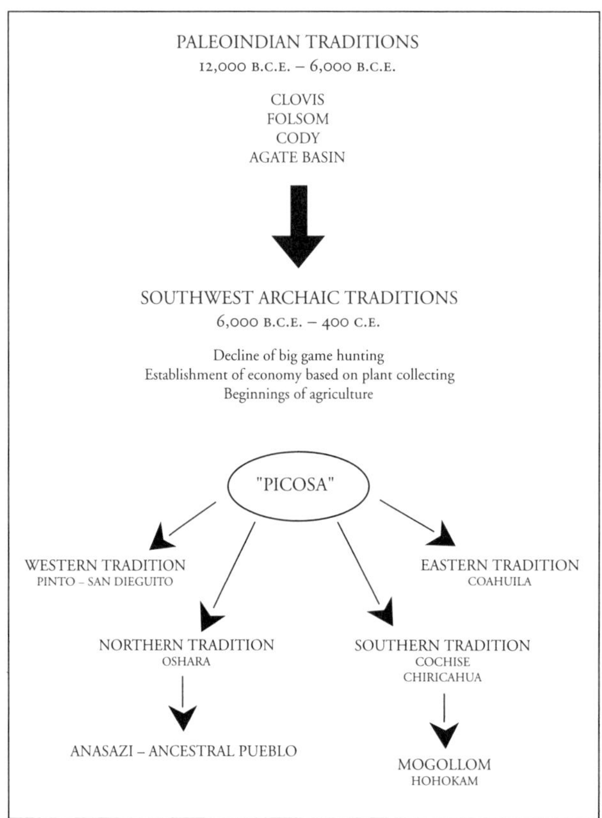

Fig. 28. Cynthia Irwin-Williams's Archaic Period "Picosa" scheme. Illustration by Jason S. Shapiro.

One of the most important things that Cynthia Irwin-Williams accomplished was to bring order to and draw connections between what she defined as regional Archaic practices and the subsequent Ancestral Puebloan and other cultural traditions. The previously mentioned Oshara tradition is one of four broad sequences (Pinto-San Dieguito, Cochise-Chiricahua, Oshara, Coahuila) that describe regionally distinct populations of Archaic hunters, gatherers, and foragers who relied upon similar resource strategies but used different tactics to achieve those strategies. For example, among the four traditions there were differences in the relative reliance on plants versus animals depending upon the mix of locally available species. Not surprisingly, there were also differences in material culture, including projectile styles, tools, and settlement forms that were generally reflective of locally available raw materials. Although the expression of Archaic culture in the area around Santa Fe is almost always associated with Oshara elements, the movement or cultural diffusion of Archaic people is illustrated by archaeological finds in the Galisteo Basin and at Ojala Cave in Bandelier National Monument that archaiologists identified with the Cochise tradition that developed in southeastern Arizona – southwestern New Mexico.[18] These findings do not mean that Irwin-Williams's categories are not valid but that archaeologists may need to reconsider just how mobile some Archaic groups might have been. In some respects, the Archaic presents us with a dichotomy. In the broadest terms over the entire course of the Archaic, there were common developments such as the use of more specialized tool kits, the adoption of the bow and arrow, the construction of larger and more substantial domestic structures, the use of larger storage pits, and the digging of wells. Viewed from narrower and more localized perspectives, one begins to see the kinds of cultural differentiations that ultimately split into the three major cultural traditions summarized in Chapter 1. From that standpoint, it is interesting to see how the broad regional distinctions became discernible over the course of some thousands of years.

Fig. 29. La Bajada Archaic Period site. Photograph by Jason S. Shapiro.

All Archaic foragers relied to a greater or lesser degree upon *mobility*. The earliest hunter-gatherers seem to have been more dependent upon "encounter-based" strategies where the ability of small groups migrating over large areas to find enough to eat was somewhat chancier ("Gee, I sure hope we run into some bison."). As people became more familiar with smaller territories, they modified this approach. Rather than constantly moving an entire residential band, people set up base camps and dispatched small collecting expeditions that covered as many as 20 miles in a single day. Later Archaic groups were very familiar with all aspects of their locales and knew what plants and animals would most likely be available at specific locations during particular times of the year ("I know exactly where the antelope herd hangs out."). Nature was not always cooperative and sometimes being a good ecologist was not enough to keep the entire band fed, but some areas in the Southwest were more biologically rich and productive than others. If persistence of the Archaic lifestyle is a proxy measure for the long-term availability of wild foods, then Santa Fe may have been one of those locally productive areas.

The Archaic tradition in and around Santa Fe is both extensive and long-lasting, with some Archaic sites dating to more than 7,000 years ago[19] while others have been dated to a mere 1,500 years ago. One of the most significant local Archaic Period sites is located less than fifteen miles southwest of downtown Santa Fe within close proximity to Tetilla Peak, a prominent piedmont landmark. Cynthia Irwin-Williams excavated the La Bajada site[20] (fig. 29), the source of a distinctive projectile style called "Bajada points" that also supplies the name for one of the earliest Archaic phases (Bajada Phase 4800 – 3200 B.C.E.). Examples of these points have been found as far away as southern New Mexico and west Texas.

As is typical of many early Archaic sites, La Bajada is located on a mesa top near a canyon head with good views in all directions, and could have functioned easily as a temporary base camp from which smaller groups could make short collecting trips. The local geology is characterized by volcanic basalt, a good material for making a variety of stone tools. In addition, the site is close to the mesa edge, which slopes down to a flat, well-watered valley floor. Both the mesa top and valley floor would have contained a variety of exploitable plant and animal species, and the site was within walking distance of the Santa Fe River, the Rio Grande, and the Jemez and Sangre de Cristo Mountains. Unlike sites in which the prehistoric living surface is buried under substantial amounts of wind or water-borne soil, the La Bajada site is characterized by a wide scattering of surface deposits that suggest repeated use of the same general locale over several thousands of years. Stone tools, flakes, and finished points are not hard to find on this site, but there is an interpretive problem because the exposed location and consequent wind erosion has limited the formation of stratigraphic layers of soil. In lay terms, the site has mixed deposits of artifacts that cover several thousand years of prehistory and are all located at or very near the ground surface. Consequently, there is no accurate way to distinguish the chronology except by identifying specific point types that have been dated in other locations.

The area around the La Bajada site looks pretty barren today, but when looking at contemporary surroundings in the Rio Grande Valley readers should bear in mind the impact of a few hundred years of sheep, goats, and cattle in denuding the landscape. Around 5,000 years ago, the Southwest climate shifted and became warmer and wetter. Permanent springs were more numerous as were locally available wild foods. Culturally, we see these changes reflected in what is called the "San Jose Phase," defined by a different and more refined style of projectile point than what people produced during the earlier Bajada Phase.

During the San Jose Phase people expanded their use of the broad, flat floodplains that stretch west and south from Santa Fe, as well as the foothills north of the city that stretch into the Tesuque Valley.[21] Many Archaic sites have been identified within the past ten to fifteen years as the direct result of numerous road construction and housing projects. Aside from road cuts, most of these sites have been found on

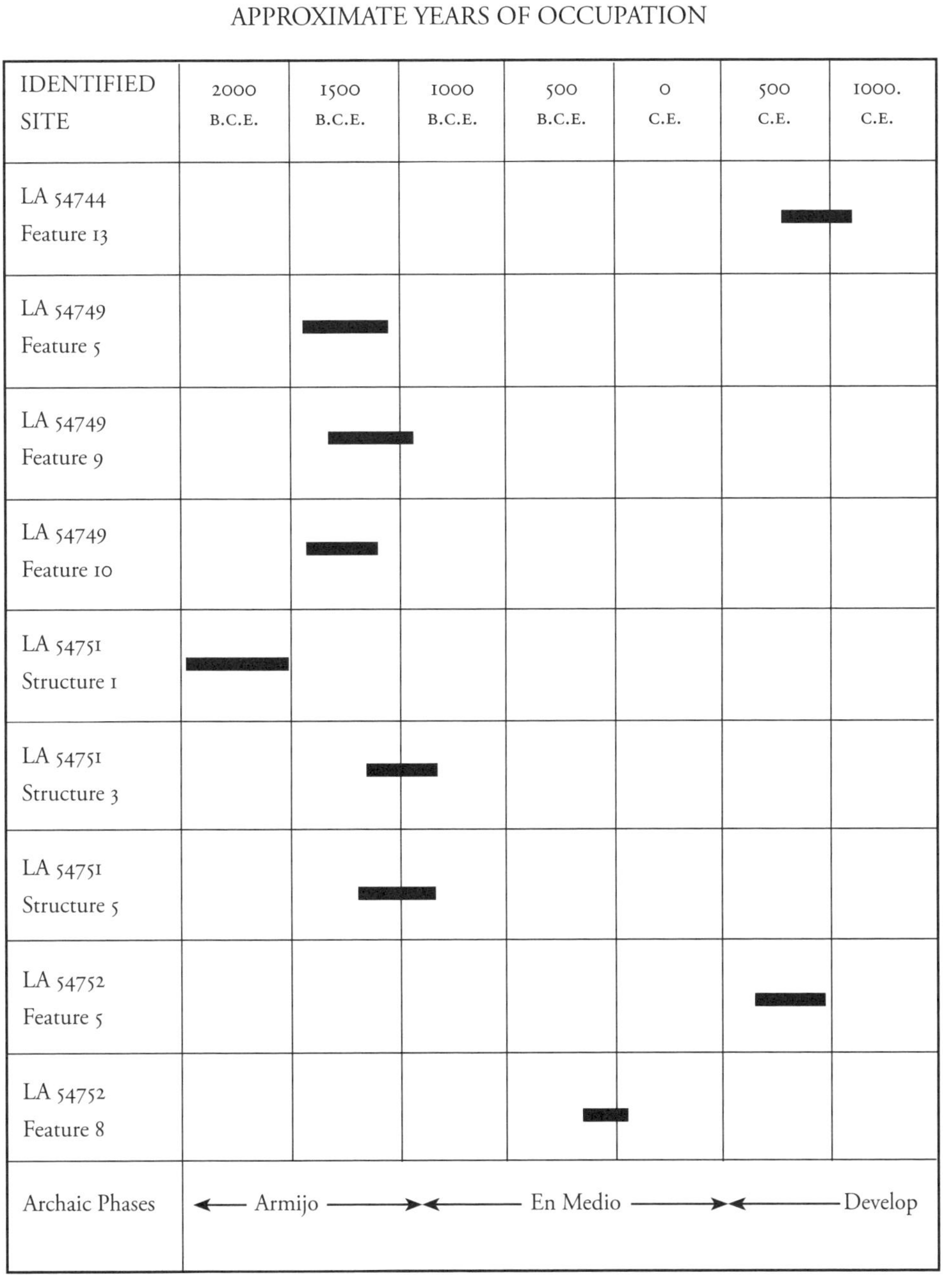

APPROXIMATE YEARS OF OCCUPATION

IDENTIFIED SITE	2000 B.C.E.	1500 B.C.E.	1000 B.C.E.	500 B.C.E.	0 C.E.	500 C.E.	1000. C.E.
LA 54744 Feature 13						▬	
LA 54749 Feature 5		▬					
LA 54749 Feature 9		▬					
LA 54749 Feature 10		▬					
LA 54751 Structure 1	▬						
LA 54751 Structure 3		▬					
LA 54751 Structure 5		▬					
LA 54752 Feature 5						▬	
LA 54752 Feature 8				▬			
Archaic Phases	← Armijo →		← En Medio →			← Develop	

Fig. 31. Occupation periods for selected Tierra Contenta Archaic sites.
Table by Jason S. Shapiro (adapted from Schmader et al. [1994]).

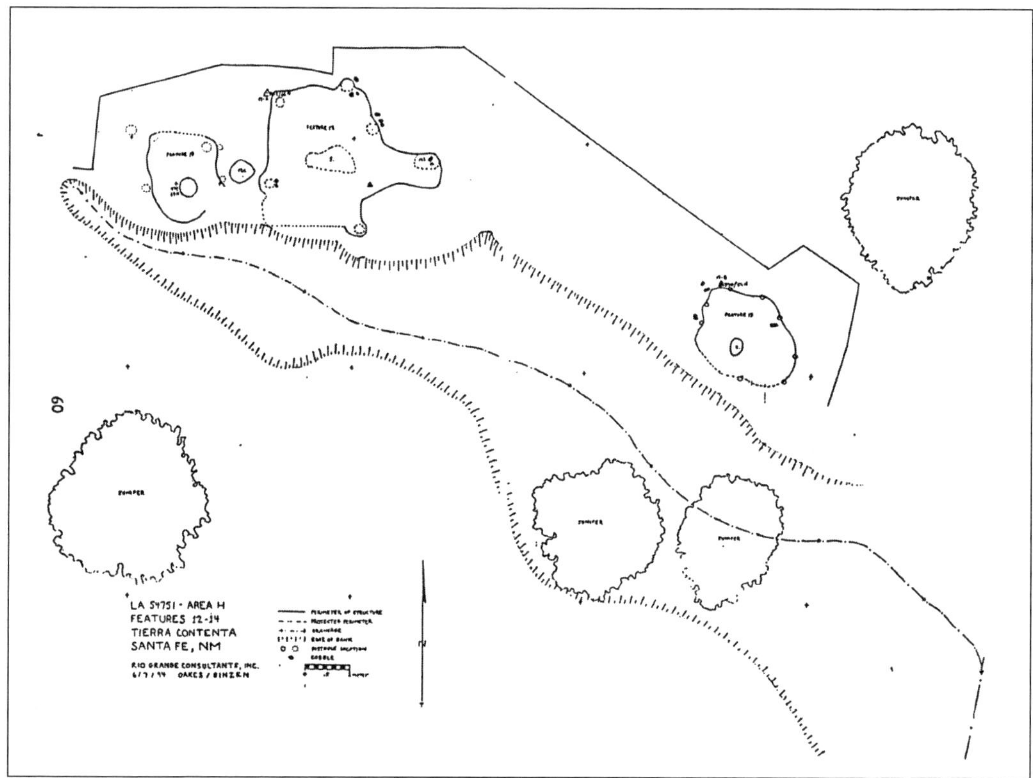

Fig. 32. Site map of LA 54751 showing the arrangement of three Archaic Period structures. Schmader et al. (1994), courtesy City of Santa Fe Planning Department.

eroded surfaces cut by arroyos, along exposed canyon rims, or on low foothills.[22] In other words, most of these sites were completely obscured and would not have been visible but for the surface disturbances associated with man-made construction or natural erosional processes. "So What?" The overall density of Archaic occupation was certainly more extensive than virtually all early studies allowed for, and while the number of still-buried sites is unknown, the Archaic presence was probably more widespread than even our best contemporary data suggest. The idea of a substantially "invisible" Archaic occupation should not come as a surprise as almost fifty years ago an Archaic site just north of Santa Fe was discovered buried under approximately ten feet of alluvial deposits.[23] Numerous subsequent studies in areas south, west, northwest, and north of the city, including recent work at the Tesuque Interchange on Route 285 north of the city, have found extensive Archaic occupations several feet below the current land surface.[24]

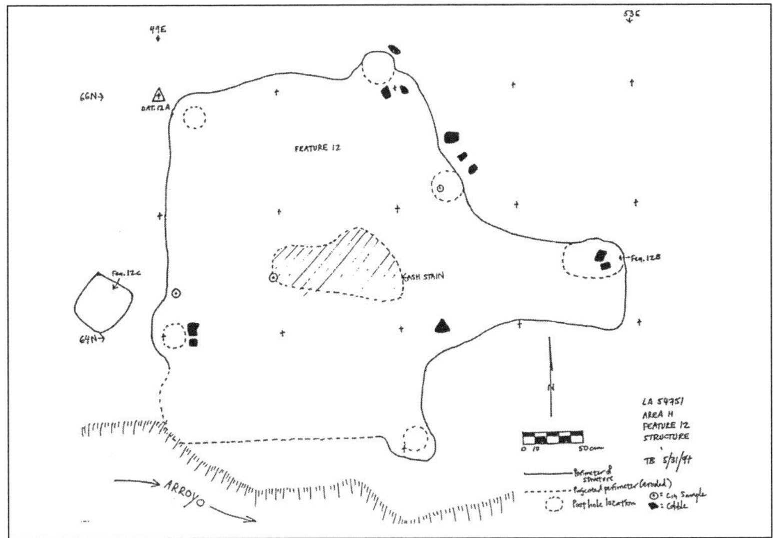

Fig. 33. Illustration of an Archaic Period structure, LA 54751 Pit Structure 3. Schmader et al. (1988). Courtesy City of Santa Fe Planning Department.

Beginning around 3,800 years ago during what has been called the "Late Archaic," there is evidence that greater numbers of people were living in the Santa Fe area. We know that groups used and reused locally productive areas because archaeologists have found their campsites. Many of these sites have been identified as small temporary hunting camps,[25] or stone quarries,[26] and one can assume that if people were creating numerous small, specialized, limited activity sites then larger base camps also must have existed. In fact, several of these semi-permanent camps have been discovered in piedmont areas to the northwest of Santa Fe near Las Campanas[27] and southwest of the city as described by Schmader, Oakes, and Binzen in their Tierra Contenta Survey report.[28]

In terms of some background, the Tierra Contenta subdivision was comprised initially of almost 1,500 acres located south of Santa Fe, immediately to the west of Cerrillos Road and the Cerrillos Road interchange with Interstate 25. As described by Schmader and others, "The project area is situated on relatively level terrain dissected by minor drainages of the Arroyo de los Chamisas and the local terrain generally slopes downhill from the northeast to the southwest, the direction of flow for the arroyo. . . ."[29] Within that area archaeologists investigated a series of sites that produced radiocarbon dates indicating occupations from the Armijo Phase, the En

Medio Phase, and extending into the Early Developmental Period.[30] A Late Archaic occupation spanned more than 2,600 years (fig. 31). As with the Chapter 3 discussion of the Paleoindian Caja del Rio site, archaeologists do not believe that these areas were continuously occupied during the subject time span but have concluded that these locales were sufficiently attractive so that people wanted to return to the same general area over and over again.

The Tierra Contenta Survey identified eight Late Archaic structures at four different sites. Some of the most noteworthy findings occurred at site LA 54751, where archaeologists excavated three pit structures dating to the Armijo Phase (1800–800 B.C.E.) (fig. 32). The actual radiocarbon dates associated with each structure indicates that they were occupied at different periods separated by a couple of hundred years, but of more importance is the indication that not only were people visiting Santa Fe on a regular basis between three and four thousand years ago, they were also staying long enough to justify the construction of some fairly substantial residential structures. What is striking at LA 54751 is the spatial arrangement of the three structures. As Schmader noted in his report, "the structures are placed in such a way as to suggest interior and exterior uses of space and possible different functions of the structures themselves."[31] Clearly the small (probably familial) group who built this residential cluster knew exactly where they wanted to be and how they wanted their living arrangements to look. Three thousand years ago this was a good spot to live because people had easy access to water, game, wild plants, and suitable material for stone tools. While this pit house cluster may not have been a permanent, year-round residence, its appearance supports the notion that around 3,000 years ago people were making fewer moves and staying for longer periods near Santa Fe.

A more detailed plan view of pit structure 3 illustrates the nature of Late Archaic residential architecture (fig. 33). Structure 3 was oriented with its doorway facing east and measured approximately 2.5 by 3 meters, providing a living area of 7.5 square meters or about 81 square feet. Now, many contemporary Santa Fe houses contain closets substantially larger than this 9 by 9 foot shallow pit house but the planning, construction, and maintenance of this and other similar structures represent a marked change in how people were living in Santa Fe because they imply a greater sense of *permanency*. In addition to the pit structure itself, several features identified as hearths were found to contain a variety of edible wild plant remains, including *chenopodium* seeds, amaranth, *portulaca*, grama grass, and piñon nuts.[32] Information obtained through the excavation of additional structures together with scientific analysis of more than a dozen groundstone tools (one-handed manos and metates) suggests that there were sufficient volumes of wild foods to allow Archaic bands to live close to Santa Fe for substantial parts of the year. The discovery of several projectile points and two scrapers supports an inference that people were not merely hunting animals for food but were processing hides for clothing, containers, or perhaps tent covers.[33] It is worth mentioning that at none of the sites examined by Schmader was there any evidence of maize or other domesticated plants. This finding is consistent with other contemporaneous local sites[34] but contrasts with evidence that Late Archaic groups in other parts of the northern Southwest already were experimenting with agriculture. Overall, Schmader's findings illuminate one small part of a widespread pattern that characterized Late Archaic lifeways around Santa Fe.[35]

The "big picture" view is that towards the end of the Archaic Period the number of sites in the vicinity of Santa Fe proliferated. Archaeologists have discovered long-term and short-term base camps as well as numerous special use hunting and raw material collection sites, some of which were used multiple times. The appearance of numerous small sites may have been the result of a general population influx with more people creating more sites as groups moved up the Rio Grande corridor and its tributaries. An alternate and not necessarily inconsistent explanation is that local populations expanded and used more and different environmental settings and so created sites in many new locations.

Some local bands may have adopted a *transhumant* lifestyle, meaning they moved from lowland areas to highland and even mountain areas, taking advantage of different ecozones within more circumscribed areas instead of following an annual round across much more extensive geographic regions. This type of adaptation has been hypothesized for Late Archaic groups living in the eastern Galisteo Basin that is neither very far from nor as biologically rich as the areas around Santa Fe.[36] People living near Santa Fe could have shifted their temporary residential camps from the riparian areas near the Rio Grande and lower Santa Fe Rivers, where fish, turtles, and water-loving plants such as cattails and arrow-weed would have been available in the spring, through the grassland savannah on the broad floodplains west of the city, where Indian rice grass, amaranth, dropseed, goosefoot, and other small seed plants provided early summer greens and, later in the summer, ripe seeds. In the fall, people would have moved into the piñon-juniper woodlands located to the north and east of the city for the collection of piñon nuts, cactus fruits, and juniper berries, and finally into the higher Ponderosa pine and mixed conifer forests of the Sangre de Cristo Mountains for fall deer and elk hunting. Finally, they would return to the lower valley of the Santa Fe River near the Rio Grande.[37] Winter was probably the time when food sources were most limited and least predictable, and people would have relied on a combination of hunting, stored foods, and edible roots such as wild potato (*Solanum* spp.), wafer parsnip (*Cymopterus* spp.), and nodding or wild onion (*Allium* spp.).[38] Support for transhumance is found in the range of Late Archaic site locations that include areas near the Santa Fe River,[39] piedmont plains west and southwest of the city,[40] foothills and piedmont areas to the north, south, and southeast of Santa Fe,[41] and finally, sites within the Sangre de Cristo Mountains, including some at altitudes above 11,000 feet.[42] Seasonal transhumance was just another kind of annual migration that constituted a vertical rather than a horizontal connection to the landscape. It was tied to the cyclical availability of ripening nuts, berries, and seed grasses as well as changing concentrations of game animals.

Was Santa Fe a magnet for Late Archaic development because of its high concentration of local resources? Some archaeologists have suggested that the ecologically diverse vegetation in the area of Cochiti Reservoir, less than 25 miles south of Santa Fe, made that area sufficiently productive to supply groups of hunters and gatherers with enough collectible foods so that they could "avoid the labor intensification of early horticulture."[43] With literally hundreds of wild plants potentially available for food, clothing, medicine, and other uses,[44] I believe that a similar argument applies to Santa Fe, a locale with substantial natural productivity. The relatively short distance between Cochiti Reservoir and the broad floodplains and piedmonts to the west of the city, coupled with growing evidence for extensive usage of the entire Santa Fe area during the Late Archaic, supports a view of Santa Fe as an attractive place for foragers and collectors.[45] Whether the increased Archaic site density was related to the above-average precipitation estimated to have fallen for the several hundred years prior to 1 c.e. may not be determinable, but information obtained during the past two decades of archaeological research has demonstrated that the local landscape was becoming more crowded.

The thoughtful reader might ask, "What exactly does 'more crowded' mean for the Late Archaic?" Nicholas Chapin has observed how "the distribution of radiocarbon dates [of Archaic Period sites] indicates that there was a low population density during the Early Archaic in northwestern New Mexico until around 4,300 years ago after which time population levels rapidly increased,"[46] but he does not provide any solid numbers for local populations. Calculating prehistoric populations is notoriously difficult for archaeologists. This is especially true with hunter-gatherers whose mobility, use of small, temporary camps, and relative absence of burials makes demographic estimations a challenging exercise in *guesstimation*.[47] Using population density estimates from historic hunter-gatherer populations as a guideline, I calculate that there may have been somewhere between 40 and 120 people regularly living in the middle northern Rio Grande, with the smaller number possibly reflecting the Early Archaic population and the larger number possibly reflecting the Late Archaic population.[48] These numbers suggest that somewhere between two and five bands of variable size would have been able to successfully support themselves in and around Santa Fe. Inasmuch as the region that I defined in Chapter 1 has somewhat arbitrary boundaries, it is likely that some Archaic bands were exploiting larger areas, implying that the foregoing population estimates may be somewhat low. In addition, the adoption of seasonal transhumance would have resulted in smaller band territories with the potential for more bands being able to sustain themselves locally. In any event, while Archaic numbers appear minuscule when compared with contemporary population densities, readers need to remember that seasonally nomadic foragers were completely dependent upon the natural productivity of a given area. Even Santa Fe, located within one or two days' travel from riparian, plains, uplands, and montane resource zones, could be a precarious place to live for hunters and gatherers.

As a general assertion, one can say that by the end of the Archaic, people throughout the Southwest had adopted lifestyles that varied according to their degrees of population density, mobility, and reliance upon wild versus domesticated plants. Ancient people in the vicinity of Santa Fe successfully maintained a way of life based upon foraging and collecting for longer than most other groups living in the northern Southwest, but as we will see in the next chapter they eventually adopted the maize-based subsistence system that had already swept across most of the Southwest.

Unidentified view of the Northern Rio Grande Valley by Nels Nelson, ca. 1912. Courtesy American Museum of Natural History.

Chapter 5

❧

Santa Fe Horticultural Societies

THE DEVELOPMENTAL PERIOD — 600–1200 C.E.

Mention the term "horticultural societies" to non-archaeologists and they will probably paint a mental picture of "ladies of a certain age" wearing large straw hats and puttering about in immaculate gardens. However inaccurate that mental picture may be, there is no question that Santa Feans are proud of their gardens. Every June the Santa Fe Botanical Garden sponsors a garden tour when all manner of justifiably flattered gardeners open their yards and patios to admiring masses of "green-thumb wannabees." I have been on those tours and I am always impressed by the varieties of plants that can be grown in the high desert of Santa Fe with a little bit of water and a great deal of ingenuity.

Conversely, mention "horticultural societies" to an archaeologist and you may receive a lengthy discourse on the evolution of incipient agriculture and the sundry ways in which indigenous societies learned to cultivate a wide assortment of plants on small plots of land without using draft animals, plows, or other forms of complex technology. As we saw in Chapter 4, hunters and gatherers often followed an annual round of food collecting as seasonal changes provided a continuum of opportunities closely tied to the availability of wild foods in dispersed habitats. The shift from food collection to food production not only limited mobility but also redirected group energy into a circumscribed set of activities in specific places. This shift presented questions to food producers that hunters and gatherers never had to

69

FOOD CATEGORY	ENERGY (Calories per 100 grams)	PROTEIN (per 100 grams)	CARBOHYDRATES (per 100 grams)
DOMESTICATED CROPS			
Beans (raw)	340	23.5	61.9
Corn	348	8.9	72.2
Squash, summer	19	1.1	4.2
Squash, winter	50	1.4	12.4
Squash blossoms	72	3.4	—
Pumpkins	26	1.0	6.5
WILD FOODS			
FRUITS			
Cholla	393	12.2	79
Prickly pear	42	9.7	7.3–10.9
Prickly pear (dry)	280	1.7	62
Saguaro (dry)	499	10.3	70
Groundcherry	148.6	1.9	11.1
Currant	44	8.8	10.9
NUTS			
Piñon	568–635	11.6	19.3
Black walnut	628	20.5	14.8
SEEDS			
Amaranth	138.8	15.2	63.9
Beeweed	427.4	23.0	15.6
Lamb's quarter	32–45	3.2–4.2	5–7.3
Pigweed	360–372	16.8	42.4
Purslane (leaves)	31	1.7	3.8
Saguaro (dry)	609	16.3	540
Sunflower (dry)	570	23.9	19.3
Tansy mustard	554	23.4	71
ANIMALS			
Deer (raw)	126	21	0
Rabbit (raw)	162	21	0
Turkey (raw)	162	24	0

Fig. 34. Nutritional contents of some common domesticated and wild foods consumed in the Southwest. Table by Jason S. Shapiro, adapted from Cordell (1997) and Cummings (1995).

consider. "What do we plant? When, how, and where do we plant? When do we harvest? How much seed do we store for next year? How do we water and maintain the growing crops?" Agriculturalists needed to answer these critical questions correctly every single time because their survival depended on it. In that vein, here are some questions I will address in this chapter: "How and why did people in the Southwest adopt agriculture and why did people in the vicinity of Santa Fe wait so long to do it?" A related question is "How did ways of life change in Santa Fe after the adoption of agriculture?"

I suggested in the preceding chapter that there were times when even successful hunter-gatherer populations were nutritionally stressed.[1] Many different wild foods found in the Southwest can provide comparative nutritional value to the most common cultivated plants (fig. 34), but the inescapable problem with wild foods is their availability, or lack thereof. No matter how much ecological knowledge people accumulate about the locations, ripening times, and means of collecting wild foods, sometimes nature just does not cooperate. There are times when piñon groves do not always produce nuts,[2] the wild grasses do not always grow or ripen, and animal populations rapidly decrease in what is called a "population crash." More than anything else, the ability to produce food gives people a measure of predictability and control over their food supplies, but the transformation from a system of collecting to one of producing also has major implications for the social, political, technological, and even religious aspects of a society.

Archaeologists call the process of plant domestication "independent invention" because that is precisely what happened in several places on four continents, including the Near East, Asia, Africa, the Andean Highlands in South America, central Mexico, and eastern North America. During what is called the Neolithic Period or New Stone Age, people in those diverse areas separately invented agriculture within the time interval of roughly between 6,000 to 12,000 years ago.[3] All of the major crops upon which much of the world's population currently depends — wheat, barley, oats, corn, rice, sorghum, and potatoes — were domesticated during those six millennia. Within the fields of archaeology and geography exists a vast literature concerning the reasons that some foragers became farmers,[4] but virtually every theory about the origins of agriculture involves the same group of variables: increasing population numbers and densities, changing environmental conditions, human responses to those changing conditions, and good old-fashioned opportunism. One group of scientists has expressed the view that the intense climatic fluctuations experienced towards the end of the Pleistocene, including extremes of hot and cold temperatures, extensive periods of dryness, and low levels of carbon dioxide in the atmosphere that limited photosynthesis, literally would have made agriculture impossible until the arrival of the Holocene with its minimal fluctuations between climatic extremes.[5] The one thing that all contemporary theories eschew is *intentionality*, the idea that people were getting hungry and running out of wild foods so they cogitated for a bit and *voilà*, agriculture was born. On the contrary, it is more likely that the earliest examples of domestication were the result of lucky accidents.

As far as domesticates in the Americas are concerned, squash (*Curcubita* spp.) may have been domesticated in Central America as early as 10,000 years ago. For a long time archaeologists believed that maize (*Zea maize*) was domesticated in highland Mexico between 7,000 and 8,000 years ago.[6] Recent radiocarbon redating has altered these dates, and domesticated maize is now seen as no more than 5,400 years old,[7] practically yesterday in archaeological terms. Both crops moved into the Southwest through the relatively warm and arid Upper Sonoran zone and were well established in the Southwestern Borderlands by 1000 B.C.E. Beans (*Phaesolus* spp.) and a host of other crops came several hundred years later, but the point is that agriculture was not independently invented in the Southwest but came in from other regions.[8]

Agricultural systems do not transport themselves like animal herds, and there has been an ongoing debate among archaeologists as to how agriculture entered the Southwest. Some suggest farmers coming north from Mexico brought their seeds and tools with them as the Europeans brought wheat, fruit trees, and domesticated animals into the Southwest in the 16th century. Others think the powerful "idea of agriculture," the technical knowledge of how to grow and care for plants together with the actual seeds, was transferred to mobile hunting and gathering groups, who in the course of their annual movements came into contact with farming groups. Archaeologists have gone back and forth on this issue for decades, but the latest evidence reveals a narrowing of the time gap between the dates for maize domestication in Mexico and the establishment of agriculturally based villages in both central Mexico and the greater Southwest. The compressed time frame reflects a rapid spread of crop growing and suggests that there must have been a movement of actual farmers into the Southwest, not just their technological ideas.[9]

The adoption of agriculture offered early farmers a whole suite of positive reinforcements. The most important consequence was that food production became more reliable and predictable. I am not suggesting that agricultural societies never faced food shortages, but people who rely on crops have much more control over their food supply than mobile foragers. The element of control includes the ability to expand the resource base by bringing additional land into production. A farmer cannot force a piñon tree to produce more nuts, but that same farmer has the option of cutting down the piñon tree and planting more maize. Agriculture provides storable food supplies that ensure food during "lean" times of the year, but because successful farmers have extra crops to trade, agriculture also increases a group's ability to maintain social ties with other communities, secure mates, and participate in ceremonial activities (a kind of "resource banking"). Food surplus eventually leads to what archaeologists call "occupational specialization." When a community can routinely produce food beyond what is needed nutritionally, then not everyone needs to be a full-time food producer. In those situations, some people can spend part of their time developing specialized abilities or knowledge in such practical techniques as pottery production and weaving, or in more abstract areas such as political and religious leadership. Finally, there is usually a connection between agriculture, sedentism, and population growth. Because agricultural groups can meet most of their nutritional needs without constantly moving across the landscape, life is less rigorous, especially for the very young and very old.

For all its benefits, agriculture is a double-edged sword with some negative consequences. Agriculture creates simplified ecosystems in which only limited species are cared for, and so they are more susceptible to violent weather conditions, insect infestations, and plant diseases. Species diversity contributes to the ecological health and strength of natural environments. Many Santa Fe gardeners have watched in utter helplessness as a summer hailstorm shredded their garden. If you had to depend on that garden to feed your family, your options would be seriously limited. Early farmers tended to rely on fewer food items than late Archaic foragers, who were exploiting virtually every local edible plant and animal. Farmers put their energy into their crops and do not have as much time for repetitive resource collecting. Although farmers can produce lots of cheap carbohydrate calories, they are also subject to "nutritional narrowing" when reduced dietary variability increases the risk of malnutrition. The skeletal remains of early agriculturalists typically reveal that they were not as healthy as preceding populations of hunters and gatherers.[10] Farming not only requires sustained labor in order to ensure continued productivity but also labor that is directed and organized in very particular ways with both social and political implications. Hunter-gatherer bands maintained general divisions of labor primarily based upon age and, to a lesser degree, gender. Among agriculturalists, these divisions became more marked and even institutionalized.[11]

One more thing that agriculture does is to turn well-watered arable soil (also known as "dirt"!) into a valuable resource for which people will compete, using violence if necessary.[12] In contrast with areas in the eastern United States or parts of Mesoamerica, there is not that much really good soil in the Southwest. People who grew crops tended to locate their communities in close proximity to the best available soils. The continued use of limited pieces of arable land leads to the problem of long-term degradation of the landscape. Coincident with their production of maize, beans, and squash, farming cultures also produced more people, which required even more environmental modifications to keep everyone fed. Clearing land results in deforestation, which increases erosion and decreases the amount of productive land. The result is that farmers have to clear marginal lands that require more energy to prepare, plant, and maintain relative to the crop yield, all of which exacerbates a cycle of diminishing productivity. Ancestral Puebloan populations were never completely sedentary. After a few generations of living in one place, difficulties associated with population growth, water supply, variations in lengths of growing seasons, soil nutrients, or crop pests would become sufficiently problematic that villages would relocate. Despite these problems, the overall productivity and predictability associated with maize agriculture made it the dominant subsistence system across the entire Southwest.

Accordingly, if agriculture is so useful, why did it take such a long time for it to become established in the middle northern Rio Grande? The glib answer is that people living here didn't need it, didn't want it, and weren't forced by their circumstances into adopting it — and there is probably some truth to this. As I've suggested, Santa Fe and its environs really were different from other parts of the Southwest in terms of the subsistence options they provided for hunters and gatherers. This may explain part of the cultural reticence surrounding the adoption of agriculture.[13] By the time that agriculture became entrenched around Santa Fe, it had already existed in parts of the Southwest for close to 2,000 years. Surprisingly, the earliest local examples of domesticated crops, corncobs recovered from Jemez Cave in the Jemez Mountains southwest of Santa Fe, have been dated to 2990 B.P.,[14] so, despite the exposure that some local residents had to the concept of growing crops, people were not buying into the program. The initial response to agriculture in the vicinity of Santa Fe can be described as hesitant at best, perhaps because of climatic limitations or perhaps the locals were simply not amenable to becoming farmers. Being a full-time farmer is hard work, harder than being a forager and collector, and maize growing is sufficiently demanding that the model of part-time "farmer-foragers" has never made sense to me as an effective long-term subsistence strategy in this region. My statement in Chapter 4 that Santa Fe offered reasonably productive surroundings for the collection of wild plant foods supplemented by hunting, implies that the locals did not feel much pressure to change because the potential costs appeared to outweigh uncertain benefits. It has been suggested that while there was a period of increased precipitation between the fourth and tenth centuries (300 – 900 C.E.) this precipitation was accompanied by cooler temperatures. That would not have necessarily prevented the wild plants traditionally used by Rio Grande residents from continuing to thrive but could have jeopardized maize and other crops grown at 7,000 feet.[15] It is not that people would have been philosophically opposed to developing a nutritious new food source, but if environmental conditions were not sufficiently benign to grow crops successfully in most years, then the locals may have considered it too risky. Once again I admit to painting with a large brush. There are sites from which substantial amounts of maize have been recovered, such as a pit house excavated on the Rio Nambe a few miles north of Santa Fe or the Pena Blanca sites at the foot of the La Bajada escarpment. Most recently, archaeologists working at the site of the former Sweeney Civic Center excavated a series of pits that may have been used to store domesticated seeds or grains.[16] All of these sites were occupied within the time frame of roughly 300 – 700 C.E. and demonstrate that some people became farmers at the same time that other people were still foraging for a living.[17]

I explained in Chapter 2 that although archaeologists work diligently at refining cultural chronologies, most of the time the periods we discern have fuzzy edges. I am about halfway through this chapter and only now describing the next cultural period, the *Developmental*, which is often divided into the Early (400/600 – 900 C.E.) and late (900 – 1175/1200 C.E.) stages.[18] During this 600-year slice of time, the triumvirate of Puebloan traits, namely agriculture, sedentism, and village-scale organization, began to take hold.[19] Just as the Archaic has been viewed as a linkage between the Paleoindians and the Puebloans, so too has the Developmental been viewed as a linkage between the last Archaic foragers and the first full-time Puebloan farmers. During this period, Pueblo life really *developed* in Santa Fe.

At this juncture I want to address two problems associated with the transitional Late Archaic-Early Developmental Period. First, how do archaeologists recognize the

Fig. 35. Example of early pottery imported into the Santa Fe area. Museum of Indian Arts and Culture/Labroratory of Anthronpology (8817).

transition? And second, how do archaeologists explain the transition? I noted in Chapter 4 that some sites south of Santa Fe that date to the Developmental Period look much like Archaic sites in terms of their locations, layouts, and artifacts. The excavation of one site in particular, dated as being occupied between 855–990 C.E., found neither ceramics nor evidence of corn.[20] Ever since Wendorf and Reed defined the Developmental Period more than fifty years ago,[21] the critical marker for its beginning has been the presence of pottery.[22] Certainly chronology is important and archaeologists need to know when a particular site was occupied, but, ultimately, I think it matters less what chronological label we put on a site than what we can learn about the people who created the site. Is a 1,600-year-old pit house with some cord-marked pottery sherds but no corn kernels or squash seeds more Puebloan than Archaic? What about a similar site with some corn pollen but no pottery? What about the Tierra Contenta site that may only be 1,000 years old but has neither pottery nor corn pollen? Obviously it is easier to excavate and analyze concrete elements such as pottery sherds and kernels of corn than to understand behaviors like "sedentism" that exist along a continuum from extremely mobile to completely sedentary. However, archaeologists are trained to marshal "hard data" in order to support their more abstract inferences. All three of these sites would probably be labeled "Developmental" as a matter of convention. My point is, throughout time people have adopted new traits unevenly, and there never was someone running around blowing a whistle yelling, "OK, the Archaic is over in Santa Fe; we are all Puebloans now!" All I am suggesting is that we do not lose sight of the big picture. The archaeological evidence does support the existence of a cultural continuum in and around Santa Fe between pre-agricultural aceramic groups and early horticultural ceramic users. Part of the "received archaeological wisdom" about the Early Developmental Period in Santa Fe echoes the same kinds of comments that people made about the Archaic, namely an assumption of a relatively light occupation with small populations.[23] In fact, there seems to have been a widespread, if patchy, Early Developmental presence in areas north, west, south of the city, and possibly downtown.[24] The absolute numbers may not have been large, but apparently Santa Fe was home to more early "crop growing pottery users" than has been assumed.

I said that there are similarities between Late Archaic and Early Developmental sites, but there are also differences. For example, Developmental Period residents put more investment in their domestic architecture than did their Archaic forebears. Pit houses became slightly larger, deeper, and more permanent and were located in more predictable places. Several of these pit houses grouped together would have constituted a typical hamlet. Settlement locations with "access to arable land and dependable water" indicated the growing importance of agriculture. The archaeological evidence reveals that Early Developmental Period farmsteads and hamlets[25] were often located on ridges and terraces that overlooked perennial or seasonally intermittent streams where residents could engage in either floodwater or irrigation-supported agriculture.[26]

The Developmental Period is partially defined by the appearance of pottery, most of it undecorated utility ware, but also several types of slipped and decorated whiteware that were imported from other areas (fig. 35). Why is pottery so significant? For one thing, it eased the preparation of corn porridge that both the very young and very old could eat more easily. In addition, sealed pottery containers offered better protection against moisture, insects, and rodents than even the best slab-lined pits so farmers were able to retain more grain from their efforts because there was less waste. Pottery-using hamlets were able to get more energy from a given volume of corn than non-pottery-using hamlets because pottery provided more options for preparation and storage. This functional distinction created the conditions for healthier (and larger) families, more surplus, and potentially more influence over local decisions such as settlement locations or the acquisition of arable land. Everyone agrees that pottery is terrific for both storing and cooking grains, but the appearance of nonlocal pottery suggests either the arrival of nonlocal people or the operation of wide-ranging trade or other kinds of social networks.

In Chapters 3 and 4 I discussed how Paleoindian and Archaic groups learned to buffer risk by exploiting a wide diversity of wild foods and by maintaining a highly mobile way of life. For instance, droughts could be extremely problematic for hunters and gatherers when wild foods became unavailable, but those people carried their

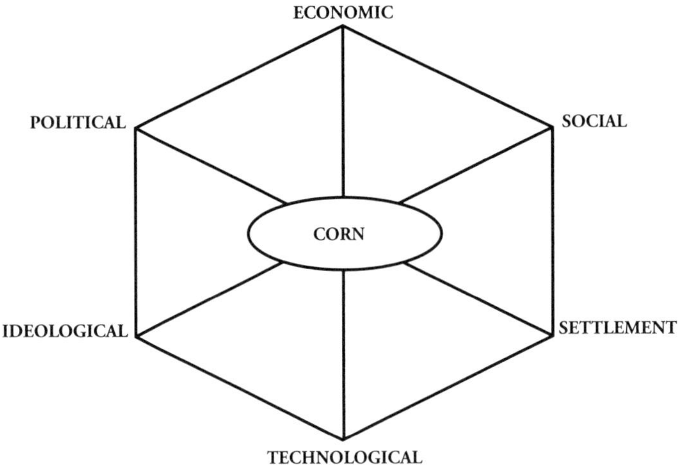

Fig. 36. A graphic portrayal of the critical significance of corn. Illustration by Jason S. Shapiro.

own "Get Out of Jail Free" cards. Because their subsistence systems were based upon the ability to move among multiple food sources, they were relatively unencumbered with stuff, and the stuff they did have was lightweight and portable. New farmers also needed to buffer environmental risks such as droughts, but their commitment to their crops limited their own mobility so they substituted a form of commodity mobility. Without oversimplifying the social, economic, technical, and even ideological complexities associated with the production and distribution of pottery, I want to propose that the increasing prevalence of non-local pottery was less about the functional usage of pots than about the external relationships the pots signified. Local settlements were relatively small and dispersed during most of the Developmental Period. Although I have not analyzed the density of non-local pottery on a site-by-site basis, I suspect that this pottery signifies efforts by individual households to make their own connections with people beyond Santa Fe, rather than evidence of some community-wide networking plan. In addition to foreign pottery from the west, local discoveries of flaked stone tools made from west Texas alibates chert probably signifies some kind of links with groups living on the Great Plains.[27] When harvests were meager, some people may have been able to call on their non-local trading partners to help bail them out. While not foolproof, this plan represented a new kind of adaptation to a new kind of life based on agriculture and reveals how even very localized populations connected with much larger economic spheres.

Middle northern Rio Grande Valley residents may have been both fitful and late relative to the rest of the Southwest in adopting maize as *the staple crop,* but just after 900 C.E. maize agriculture became so pervasive that it represents one of the few "bright line" events that define a cultural transformation. Maize was not just something to eat but constituted a fundamental change in how people behaved. Over the course of several hundred years, an entire cultural system built around corn developed in the northern Rio Grande. Those systems included a lot more than the corn itself. There were special tools (digging sticks, hoes, etc.); practical knowledge about how to grow and harvest corn, the ways to process, prepare, and store corn, and the kinds of settlement systems that facilitated and reinforced this agricultural focus; the web of social relationships, including gender roles, embodied by this new system; and an overriding ideology designed around the annual agricultural cycle and centered on fertility and precipitation that gave meaning to all those other activities. In other words, the adoption of maize agriculture resulted in a series of countless behavioral changes that transformed life in this region in the same way that it transformed life throughout the Southwest.[28]

Between the years 800 to 1000 C.E., the northern hemisphere became warmer and experienced higher levels of summer precipitation.[29] Not coincidently, this was also a period of Ancestral Puebloan expansion throughout the northern Southwest. It is almost as if people were trying out every potential area where agriculture might be possible with everyone looking for the most productive locations. In the area around Santa Fe, people began moving their small farmsteads and hamlets into upland areas that had previously been unoccupied. The apparent speed with which maize-based agriculture, pottery usage, and more sedentary village life coalesced after 900 C.E. into a widespread "Puebloan lifestyle" leads to another question. Can we attribute that coalescence to migrant groups who brought shiny new ideas into the "boondocks" of the northern Rio Grande, or to some innovative locals who pulled all the separate threads together?

In that vein there are archaeologists who propose that a group of immigrants physically brought to the Santa Fe area what has been called the "Neolithic package"[30]—maize, pottery, and the concept of sedentary village life. According to this hypothesis, small groups of "corn-growing pottery-makers" arrived in the Rio Grande Valley from the south or west, possibly from the Four Corners region or the San Juan Basin.[31] Eventually the immigrant populations became so successful they absorbed or displaced the existing Late Archaic-Early Developmental groups so that the subsequent Puebloan populations were mostly the descendents of the immigrant farmers. Support for this idea is based on timing, namely the sudden appearance of the full 'Neolithic package' around 900 C.E., coupled with what looks like a relatively slow spreading out of these sites throughout the Santa Fe area.[32]

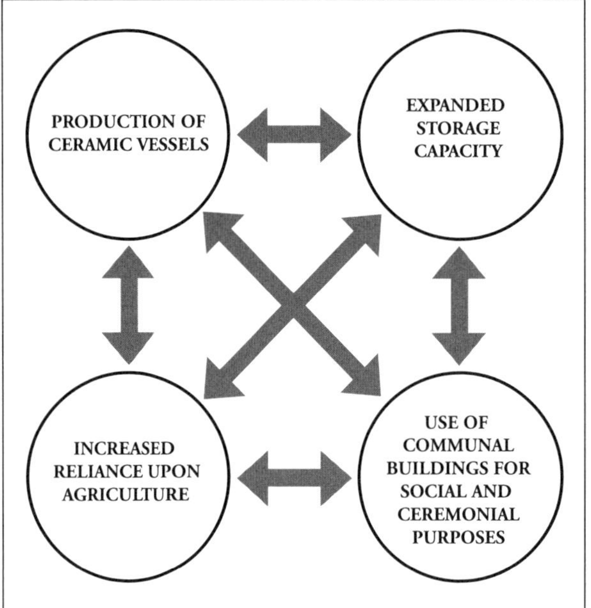

Fig. 37. Technological and economic changes associated with the expansion of Ancestral Puebloan village life. Illustration by Jason S. Shapiro.

Other archaeologists think that the appearance of "maize-and-pottery hamlets" was not quite so sudden and had more to do with local populations changing how they lived than with the arrival of immigrant farmers. Archaeologist Regge Wiseman's reanalysis of the Pojoaque Grant site several miles north of Santa Fe securely dates the presence of the "Neolithic package" of traits prior to 900 C.E. and possibly as early as the mid-700s.[33] Although the most intensive occupation of two pueblos at the Pojoaque Grant site occurred in the tenth and eleventh centuries, Wiseman's findings suggest a long, sequential occupation of this particular place that extended for more than three hundred years. Archaeologists have also investigated Altar Mayor, a pueblo with as many as 250 rooms that was located several miles south of Santa Fe on the lower reaches of the Santa Fe River[34] and occupied at the same time as the earliest occupation at Pojoaque Grant (700 – 900 C.E.). The size of these two settlements was in such marked contrast to the small hamlets where most people were living that each settlement may have constituted some kind of small regional center. More illuminating perhaps is Wiseman's observation that "many (most?) cultural events in the Rio Grande were essentially contemporary with developments in the Four Corners area. Thus, they could not have been solely the result of "diffusion" from that region. The best example is the shift from pit houses to pueblos as primary habitations."[35] In other words, if people in Santa Fe were growing corn, making pottery, and building villages at the same time people were doing these same things out on the Colorado Plateau, then it becomes harder to argue that Rio Grande Puebloan culture was derived from other areas. Every archaeologist knows that it is easier to describe a problem than to resolve it, and "it may be that there is not yet any clear-cut support for either the immigrant or indigenous development model for Puebloan

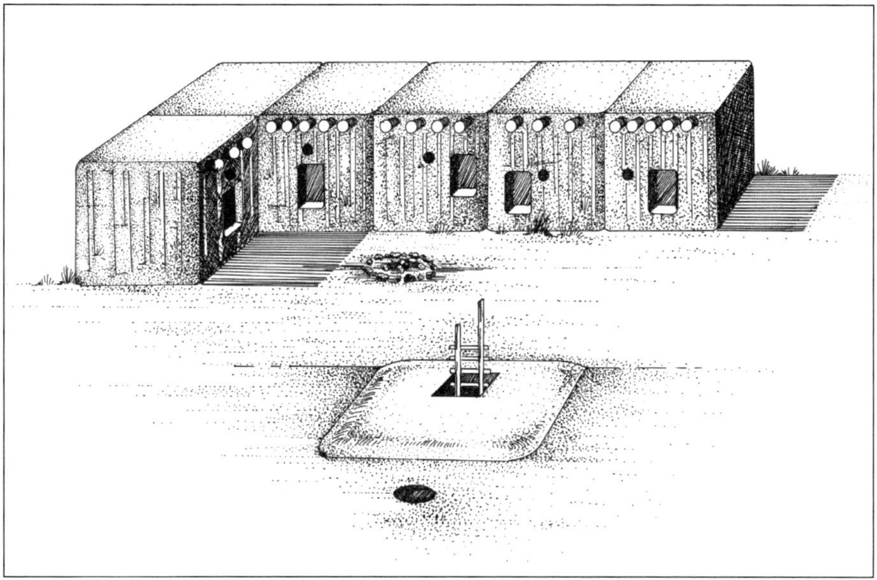

Fig. 38. Artist's reconstruction of Ancestral Puebloan unit pueblo of the Pueblo Developmental Period. Illustration by Ferguson and Rohn (1991), courtesy of Lisa Ferguson.

farmers in the Santa Fe area."[36] I do think that most archaeologists would agree that by 1,000 years ago the elements we associate with Ancestral Puebloan culture were firmly in place in the northern Rio Grande. Mutually reinforcing processes fostered the development and expansion of village life in Santa Fe as well as across the entire northern Southwest (fig. 37).

Wiseman's comment about the shift from pit house to pueblo residences is a good lead in to a brief discussion about another one of those transforming processes in Southwest prehistory. The "pit house–to-pueblo transition" occurred among all of the major cultural groups (Ancestral Pueblo, Mogollon, Hohokam) as people ceased to live in pit-like structures and instead began living in aboveground structures built of jacal, masonry, or adobe (fig. 38). This transformation occurred at different times in different areas. In the northern and mountainous areas of the Southwest, such as the Mogollon Highlands and the Colorado Plateau, this shift in architectural arrangements occurred between 700 – 1000 c.e. In the desert areas of central Arizona it did not occur until after 1100 c.e. In Santa Fe, the residential use of pit structures continued into the 1200s.

Archaeologists are a curious lot. When we find evidence that people gave up a long-standing and well-adapted house type for something entirely different, we want to know why. Consistent with some of the other cultural changes I have discussed, there were probably several factors that contributed to this major conversion in residential living. I have mentioned how periods of increased precipitation and favorable environmental conditions resulted in increased agricultural productivity and population growth, all of which put more demands on limited items such as food, arable land, timber, and space. Pit houses are perfectly adequate structures in which to live. They are easy to build, cool in the summer and warm in the winter, but they do have limitations. Existing pit houses cannot easily be expanded to accommodate more people, and there is limited space available for storage and other activities. If substantially larger pit houses are dug, it becomes more difficult for small groups to cut and transport trees that are long enough for roofing beams. For one or two larger communal buildings, this may not have posed a problem, but roofing an entire village of large pit structures to house growing families would have been a major challenge.

The adoption of sedentary village life also meant that more people were available for work, including the multiple jobs associated with food preparation. Tasks such as grinding corn became separated from other household tasks for practical reasons such as the production of clouds of corn dust, the need to keep children and dogs away from the cornmeal, and the desire of women to socialize during these food preparation activities. These changes were initially reflected in the presence of what appear to be specialized grinding rooms associated with some pit structures. The thought of spending several hours a day in a small, low-ceiling pit structure surrounded by cornmeal dust would convince me that a separate surface room made of jacal or adobe would be an attractive alternative. Similarly, as agriculture became more important to group well-being, better ways had to be found to protect maize, beans, and other grains from contamination, spoilage, and rodents. I mentioned that pottery is one very good way, but there are practical limits on the size of pottery containers. Aboveground storage rooms with large, covered adobe bins are much better than slab-lined pits in terms of their ability to protect against rainwater seepage and burrowing rodents.

One of the downsides to larger and more densely packed populations was the increased opportunity for social friction. All groups have an ongoing need to develop mechanisms for reducing conflict, but they do not always work. Some groups created intermediate-level organizations, such as clans or moieties, that interceded between the family and the village.[37] Even with such mechanisms, disputes still occur and communities can sometimes split apart, as in the historical events at the Hopi settlement of Orayvi.[38] Easily constructed and modified architectural devices that provide a greater level of privacy than single, open pit rooms (adobe is a very good sound absorber as well as an insulator) may also have encouraged the transition away from pit houses. At least one study has suggested that the architectural changes associated with the shift to pueblos reflected an increased desire for more individualized food storage because of threats from warfare and unpredictable agricultural production.[39]

Another factor to consider in connection with the evolution of Puebloan lifeways in Santa Fe is the worldwide climatic event known as the Medieval Warm Period.[40] During the time between the eighth and the thirteenth centuries, temperatures in the northern hemisphere became extraordinarily mild and facilitated diverse phenomena such as the Norse expansion into Iceland, Greenland, and North America, and the growth of grapes in England leading to a highly successful wine industry. For the Southwest, this warming event meant longer growing seasons and changes in precipitation patterns that made the area around Santa Fe a much better place for cultivating plants. What was probably more important than increases in the volume of rainfall was the stabilization of annual rainfall cycles. Spring seed germination is generally associated with available groundwater, but late summer plant growth and productivity is tied to the timing and volume of summer monsoons. When the Ancestral Puebloans living on the Colorado Plateau and in the Four Corners region recognized that the large fluctuations in both the predictability and intensity of rainfall were improving, enterprising farmers expanded their croplands onto mesa tops and other areas with the reasonable expectation that the seasonal rains would arrive on time and in the right amount. During the roughly 430 years between 700–1130 C.E., the farmers were not disappointed as rains arrived on schedule. Ancestral Puebloan populations in the Four Corners region and on the Colorado Plateau increased in large measure because of their increasing success with and growing reliance upon maize.[41] This entire period was not an unremitting cornucopia for farmers—tree-ring studies have revealed the occurrence of periodic and severe decreases in precipitation beginning during the eighth century. Serious droughts occurred in Santa Fe between 1005–1020 C.E., 1090–1095 C.E., and one of the worst occurred between 1130 and 1150 C.E.[42] This mid-12th-century drought

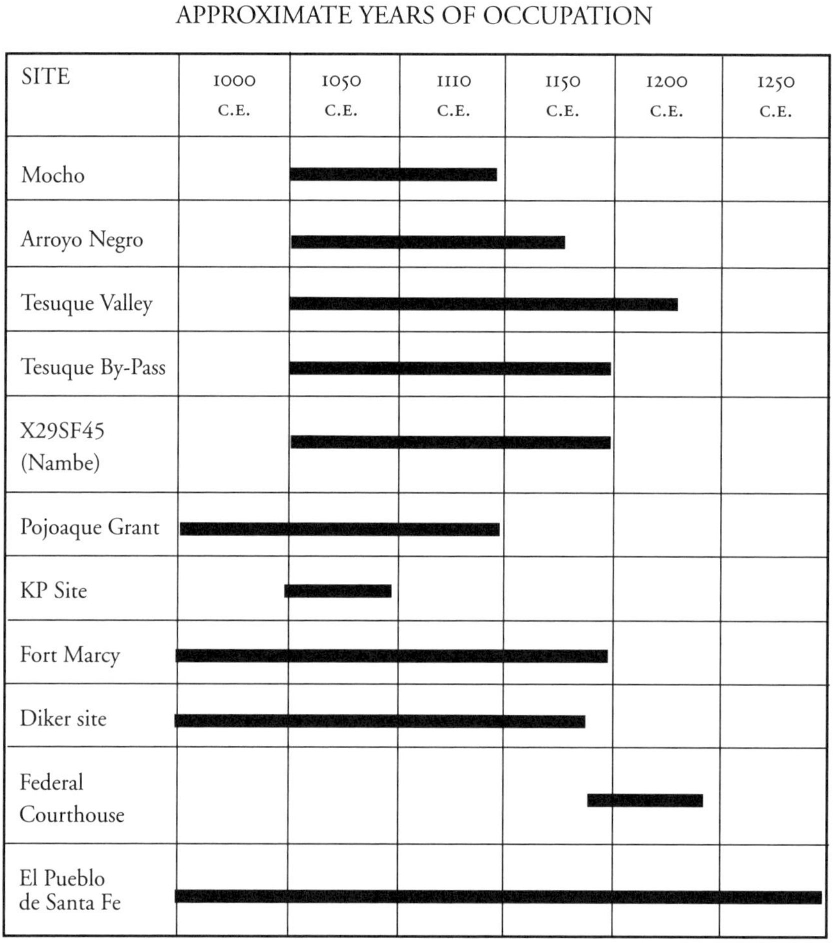

APPROXIMATE YEARS OF OCCUPATION

SITE	1000 C.E.	1050 C.E.	1110 C.E.	1150 C.E.	1200 C.E.	1250 C.E.
Mocho		█	█			
Arroyo Negro		█	█	█		
Tesuque Valley		█	█	█	█	
Tesuque By-Pass		█	█	█		
X29SF45 (Nambe)		█	█	█	█	
Pojoaque Grant	█	█	█			
KP Site		█				
Fort Marcy	█	█	█	█	█	
Diker site	█	█	█	█		
Federal Courthouse					█	
El Pueblo de Santa Fe	█	█	█	█	█	█

Fig. 39. *Occupation dates for selected Developmental Period sites in and around Santa Fe. Table by Jason S. Shapiro (adapted from Wiseman, 1989).*

caused major dislocations in the complex Puebloan cultural phenomena centered at Chaco Canyon in New Mexico's San Juan Basin. Santa Fe suffered along with the rest of the Southwest, and even though local precipitation fluctuations improved somewhat in the early 1150s and early 1160s, several local pueblos, such as Mocho, Pojoaque Land Grant, and Pueblo Negro, were abandoned around this time (fig. 39).[43] Looking at the big picture, when compared with the climatic record before the eighth century and after the thirteenth century, this Medieval Warm Period in between was relatively benevolent for early agriculturalists.[44]

The combination of elements associated with farming — more sedentary living, population growth, and the need to locate settlements close to water and arable land — are all reflected in Late Developmental Period settlement growth. By the mid-1100s there appear to have been several centers of village growth around Santa Fe. One focal point was along the Santa Fe River, two to five miles west of the city. Another focal point was downtown in the area of Fort Marcy Hill and Federal Place, and a third was north of the city towards Tesuque.

Arroyo Negro, located on a small ridge about six miles west of Santa Fe, typifies the settlements there along the Santa Fe River. When H. P. Mera first excavated Arroyo Negro in the 1920s, he found it was composed of seven small to medium roomblocks that incorporated more than 100 rooms and three kivas. Subsequent tree-ring studies found a range of dates between 900 – 1145 C.E., although the earliest dates associated with a pit structure identified as kiva C reached back into the 700s and 800s.[45] These findings suggest that this pueblo began as a small pit house community. A similar process was observed at the much larger Pindi Pueblo, which although usually associated with the subsequent Coalition Period, appears to have begun as a Late Developmental hamlet that included at least one pit house, two jacal structures, and some associated trash deposits.[46] This "Agua Fria corridor" along the Santa Fe River would continue to be occupied well into the 15th century, and after a brief hiatus, during the 16th century as well.[47]

As far as downtown Santa Fe is concerned, there are strong indications of some kind of early (400 – 600 C.E.) settlement at El Pueblo de Santa Fe, located at the site of the new convention center. The nature and full extent of that particular settlement is currently being unraveled,[48] but by the tenth century there was evidence of substantial residential use of areas just north of the city, including the large village of Kwapoge centered on Fort Marcy Hill. The village overlooked the Santa Fe River, a typical location for Developmental Period sites that tend to be found on the first terraces above the Santa Fe River floodplain.[49] The eight-foot depth of the trash midden associated with the site supports the inference that this was a fairly large settlement whose primary period of occupation was 1050 – 1150 C.E.[50] One of the noteworthy elements of this excavation was that within the limited ceramic sample collected, Red Mesa Black-on-white pottery was the most common decorated ware.[51] This particular ceramic type was manufactured between roughly 900 and 1125 C.E. in the Cibola Region near Gallup, New Mexico, and its presence supports the ideas regarding long-distance trade connections that I introduced earlier in the chapter.

Fig. 40. View from Fort Marcy, northeast of the city. Photograph by Nels Nelson, courtesy American Museum of Natural History.

Archaeology can be serendipitous, and sometimes archaeologists find unexpected opportunities to fill in blank spaces on the cultural landscape. Three small sites in downtown Santa Fe that were inadvertently discovered in connection with construction activities have sufficient overlap in their occupation dates that we now have a much better idea of what village life was like in Santa Fe between the late tenth and early thirteenth centuries. The KP (Kearney Partners) site is a good illustration of an early Late Developmental Period residential structure in downtown Santa Fe. The site itself was a pit house with some associated surface rooms that appear to have been occupied between 1047 and 1093 C.E., or around the same time as the earliest components of Arroyo Negro.[52] The pit house was discovered and excavated just ahead of a condominium construction project not far from the Scottish Rite Temple. Although part of the structure was destroyed, archaeologists estimated that the complete pit house had a diameter of roughly four meters, which would have provided a floor area of approximately 12.56 square meters or 135.2 square feet (think of a room 11 x 12 feet in size). For comparison purposes the Late Archaic pit house illustrated in Figure 33 had a floor area of approximately 81 square feet, or only about 60 percent of the size of the KP structure. The larger size of the KP site pit house suggests several plausible changes from the preceding Archaic Period. People may have put more effort into pit house construction because they were spending a greater part of the year living in one place. It also is possible that agriculture-based sedentism resulted in more children so that domestic groups became larger than analogous groups during the Late Archaic. Finally, Late Developmental Period groups lived a more complex lifestyle that included agricultural products and tools as well as pottery, so perhaps they needed larger places to store their stuff. It may have been just like comedian George Carlin said, "Sometimes you gotta move, gotta get a bigger house 'cause you have more stuff."[53] Some contemporaneous settlements had already abandoned pit house living for aboveground pueblos,[54] but locals in downtown Santa Fe continued to use both residential forms simultaneously for some time. (fig. 41)

An analysis of the plant remains from the KP site revealed that the residents were eating some of the same wild foods used by Late Archaic groups, including grasses, cacti, amaranth, goosefoot, and pigweed, as well as maize and squash.[55] Although absolute evidence of formal connections is lacking, the KP site was close enough to Fort Marcy Hill to have been associated with that large settlement. In other words, the people living at the KP site were not residing in some isolated farmstead but were instead part of a larger community.[56] Clearly, by the end of the 11th century Santa Feans were living in physical groupings that could be called either large hamlets or small villages, and the KP site was one structural element of a developing community with one foot in a foraging past and the other foot in an agricultural future.

The second downtown site of interest is the Diker site excavated by archaeologist Cherie Scheick and her associates at Southwest Archaeological Consultants. The site, located on a private lot just north of the downtown area, consisted of a small adobe roomblock with several associated pit structures and trash middens.[57] A combination of radiocarbon dates placed the occupation of the Diker site between 990–1190 C.E., a time frame that overlaps the occupations at the KP and Fort Marcy sites. The largest Diker pit house had a floor area of 13.86 square meters or about 149.2 square feet, slightly larger than but comparable to the KP site pit house. This pit house was more structurally complete than the KP site, making some comparisons difficult, but small corncobs were recovered from the excavation together with the remains of numerous faunal species, including fish, snakes,

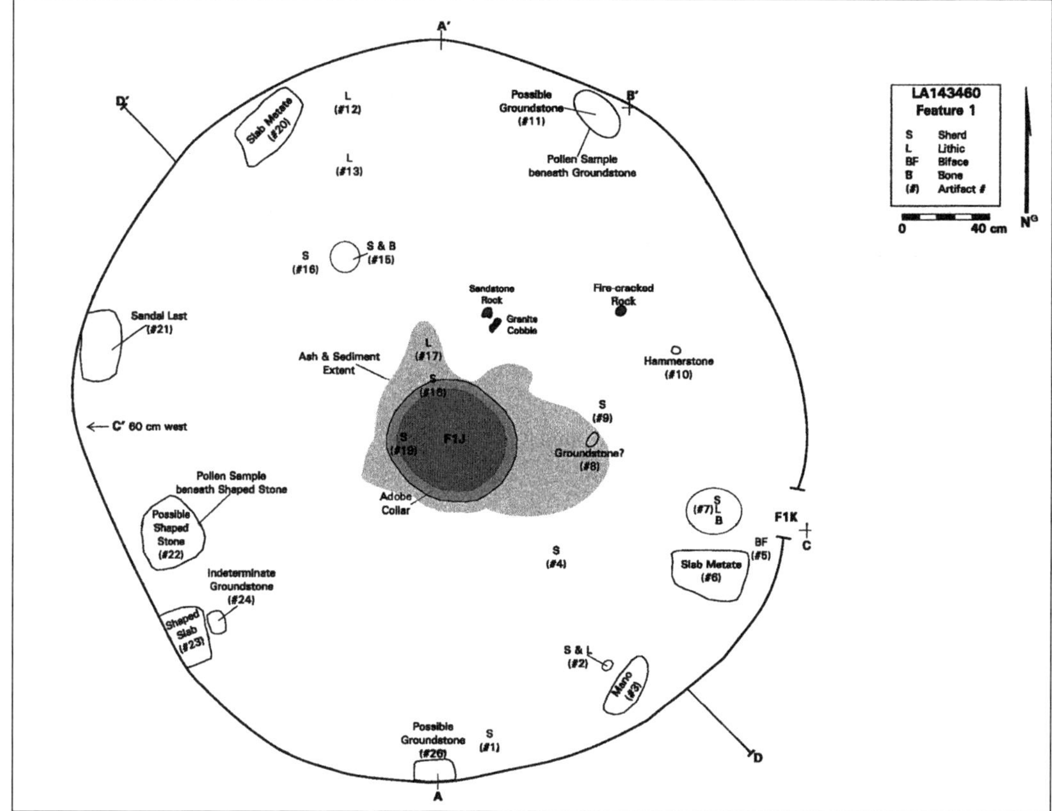

Fig. 41. Plan view of Federal Courthouse Developmental Period pit house showing floor features. Illustration courtesy of Cherie Scheick, Southwest Archaeological Consultants.

birds, and a variety of mammals ranging from prairie dogs to bison.[58] Even without a detailed botanical analysis, it looks as if the Diker folks lived in similar structures as the KP folks and ate from a similar smorgasbord of cultivated and wild foods.

Less than a long stone's throw from the KP site sits Santa Fe's Federal Courthouse, built in 1853. Because this building is listed on the National Register of Historic Places, when the General Services Administration initiated a construction project in 2003, the agency was required to conduct an archaeological survey and testing program. As with the Diker site, the Federal Courthouse project was excavated by Southwest Archaeological Consultants. Among the things they unearthed was a Late Developmental-Early Coalition Period pit house (1195–1240 C.E)[59] that was occupied not long after the Diker site and only about a century after the KP site (fig. 41). The subject pit house had a floor area of 10.73 square meters or 115.5 square feet, and so was midway in size between the late Archaic pit house described in Chapter 4 and the slightly larger KP and Diker site pit houses. The occupation dates place it on the cusp between the Late Developmental and Early Coalition Periods, but as I have previously explained, archaeology is more concerned with understanding what people were doing and how they were living rather than slotting them into a particular cultural cubbyhole. Among other things, the importance of this discovery is that the "pit house-to-pueblo" transition essentially complete in other parts of the northern southwest by the 11th or 12th centuries was still an ongoing process in Santa Fe well into the 13th century. During the early 1200s, there were no Ancestral Puebloan realtors putting up signs inducing everyone to move out of their antiquated pit houses and into fancy new pueblos. Even if there were, not everyone was paying attention.

The analysis of floral and faunal remains from the Federal Courthouse site showed that the residents relied upon a mixed food strategy that combined agriculture, wild plant collecting, and hunting not appreciably different from what the occupants of the KP site had been doing a hundred years earlier. On the other hand, aside from domesticates like maize and squash, the majority of wild plant and animal foods from the Courthouse site came from nearby mountain locations. Standing alone, that information is not remarkable. However, when combined with similar information from Pindi Pueblo that revealed the presence of numerous piedmont but very few mountain species, there is an intimation of emerging territorial behavior and the possibility that some pueblos may have limited the free access of nonmembers into hunting grounds or other resource collection areas.[60] Over the course of several hundred years, the actions of a few thousand people engaged in agricultural pursuits meant that the very things that supported Puebloan farming, namely access to water, wood, and arable land, became limited in selected areas. Admittedly, the evidence for territorial behavior is narrow and circumstantial, but it may be an early hint of the stresses that contributed to the formation of large, defensible pueblos during the next few centuries. If nothing else, I can at least offer the tongue-in-cheek suggestion that the occasional tensions we see today between "west siders" and "east siders" in Santa Fe is really nothing new.

Fig. 42. View from Atalaya Peak looking southwest. Photograph by Jason S. Shapiro.

It Takes an Evolving Village

THE COALITION PERIOD — 1175 – 1325 C.E.

Atalaya Peak is a steep but popular hike in the Sangre de Cristo foothills just to the southeast of Santa Fe. If you climbed Atalaya Peak eight hundred years ago and had a decent pair of binoculars, you could probably pick out, or at least see the smoke from, most of the Coalition Period pueblos that occupied various parts of the city (fig. 42). Right in the center of downtown was El Pueblo de Santa Fe,[1] as well as a pueblo on Fort Marcy Hill.[2] On the south side of town one could see Mocho[3] and Upper Arroyo Hondo[4] and possibly Los Alamos Pueblo located several miles southeast of Santa Fe along state route 285.[5] Indeed, unknown to thousands of daily travelers the remnants of Los Alamos sit directly under the I-25 and route 285 interchange. Continuing on to the west side of town where Agua Fria Street and the Alameda bracket the Santa Fe River, you could see several settlements beginning with the largest pueblos, Agua Fria Schoolhouse and Pindi, and continuing with several others positioned like beads on a string for about three miles along the river.[6] These were not the small, almost tentative pueblos that appeared during the Developmental Period but were the successful results of a couple hundred years of maize-fueled village growth.

Consider that during the early twelfth century Santa Fe was home to a number of small settlements with at most only a few dozen rooms. By the mid-thirteenth century, Pindi had no less than 175 rooms (and probably many more), and Agua

Fria Schoolhouse had grown to contain upwards of 500 rooms.[7] As with many large pueblos, not all of those rooms were built or occupied at the same time, but these settlements were still larger than any that ever had been seen locally. In addition to their own expanding dimensions, Pindi and Agua Fria also anchored the aforementioned line of Santa Fe River settlements that gave the impression of a single, linear community exploiting some of the best arable land in what was to become Santa Fe.[8] By the end of the 12th century, there was no question that Santa Fe represented a thriving place, an expanding spot on the landscape where people and their descendents lived out their lives as members of something larger than small, disconnected farmsteads and hamlets. Viewed within the larger context, Coalition settlements represent a transitional stage from those small farming hamlets to the really large pueblos built during the subsequent Rio Grande Classic Period. That's a nice statement, but it does not answer the question of why a transitional stage occurred. One of the objectives of this chapter is to explain the operative forces that were suggesting "bigger is better" eight hundred years ago.

More than anything else, the Coalition Period was a time of large-scale social and economic *amplification* where the defining elements of Pueblo life that developed during the Developmental Period matured in size and complexity. This period was so named because earlier generations of archaeologists were convinced that non-local Puebloans, primarily from the Four Corners or other areas in western New Mexico, moved into the northern Rio Grande where they "coalesced" with the local populations and drove some of this cultural amplification.[9] The theory was that as the Chaco Canyon and Mesa Verde-centered systems began to dissipate in the 12th and 13th centuries, people left the Colorado Plateau for areas like the Rio Grande Valley because of its relatively low population density, arable land, and adequate water supplies. The "coalescence" may also refer to the amalgamation of local populations into larger settlements. Archaeologists have subdivided the Coalition into earlier stages (Pindi Phase 1200–1300 C.E.) and later stages (Galisteo Phase 1300–1325 C.E.) based upon changes in pottery styles and architecture that were less dramatic than the kinds of changes that distinguish broader cultural periods.

For those readers who by now are wondering if absolutely every period of significant cultural change results in a debate between archaeologists who favor immigration as a root cause as opposed to archaeologists who favor in-place development, the answer is, for the most part, "yes." These positions are not mutually exclusive, and while I have always been more persuaded by the arguments made by "immigrationists,"[10] in conducting the research for this book I have been impressed with the sheer numbers of Late Archaic and Developmental Period sites discovered recently in the vicinity of Santa Fe. I do not believe that any archaeologist would take the position that no immigration occurred during the late 12th, 13th and early 14th centuries, but this recent evidence of the demonstrable existence of more extensive pre-Coalition indigenous populations strengthens the case for local explanations for expanding populations. The most likely suspects for local population growth are ecological and include an onset of favorable environmental conditions combined with the use of more drought-resistant and productive strains of maize. These strains initially arrived in the northern Rio Grande sometime after 700 C.E. and contributed to caloric stability among the local groups.[11] Translation: more and better corn + favorable growing conditions = more food energy = population growth. Despite the appeal of such a simple and direct explanation, there also is a case to be made for some immigration. A number of archaeologists subscribe with varying degrees of adherence to the idea of 13th century population infusions from the Mesa Verde or Gallina areas.[12] Stuart and Gauthier discuss site survey results from the Cochiti Reservoir area indicating a tenfold increase in identifiable sites (and by extension, population) during an interval extending from the Late Developmental into the mid-Coalition Period.[13] Such numbers suggest extraordinarily prolific locals, some in-migration, or both.

In trying to reconcile these views, archaeologists who support an immigration model, as well as those who rely upon an indigenous development model, confront some awkward facts. For example, to immigration theorists, the presence of Mesa Verde-style ceramics in the northern Rio Grande region implies that migrants carried these items or the techniques involved in their production, as predictable "cultural baggage."[14] Then again, archaeologists who question the purported Mesa Verde connection explain the presence of foreign ceramics merely as the diffusion of design motifs rather than actual people carrying their pots when they moved in. The skeptics assert that even if some people did arrive from the west, they literally would have looked like ragged remnant groups of refugees moving away from an agriculturally diminished Four Corners region rather than the robust hordes of thousands about which archaeologists have long speculated. Furthermore, those who favor indigenous population expansion point out that no site has been discovered where a complete assemblage of material has revealed the presence of an immigrant community.[15] In other words, if Mesa Verdeans entered this region in substantial numbers, we should see a lot more

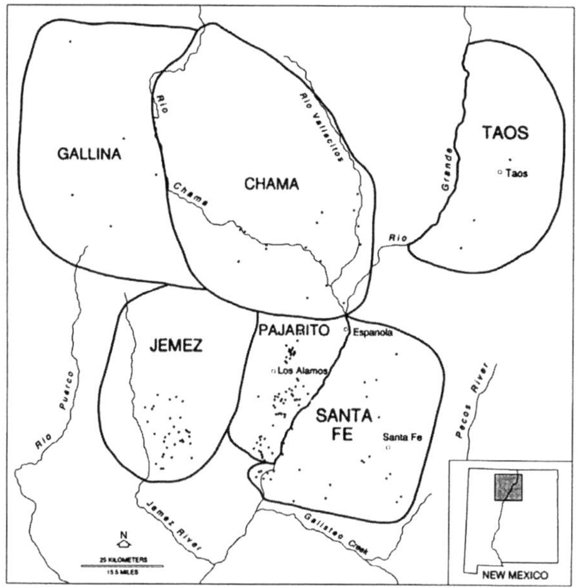

Fig. 43. Cultural districts identified in the Northern Rio Grande in the 13th century. Illustration by Crown, Orcutt, Kohler (1996).

of their stuff, particularly Mesa Verde-style architecture, a trait that is as fundamentally embedded in any culture as its pottery types and motifs. As an example of the sort of intrusive architecture I am talking about, consider the Pinnacle site located on Alamosa Creek south of Socorro, New Mexico. Archaeologist Stephen Lekson, who has excavated portions of the site, has proposed that the architecture at that site is different from the typical local Mimbres-Mogollon styles and is strongly suggestive of Mesa Verdean masonry.[16] This kind of an architectural intrusion is not clearly evident in the Santa Fe area.

In response to the foregoing, migrant groups do not necessarily replicate their old lives in their new host communities but attempt to blend in. Because of this, archaeologists may have to "dig deeper" in order to find unmistakable evidence of foreign site intrusions. One foreign architectural element that did appear in the 13th century was the D-shaped kiva, a form easily distinguishable from the circular style typically built in the northern Rio Grande. The appearance of these distinctive structures at Pindi and Arroyo Hondo Pueblos, as well as at a plethora of sites throughout the Rio Grande Valley, adds weight to the arguments in favor of some kind of influx of newcomers into the region. Ultimately, population growth had some source, and if in fact a tenfold increase occurred between 1150–1250 C.E.,[17] it must be acknowledged that there has never been a reported or observed historical case in which natural in-place increases have accounted for such numbers in such a short period of time.[18]

If archaeologists seem to know more about the Coalition Period than the Developmental Period, it is because there is much more material available for study. Villages became larger and were built in previously unoccupied upland zones. Pottery usage became pervasive, pottery forms and designs became more elaborate, and maize-based agriculture became the dominant means of subsistence. All of these elements combined to create a more extensive and visible archaeological record and "in recent years alone archaeologists have documented hundreds of sites."[19] The "cultural triumph" of sedentary agriculture did not mean that people no longer went out to forage and hunt, but it clearly meant that more energy was directed into the growing, care, and processing of domesticated crops. This late 12th and 13th century extension and expansion of Puebloan culture was not limited to the area in and around Santa Fe but occurred throughout several contiguous districts within the northern Rio Grande Valley. None of the six districts (Chama, Gallina, Jemez, Pajarito, Santa Fe, and Taos) exhibited exactly the same patterns of new construction, agricultural intensification, and population growth, but they all exhibited growth in all three categories.[20] As with other kinds of cultural changes, the transformation of settlement structure and village life was neither intended nor directed but was another type of adaptation that balanced the increased demands of expanding populations with the opportunities presented by an unpredictable environment.

From a climate standpoint, the people who lived in Santa Fe during the hundred plus years that define the Coalition Period struggled with extreme swings in precipitation. Using tree-ring analysis, archaeologists have learned that for the period 1195 to 1210 C.E. precipitation was, like all the children in Garrison Keillor's Lake Wobegon, definitely above average. This bountiful period was followed by fifteen years of below-average rainfall (1215–1230 C.E.). The good times rolled again from approximately 1230 to 1240 C.E. with higher than average rainfall. Sometime after 1240 C.E. the pendulum swung back, and the years 1245–1265 C.E. were again marked by below-average rainfall.[21] If some readers are getting dizzy trying to follow these periodic cycles, consider what they meant to the Puebloan farmers. In most years people produced enough food, but even under the best conditions it was not an easy process, and there were years when food production was precarious. In addition, I do not think that archaeologists have definitively answered the question concerning how much stored food might be available during bad years.[22] One way that people responded to these cycles was by adopting more water management technology. Archaeologists have discovered that during the 1200s local farmers tried to keep their crops well watered through the use of irrigation ditches, checkdams, reservoirs, and pebble mulch gardens (fig. 44). They integrated these features into larger and more complex agricultural systems that squeezed more production out of available farmlands.[23] Irrespective of how many migrants did or did not move into the northern Rio Grande, local populations increased because people had learned how to become better farmers.

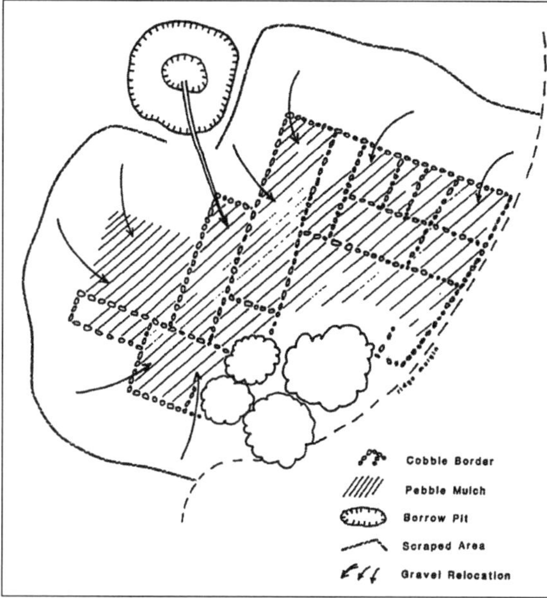

Fig. 44. Pebble-mulch grid gardens. Illustration by Dale Lightfoot (1993).

Fig. 45. Examples of Santa Fe Black-on-white pottery. Museum of Indian Arts and Culture/ Laboratory of Anthropology (1914,3676).

Following the relatively benign climate of the eighth through the thirteenth centuries, higher-than-average temperature trends resulted in worsening drought conditions across the entire Southwest.[24] Probably the most well-known and intense episode was the so-called "Great Drought" that occurred between 1276 and 1299 C.E. This "event" is really an amalgamation of a number of below-average precipitation years. While it was neither the longest nor most severe period of below-average rainfall, it is widely credited as one of the probable factors that resulted in a general movement of Ancestral Puebloans out of the Four Corners and Colorado Plateau regions. Deteriorating environmental conditions, warfare, and population instability contributed to this movement as well. Santa Fe also experienced the "Great Drought," but it was less intense locally than on the Colorado Plateau, and not as severe as earlier droughts in the 1220s and 1250s. Inasmuch as both Pindi and Agua Fria Schoolhouse pueblos "were quite successful during the years of the Great Drought,"[25] it appears as if Santa Fe skated through one of the most severe environmental challenges faced by Ancestral Puebloans.

Overall, the Coalition Period began with a scattering of local groups operating as small-scale farmers who still spent some time hunting and gathering. At the end, virtually everyone was living as settled, full-time agriculturalists. It was also the period when small pit house and jacal hamlets expanded to become larger villages, a process that entailed many changes, including the ways in which the people within these villages learned to hold their communities together and interact with other communities. The accepted material marker for the changeover from the preceding

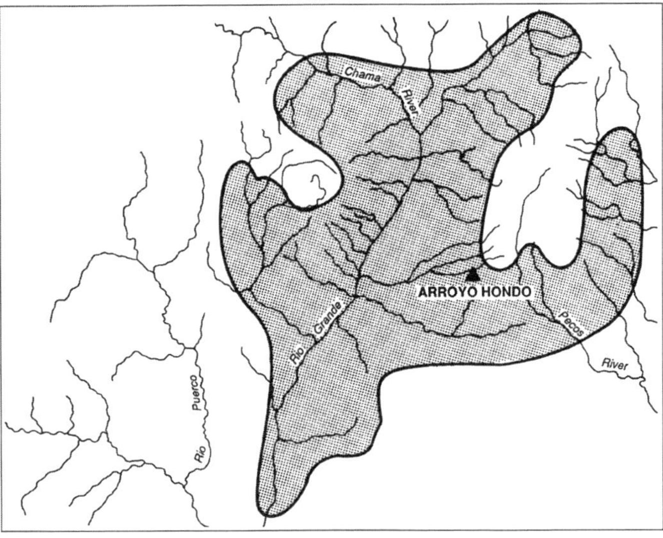

Fig. 46. Distribution of Santa Fe Black-on-white pottery during the 13th century. Adapted from Habicht-Mauche (1993). Illustration courtesy of the School for Advanced Research.

Developmental Period to the Coalition is the appearance of organic, carbon-based paint that replaced mineral-based paint on black-on-white pottery.[26] This black paint was not invented in Santa Fe but probably came with "westerners," people from the Four Corners region and the San Juan Valley. Although the older local Kwahe'e Black-on-white designs were generally retained, the new carbon-painted pottery is called Santa Fe Black-on-white (fig. 45). It is not clear precisely why this new paint became so popular, although from a technical standpoint mineral paints tend to "fail" more often than carbon paints when applied to Rio Grande clays that fire at lower temperatures than, for example, clays found in the San Juan Valley.[27]

Regardless of its genesis, Santa Fe Black-on-white pottery became, as archaeologist Stephen Post so aptly notes, "the people's choice in 13th century Santa Fe."[28] For more than two centuries, it was one of the principal types of pottery produced throughout the northern Rio Grande region (fig. 46) and was characterized by both "stylistic uniformity" and "local compositional and technical variation." In other words, all Santa Fe Black-on-white pottery looks similar because of shared design layouts and motifs, but the tempering is different because the pottery producers were widely distributed and relied upon different clay sources.[29]

This last statement was not necessarily a hard and fast rule. One of the enduring questions concerning Santa Fe Black-on-white pottery was whether it was produced

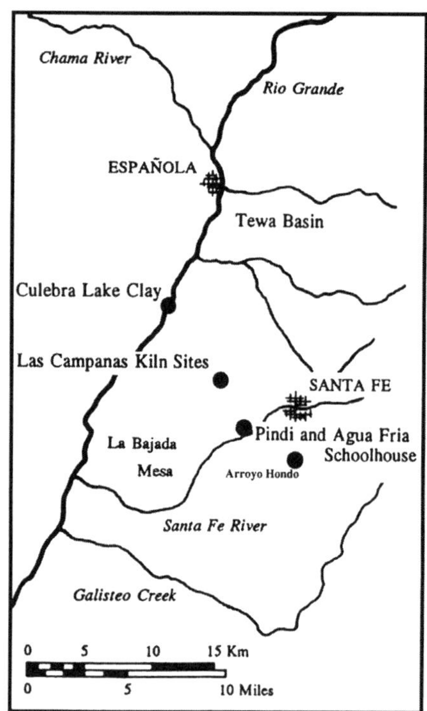

Fig. 47. Location of Las Campanas pit kilns in relation to Culebra clay source and nearby pueblos. Map courtesy of Stephen S. Post.

by many individual potters as part of localized, household-based systems, or whether there were actual centers of production from which the ceramics were distributed over a wider area. Intensive analyses of pottery recovered from Arroyo Hondo Pueblo supports the latter theory,[30] but it was not until archaeologists discovered actual kiln sites west of Santa Fe that the idea of centralized production centers received archaeological support.[31] In the early 1990s, archaeologists discovered two presumptive pit kilns during a survey of the Las Campanas area, approximately seven miles west of Santa Fe. What was most surprising was that the kilns were found at least four miles from the large communities of Pindi and Agua Fria Schoolhouse, the closest Coalition Period sites (fig. 47). If these kilns are representative structures, they are relatively small (approximately 5 by 3 feet)[32] and could easily be overlooked during a survey, so once again archaeologists must wrestle with the idea that under the rolling piedmont west of the city there may be much more than meets the eye. Why kilns would have been located literally out of sight of the nearest pueblos remains unexplained, but subsequent investigations identified a clay source at Cañada Ancha on the Rio Grande that may eventually be recognized as the single, major clay source for a substantial portion of Coalition Period Santa Fe Black-on-white ceramics.[33] This could result in a major reconsideration of the economic and social networks operating in Santa Fe from the late 12th into the early 14th centuries. If the foregoing is correct, conceivably Pindi and Agua Fria Schoolhouse may have secured a dominant position in the local production and distribution of Santa Fe Black-on-white pottery. "So what?" Nominally autonomous Coalition communities may have been tied more closely together in ways that archaeologists have not previously considered. The term "market monopoly" sounds a bit too modern, but if the archaeologists are correct about the origins of this high-quality pottery's distribution throughout the Santa Fe region, that is exactly what the people at Pindi and Agua Fria accomplished.[34]

When the pit kiln information is coupled with the notion of embryonic territoriality that I introduced at the end of Chapter 5, we may be seeing an emerging picture of rapidly growing communities proactively appropriating land for farming or other resources such as clay, and protecting it against intruders. Almost three decades ago, D. Bruce Dickson, Jr., suggested that the occupants of the middle northern Rio Grande district may have literally closed the area to immigrants from the west or south.[35] Why would local people cut off potential sources of new labor or ideas? Probably because of real or perceived shortages of arable land, water, or wood and the need to take care of "us" rather than "them." Life was indeed becoming more complicated in Santa Fe.

In Chapter 5 I discussed how the Late Developmental was a period of indisputable population growth, but it did not compare to the ways that neighborhoods filled up during the Coalition Period. The decades after 1175 C.E., particularly those after the mid-1200s, witnessed enormous demographic changes throughout the entire Southwest, and the middle northern Rio Grande Valley was no exception. The local landscape was soon characterized by the existence of pueblos whose size and form were quite different from earlier pit house villages. These newer and larger pueblos were planned and constructed around "public" plazas. On a natural bench above the Santa Fe River, archaeologist Regge Wiseman may have identified an early example of "plaza centering" at a small Late Developmental Period pueblo in which a set of contiguous, single-story surface rooms was arranged in a U-shape around an internal plaza.[36] This simple form was enlarged and adapted over the next century until Coalition Period pueblos emerged as a new and different kind of settlement structure. The presence of central plazas presumes social as well as architectural change. Plazas are associated with community-based forms of social and political organization as opposed to household-based forms. Large plazas can accommodate community-wide ceremonial events, but they tied people together as places where one could "see and be seen" even when used for ordinary domestic activities. Built space essentially became the community integrator as well as the "policeman," because unusual or unacceptable behavior could be observed, reported, and resolved by "the community."[37]

On the other hand, despite the sometimes-impressive sizes of Coalition pueblos, they can appear more like random agglomerations than carefully designed structures. Indeed, Pindi Pueblo, located within the present village of Agua Fria south of Santa Fe, does look a bit like a creeping amoeba stretched along the ridge on the west bank of the Santa Fe River (fig. 48). Pindi was occupied for more than two hun-

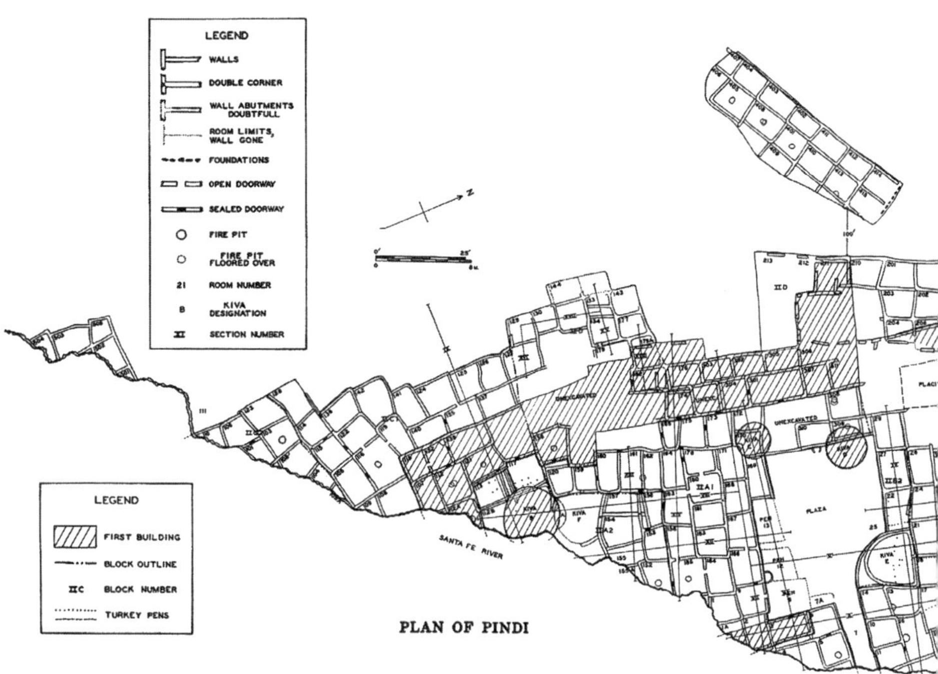

Fig. 48. Plan of Pindi Pueblo. Illustration by Stubbs and Stallings (1953), courtesy of School for Advanced Research.

dred years (1200–1425 C.E.) and its occupation history spanned the entire Coalition and extended into the Classic Period. However, readers should understand that large pueblos such as Pindi and those that followed were the result of complicated sequences of construction, maintenance, abandonment, and reuse that are not represented in the architectural summary in Figure 48. In a sense, a pueblo is as much a process as a thing. Focusing upon an "archaeological snapshot" in the pueblo's existence may not tell us very much about the sequence of growth and development any more than someone could discern my own life history by looking at my high school graduation picture. Part of Pindi is built on top of a small residential cluster dating to the Late Developmental Period. "So what?" During a time when pueblos were often abandoned after two or three generations, this settlement was occupied for at least eight or nine generations. Pindi was a large, multistoried (two or three stories) pueblo consisting of more than 175 rooms, at least two plazas, and five kivas. Notably, at Pindi two very different types of kivas were being used at approximately the same time (fig. 49). In my opinion, the architectural diversity expressed

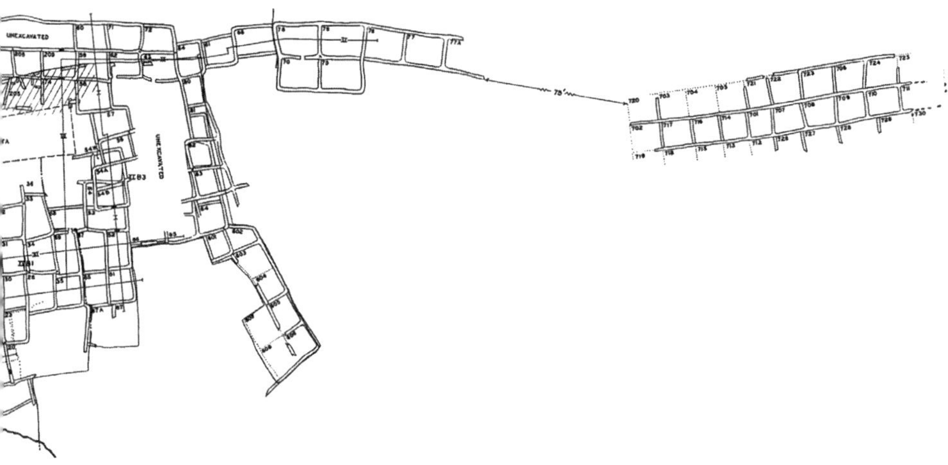

in the construction of ceremonial structures could indicate that diverse peoples with ethnic, linguistic, or even religious differences were living together.[38]

The name *Pindi* actually means "turkey" in the Tewa language. The discovery of four turkey pens, identified by the presence of turkey manure, eggshells, and bones in the main plaza, provided an apt moniker for this particular pueblo. Turkeys would have been an excellent source of food, feather blankets, bone tools, and even ceremonial items.[39] While the size of this presumed turkey-breeding operation is noteworthy, archaeologists have uncovered evidence of turkey breeding from both the prior Developmental Period[40] as well as the subsequent Classic Period,[41] suggesting that a significant level of turkey domestication was probably coincident with the local agricultural expansion that occurred after 900 C.E. The presence of turkey iconography on local rock art panels would appear to attest to the significance of turkeys (fig. 50).

Pindi was partially abandoned in the mid-14th century during a period of very high rainfall. Since there is no evidence of warfare such as substantial room burning or extensive trauma associated with human remains, the pueblo may have been vic-

KIVA	SHAPE	AREA IN in sq. feet	PROBABLE OCCUPATION DATES (from tree rings)	FIRE PIT CONSTRUCTION	SIPAPUS	ORIENTATION
A[1]	circular	?	?	?	?	?
B	circular	226	1201–1288[2]	circular, adobe rim	2	East-southeast
C	circular	132	1204–1267[3]	circular, adobe rim	none	East-southeast
D	circular	113	1269–1272[4]	circular, mud lined	1	East-southeast
E	D-shaped	?	1242–1274[5]	square, some stone, adobe rim	none	South-southwest
F	D-shaped (possibly)	256	1304–1336[6]	square, stone-lined, adobe rim	1 (with jar)	East-southeast

[1] Kiva A was effectively destroyed by the construction of Kiva B, and very little information was recovered. Stubbs and Stallings (1953:39).

[2] An outlying tree-ring date of 1157 may be the result of timber reuse from earlier construction, but there were twenty-one 13th-century dates with a mean of 1251–1252, a median of 1250, and a mode of 1278. Stubbs and Stallings (1953:156–162).

[3] Based on two tree-ring dates.

[4] Based on two tree-ring dates.

[5] An outlying tree-ring date of 1200 may be the result of timber reuse from earlier construction, and there were four other dates between 1242 and 1274.

[6] An outlying tree-ring date of 1229 may be the result of timber reuse from earlier construction, and there were four other dates between 1303 and 1336. Stubbs and Stallings (1953:156–162).

Fig. 49. Architectural summary for Pindi kivas. Table by Jason S. Shapiro.

timized by flooding that destroyed agricultural land and possibly even parts of the pueblo. Stubbs and Stallings reported "a portion of the pueblo has been washed away by the Santa Fe River, and old inhabitants of [the village of] Agua Fria report that years ago many burials were washed out by the eroding river."[42] It would not be the first or last time that a flood destroyed a village, but I have always found it ironic that in this "land of little rain" water can be such a destructive force. Clearly, the people of Pindi were persistent, had strong leadership, or both, because by the 1340s the pueblo had reestablished itself on a smaller scale and remained occupied until the 1420s.

The occupation sequence of Pindi's "sister" pueblo of Agua Fria Schoolhouse, situated on the east side of the Santa Fe River, is both similar and different from that of Pindi.[43] Detailed knowledge of this site has been limited by the fact that it was only recently that archaeologists, working in conjunction with a Santa Fe County transportation improvement plan, have understood just how much of the pueblo has been preserved. Although much of the later Classic Period sections of the pueblo have been destroyed by a couple of hundred years of construction activity, substantial portions of the earlier Coalition Period component still lie under well-traveled portions of Agua Fria Street as well as near the surface on the south side of the road (fig. 51). Ceramics indicate that occupation began around 1200 C.E. and continued uninterrupted until around 1315–1320 C.E., when a large portion of the pueblo was

Fig. 50. Turkey petroglyph at La Cieneguilla petroglyph site. Photograph by Jason S. Shapiro.

Fig. 51. Agua Fria Schoolhouse site. Photograph by Nels Nelson, courtesy American Museum of Natural History.

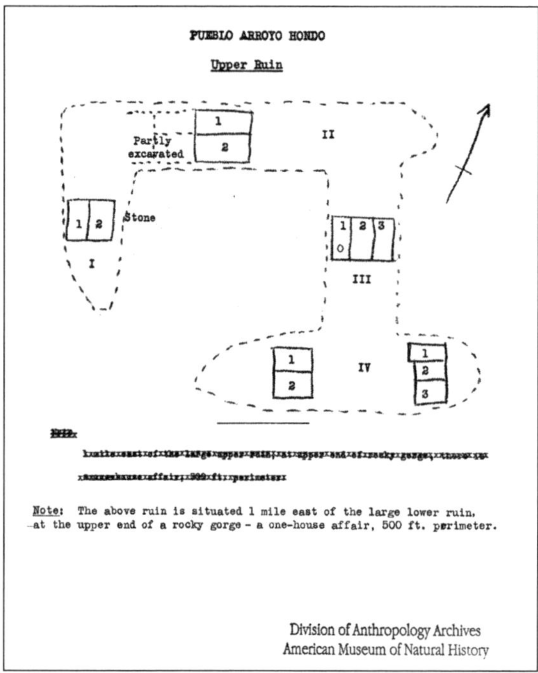

Fig. 52. Upper Arroyo Hondo Pueblo. Illustration by Nels Nelson, courtesy American Museum of Natural History.

abandoned, probably as a result of flood damage. Not everyone left, however, and tree-cutting dates from recovered beams suggest that people continued to repair the pueblo through the 1320s with evidence of new construction through the 1360s. Apparently, some people remained at the site until around 1420 when it was finally abandoned. Some archaeologists believe that at Pindi's height during the early Classic Period possibly between 1,000 and 2,000 people may have resided there and at Agua Fria Schoolhouse, making them together the largest settlement in Santa Fe.[44]

One of the things that archaeologists often associate with the Coalition Period is the expansion of settlements into areas beyond the confines of the major river valleys. However, there is evidence this trend actually began during the Late Developmental Period.[45] In the previous chapter I noted the growth of three local settlement nodes: north of the city near Tesuque, west of the city along the Santa Fe River, and downtown in the vicinity of Fort Marcy and Federal Place. Now, during the early Coalition, a new settlement node developed southeast of the city that included the pueblos of Mocho, Upper Arroyo Hondo (fig. 52), Los Alamos (figs. 53), and other pueblos slightly further afield such as Chamisa Locita[46] (figs. 55, 56), and Burnt Corn. Other archaeologists have described a fifth settlement node located further down the Santa Fe River Canyon beginning with La Cienega Pueblo in the early 1200s and eventually including La Bajada and Cieneguilla pueblos together with several smaller sites.[47] Archaeologists continue to research and debate whether these new settlements were precursors to the Classic Period expansion in the Galisteo Basin as changing rainfall regimes made some upland areas more productive, whether they were the result of a growing population base expanding into previously unoccupied and less productive zones, and even whether they represented the apex of groups moving into this area from someplace else.

At least in the case of Upper Arroyo Hondo Pueblo it appears as if people merely moved along the foothills a few miles from existing settlements and established themselves beside Arroyo Hondo Creek, not because of the proximity of Steaksmith, a popular local restaurant now located near this site, but because that creek was the only perennial water course on the south side of town. Nels Nelson excavated a handful of this pueblo's 50 rooms in 1912, but for the most part this site remains unexcavated. Unlike Pindi and some other pueblos that were built upon earlier Developmental Period structures, the "southeast node" pueblos look like new Coalition creations. For example, Burnt Corn was a moderate-sized pueblo about 15 miles south of Santa Fe, not far from the town of Cerrillos in the Galisteo Basin. A linear settlement located along a low ridge, not unlike Pindi, it is comprised of several roomblocks and plazas and consisted of perhaps 150–200 rooms. The varieties of "Black-on-white" pottery recovered on site indicate that Burnt Corn was built and occupied in the thirteenth century with no earlier or later occupations.[48] Burnt Corn was near Upper Arroyo Hondo and only a few miles away from Los Alamos Pueblo, located under the present intersection of I-25 and Route 285.[49] Both

Fig. 53. *Los Alamos Pueblo.*
Photograph by Nels Nelson,
courtesy American Museum of
Natural History.

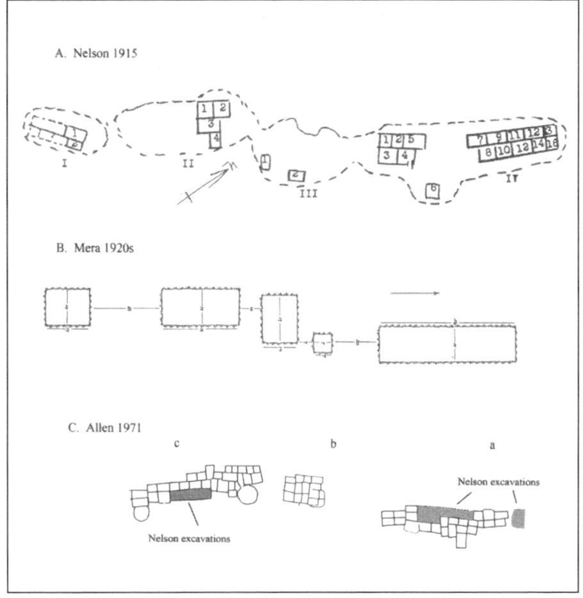

Fig. 54. *Comparative maps of Los*
Alamos Pueblo. Snead 2005.

Fig. 55. Chamisa Locita Pueblo. Photograph by Nels Nelson, courtesy American Museum of Natural History.

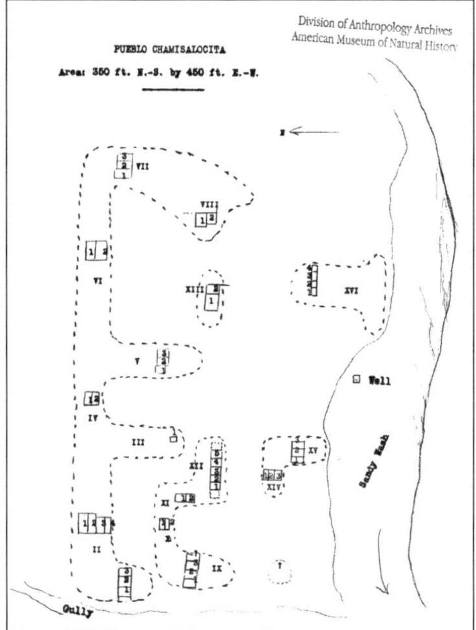

Fig. 56. Chamisa Locita Pueblo. Illustration by Nels Nelson, courtesy American Museum of Natural History.

of these pueblos were slightly smaller than Burnt Corn but were constructed and occupied during the same time frame. Chamisa Locita, built a bit later than the three former pueblos, was somewhat larger and was occupied almost twice as long as Burnt Corn.

Of particular interest for this chapter is El Pueblo de Santa Fe, only recently excavated by the Museum of New Mexico's Office of Archaeological Studies in preparation for the construction of the new downtown convention center.[50] Originally referred to by the Tewa name *Ogapoge*, literally "down at the Olivella shell-bead water," this large downtown pueblo has been the subject of both speculation and investigation for well over 100 years. Generations of archaeologists have unearthed tantalizing clues and dateable artifacts that appeared to substantiate persistent stories about a large pueblo located under city hall.[51] The central downtown location of this site, bordered today by Lincoln Street on the east, Federal Place on the north, Grant Street on the west, and Marcy Street on the south, places it in close proximity to the earlier KP, Diker, and Fort Marcy sites (fig. 57). It also is unclear what, if any, connection El Pueblo de Santa Fe had with the roughly contemporaneous Federal Courthouse site except that archaeologists have determined that both sites were probably occupied in the 12th and 13th centuries. Overall, from

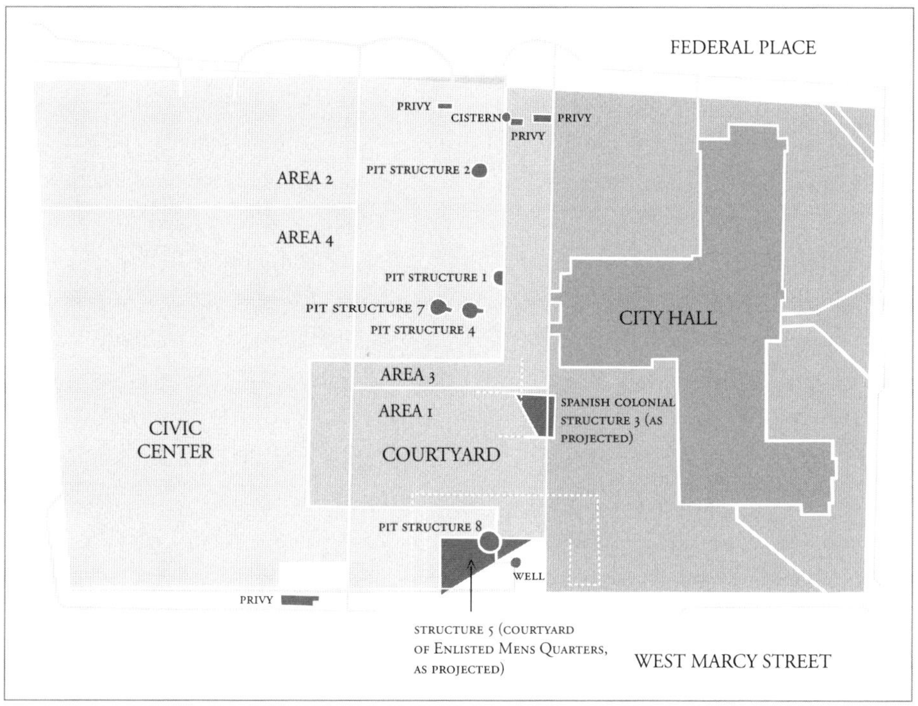

Fig. 57. Excavations of El Pueblo de Santa Fe. Map courtesy of Office of Archaeological Studies, Museum of New Mexico.

the Coalition into the early Classic Period, it looks as if El Pueblo de Santa Fe was both a focal point for the continuing occupation of the downtown area, as well as a community with broader connections.[52] Preliminary evidence suggests that the people living at El Pueblo de Santa Fe may have maintained relationships with local pueblos such as Pindi and Arroyo Hondo, as well as with unnamed "foreign" groups (producers of White Mountain red ware and Cibola white ware pottery) who were living in areas west of the Rio Grande Valley.[53]

The nature of inter-pueblo interactions within Santa Fe is another subject that needs to be studied. For example, we do not know whether these pueblos formed some kind of "Santa Fe alliance" and were connected by bonds of kinship or informal reciprocity or whether they dealt with each other on more formal, "arm's length," or even hostile footing. Similarly, we do not know if the local residents were of uniform or mixed ethnicity, engaged in any joint ceremonial activities, or even shared a common language.

Among the things we do know is that Coalition settlements seem to have developed in a couple of ways. Some pueblos, located where water and arable land remained available, were continuations and expansions of hamlets and villages that formed during the Developmental Period. Other Coalition pueblos were entirely new settlements that were established along secondary or tertiary drainages when small groups of locals or immigrants elected to move, or were pushed, into less desirable areas. Some of these new pueblos such as La Cieneguila,[54] located along the lower Santa Fe River several miles below the present municipal airport, and Cuyamungue,[55] located about 12 miles north of Santa Fe, persisted and prospered through the Coalition and continued to thrive into the Classic Period. On the other hand, smallish pueblos, such as Los Alamos (1243–1284 C.E.),[56] Upper Arroyo Hondo (1287–1313 C.E.),[57] and Burnt Corn (1272–1325 C.E.),[58] had much shorter "shelf lives." In fact, it looks as if someone came along and literally knocked Los Alamos and Burnt Corn right off the shelf, as both pueblos were abandoned after an episode of deliberate burning (fig. 58).[59]

In one sense this chapter has been a long windup for a short pitch. We have seen that by 1300 people were dealing with a much more competitive environment than they had faced only one hundred years earlier. For one thing, there were many more people living in the middle northern Rio Grande than ever before, and arable land—the Ancestral Puebloan equivalent of "affordable housing"—remained in limited supply. To complicate matters, a fickle climate caused unpredictable annual crop yields and added an element of nutritional stress to escalating social and environmental stresses. Agricultural intensification, water management technology, and increased hunting and gathering efforts worked only to a point, but there was always the option for hungry people to take what they needed from their neighbors. Without a doubt the neighbors resisted, and archaeologists have discovered evidence of burned villages. The systemic response to this kind of anarchy was for people to collect themselves into bigger settlements where larger workforces could be organized not only to plant more extensive croplands but also to protect them. Archaeologists sometimes blithely refer to this period as one of "population instability," but I do not wish to treat these matters lightly. The late 1200s were not particularly easy or joyous times. Forget about artistic expression and religious elaboration—these people were trying to grow enough food to keep from going hungry and had to protect what meager reserves they had.

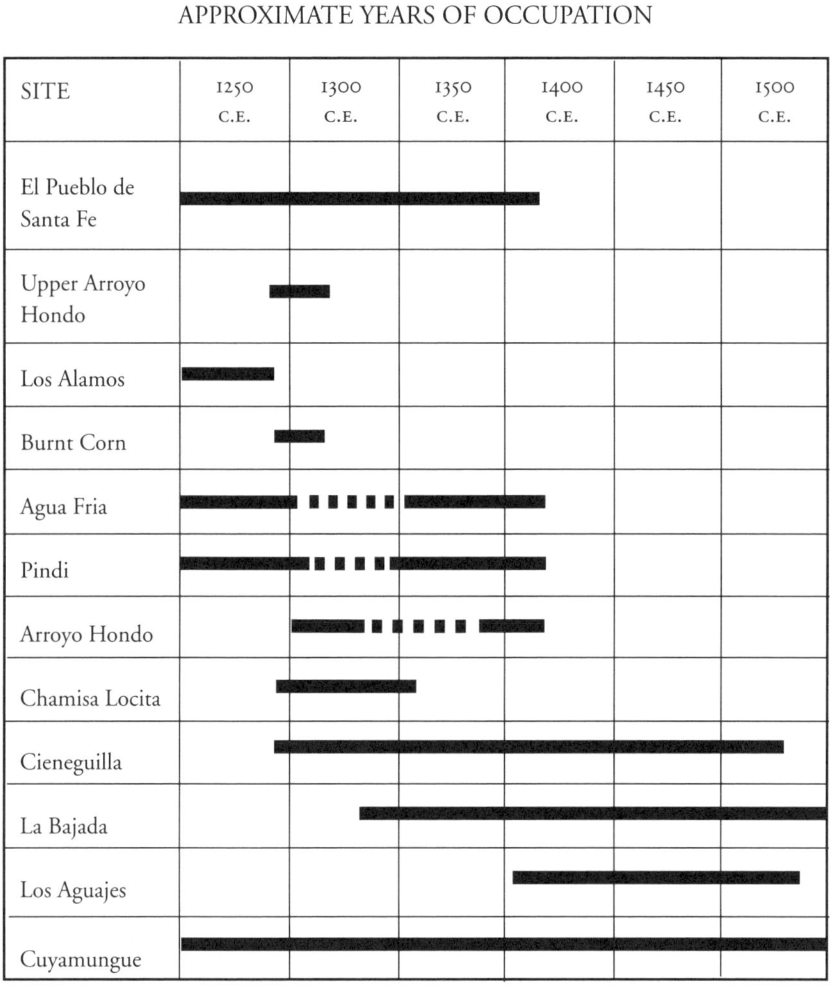

APPROXIMATE YEARS OF OCCUPATION

SITE	1250 C.E.	1300 C.E.	1350 C.E.	1400 C.E.	1450 C.E.	1500 C.E.
El Pueblo de Santa Fe	████████	████████	████████			
Upper Arroyo Hondo		██				
Los Alamos	███					
Burnt Corn		██				
Agua Fria	████████	▪ ▪ ▪ ▪	████████			
Pindi	████████	▪ ▪ ▪ ▪	████████			
Arroyo Hondo		████ ▪ ▪ ▪	████			
Chamisa Locita		█████				
Cieneguilla		████████	████████	████████	████████	
La Bajada			█████	████████	████████	████████
Los Aguajes				█████	████████	████
Cuyamungue	████████	████████	████████	████████	████████	████

Fig. 58. Occupation dates for selected Late Coalition and Classic Period sites in and around Santa Fe. Table by Jason S. Shapiro.

A Nels Nelson photograph identified as "New Mexico, 1912," possibly Tesuque Pueblo. Courtesy American Museum of Natural History.

Chapter 7

Big Box Zoning

CLASSIC PERIOD TOWNS 1325 – 1540 C.E.

If one drives south from downtown Santa Fe on the main commercial thoroughfare known as Cerrillos Road, within a few miles one enters the Realm of the Big Box Stores. In some respects, "The City Different" is not so different. Just like many other cities, Santa Fe has its own Wal-Mart, Lowe's, Home Depot, Target, and Sam's Club. Despite their "adobified" exteriors and competitive pricing, these stores have caused controversy, if not downright consternation, among some contemporary Santa Feans because of their sizes, traffic impacts, and real or perceived corporate policies.[1] From a different perspective, it is fascinating to consider the interplay of economic and political forces that successfully promote the aggregation of thousands of marginally related products into buildings that routinely exceed 200,000 square feet in size, are surrounded by acres of asphalt parking lots, and are clustered together in selected parts of town.

Beginning around seven hundred years ago Santa Fe, together with the entire Rio Grande Valley and other parts of the Southwest, experienced a different kind of aggregation as hundreds or sometimes thousands of individuals abandoned their small, dispersed settlements, moved in together, and built some of the largest pueblos ever seen in the region. Chaco Canyon's 800-room Pueblo Bonito is often presented as the apogee of Ancestral Puebloan building construction, yet numerous pueblos built and occupied during the 14th and 15th centuries had more than 1,000 rooms, with several having well in excess of 2,000 rooms.[2] Small farming villages characterized the earlier Ancestral Pueblo world of the 12th and 13th centuries, but by the 15th century many fewer but much larger town-sized pueblos defined this same world.[3] As we have seen throughout the previous several chapters, transformations in settlement patterns imply changes in social, political, economic, and ideological relationships but the Classic Period represents perhaps the largest scope of societal change that we have examined. Because it occurred within such a relatively short time period, it is even more remarkable.

Although no bell tolled at midnight on New Year's Eve in 1325 C.E. to ring in a new era, archaeologists use that convenient year to define the beginning of the Classic Period when virtually all of the inhabitants of the northern Rio Grande region gave up small- and medium-sized villages in favor of big settlements[4] that were sufficiently populous to be called "towns." The vast majority of those towns looked like variations of an architectural design form in which multiple plazas were enclosed by multistory roomblocks. Some of these settlements, such as El Pueblo de Santa Fe, Pindi, and Agua Fria Schoolhouse, were ongoing occupations from the Coalition Period, but many new pueblos such as Arroyo Hondo (not to be confused with Upper Arroyo Hondo discussed in Chapter 6), as well as several truly massive settlements in the Galisteo Basin, were newly built at this time. Population estimates for just the middle northern Rio Grande during this period range between 3,000–5,000 people,[5] and the estimated population for the entire region between Albuquerque and Taos was easily several times higher. The production of lead glaze-painted pottery and the appearance of *katsina* symbolism are two other often-discussed markers for this period.

At the same time that people were building BIG, they were also building small. Classic Period sites are also characterized by small structures of one, two, or three rooms, located at some distances from the pueblos. As Puebloan farmers increased the sizes of their field systems in order to feed burgeoning populations, they developed farmlands further and further away from the pueblos. Four to five miles seems to have been about the limit of reasonable travel distance from any one pueblo, but most fields were located closer to the main settlements.[6] Field houses provided temporary shelter for people charged with monitoring and protecting crops, and served as places to temporarily store harvested crops, or as limited-activity bases for hunting[7] or the collection of clay and stone. These small structures were used intermittently, although in some cases for long periods of time, and they constituted an important part of Classic Period subsistence strategy. Studies have revealed that

ENVIRONMENTAL EXPLANATIONS FOR AGGREGATION	CULTURAL EXPLANATIONS FOR AGGREGATION
Climatic changes (precipitation, temperature, alterations in growing season) resulting in movements to better sites	Defense from conflict and warfare ("Strength in numbers")
Natural processes (changes in water tables, soil depth, biomass levels; natural disasters) resulting in movements to better sites	Agricultural production and associated labor needs and specializations (multiple plantings and harvestings, water management, crop defense) ("The more the merrier")
	Access to systems of status, alliance, trade, ritual activity, or information control ("Be all that you can be")
	Population growth and density ("Bright lights, big towns")
	Reduction of competition ("When you can't beat them, join them")

Fig. 59. Selected explanations for population aggregation among groups in the Southwest. Table by Jason S. Shapiro.

areas adjacent to the middle northern Rio Grande, including the Pajarito Plateau, the Chama Valley, the Galisteo Basin, Pecos, and areas near Albuquerque, all experienced similar episodes of population growth and aggregation, the construction of large pueblos, new forms of ceramic production, and the establishment of inter-pueblo and inter-regional exchange networks. In other words, the phenomena that archaeologists associate with the Classic Period were not localized but widespread.

Readers may have grown weary of the notion that the causes behind most cultural changes are both "many and varied." Despite our overwhelming desire for crystal clarity, the idea of multiple causations is still relevant to the evolution of large, nucleated Classic Period pueblos. The fundamental question that continues to vex archaeologists is "Why aggregation?" What forces drove people across the entire Southwest to construct these enormous settlements? Archaeologists Michael Adler, Todd Van Pool, and Robert Leonard have authored a comprehensive review of the dual subjects of aggregation and abandonment and I have adapted Figure 59 from their study.[8]

Adler, Van Pool, and Leonard have reduced the fluid process of aggregation to a collection of "environmental" and "cultural" triggers. What some scholars may view as a rote repetition of concepts that have been "in the box" for a long time I think actually strengthens the explanatory value of these triggers. Virtually every examination of earlier manifestations of community aggregation in the Southwest including the 11th- and early-12th century events in the Mimbres region of southern New Mexico, the 10th-, 11th-, and 12th-century events in Chaco Canyon, and the 13th-century events in southwestern Colorado, has arrived at a similar mix of environmental and cultural causes. The widespread archaeological evidence of a near total shift towards aggregated settlements across the Puebloan Southwest in the 14th and 15th centuries looks like a large-scale version of a recurring phenomenon. As far as the Santa Fe area is concerned, all of the factors identified in Figure 59 probably contributed in some way to a process that began during the Coalition Period. It is impossible to tease out any single aspect and say, "Aha, so that's why the Puebloans built those enormous settlements in the Rio Grande Valley!" The process was not just *aggregation*, the idea of collecting people into larger units, but included *amalgamation* and *accommodation* as well. People found themselves living in communities that were both larger and more diverse than the Coalition communities of only a few generations past. Everyone needed access to land and water, and people had to be blended into the community's social fabric. There also had to be a willingness among community members to adjust their lives in some manner to the needs of others. The backdrop to aggregated pueblos is that the northern Rio Grande was filling up with people, it was a challenging area for maize-based agriculture, and there was just not that much really good agricultural land. Larger pueblos could muster more workers and warriors.

Archaeologist Eden Welker has investigated the nature of Classic Period settlement aggregation, and although her case studies of San Marcos and Pecos Pueblos involve sites located just beyond the boundaries of the middle northern Rio Grande, her observations are worth considering.[9] The essence of Welker's study is that while both San Marcos and Pecos were large aggregated settlements, the economic systems that sustained each pueblo were different and diversified, with a changing emphasis upon subsistence agriculture, pottery production, and participation in trading networks. Welker's comment that "maintaining aggregation required...effort and economic savvy to shift production, distribution, and consumption patterns in order to survive"[10] underscores the idea that "aggregation" is more of a process than either a static condition or a singular event. Welker's statement also highlights the less obvious point that despite certain superficial similarities, not all Classic Period settlements necessarily followed the same economic, social, or even political pathways. This is a reminder for archaeologists to be as careful, specific, and detailed as possible in their analyses because statements that begin "All Classic Period pueblos in the Santa Fe area…" cannot account for genuine differences between, for example, Arroyo Hondo, Cieneguilla, and El Pueblo de Santa Fe. That said, I know that being "careful and detailed" can be an elusive goal. I have visited and worked on a number of large Classic Period pueblos in the Rio Grande Valley and have found it sometimes difficult to set aside the similarities I observed among the remnants of orthogonally arranged roomblocks[11] and plazas littered with variously decorated pottery sherds, and wrap my mind around the idea that these pueblos were built, occupied, and abandoned at different times, by different people, and for different reasons.

I mentioned that one of the road signs announcing the arrival of the Classic Period was a technological development similar to the one that separated the Coalition from the Developmental Period. During the 12th century it was the shift from mineral- to carbon-based paint that signaled a significant cultural change; in the 14th century it was the production of lead glaze-painted pottery.[12] Lead glazing as pottery decoration appears to have developed in more than one place. People were making it in the Acoma and Zuni areas in west-central New Mexico by 1275 C.E. and in the vicinity of Albuquerque by around 1300.[13] By 1325, a sequence of locally produced lead-glazed pottery appeared in the northern middle Rio Grande beginning with what has been defined as "glaze A" (fig. 60), but the technique did not become widely distributed until between 1340 and 1350.[14] At that time production shifted to several pueblos in the Galisteo Basin that had relatively easy access to sources of lead ore in the Cerrillos Hills. Archaeological evidence strongly suggests the operation of both *specialization* (relatively few skilled potters controlled production) and *standardization* (relatively few kinds of forms were manufactured) in what may be called the "Galisteo glazeware industry," except that it was an industry in which local, independent potters operated at the level of individual villages.[15] The sequence of painted glaze wares changed over time but continued for several hundred years (fig. 61) and is still one of the most effective ways of dating occupational events in and around the Rio Grande Valley.

The 14th-century process of *aggregation-amalgamation-accommodation* is associated with changes in architectural style. By this time, local Puebloans had expanded

Fig. 60. Glaze A bowl, ca. 1315–1425. Photograph courtesy Museum of Indian Arts and Culture/Laboratory of Anthropology (18641).

the earlier Coalition plan of a single plaza partially enclosed by two or three roomblocks into much more outsized designs. For example, at its zenith Arroyo Hondo (not to be confused with Upper Arroyo Hondo discussed in the previous chapter) was comprised of 24 mostly contiguous roomblocks with around 1,000 rooms and 13 plazas. Not every large settlement that developed during the Classic Period was configured the same way, but, overall, the size and spatial complexity of Classic pueblos was unlike anything that had ever been built before in the northern Rio Grande. Archaeologists have increased their understanding of the relationship between architecture and other cultural elements to the point where the following quote from archaeologist Erik Reed, made fifty years ago, now seems curiously quaint in its honesty: "Interpretation of the [architectural] changes during the last few centuries in the Upper Rio Grande, from the front-directed Anasazi [construction] plan to the hollow-square layout…to [the] predominance of parallel [roomblock] alignments, except among the Tewa, is beyond me."[16]

Archaeological and architectural studies have attempted to relate the design of plaza-oriented settlements to the ability to respond to changing demographics. Architecture worked in concert with new social rules in amalgamating diverse groups of people who now found themselves living together. "Ladder-style" roomblocks[17] could be built in a relatively short period of time in order to accommodate population increases, and plazas became settings for a wide variety of both family-centered and larger group activities. Ultimately, plazas became community-integrating mechanisms in the same ways that kivas had integrated smaller groups in the past.[18] The change in architectural style and living arrangements seems to have predated the rapid increases in population, but that ongoing debate about whether the population increases beginning in the 13th century were the result of in-migration or local population increases is still with us. I won't repeat those arguments except to note that the overall growth rates, measured in numbers of newly built pueblo rooms, cannot be

GLAZE TYPE	TIME RANGE OF PRODUCTION AND USAGE
Glaze A	1315–1425 C.E.
Glaze B	1425–1450 C.E.
Glaze C	1450–1490 C.E.
Glaze D	1490–1515 C.E.
Glaze E	1515–1625 C.E.
Glaze F	1625–1700 C.E.

Fig. 61. Chronology of Rio Grande glazeware sequence. Table by Jason S. Shapiro.

accounted for by focusing only on the fertility of local populations. The local rate of increase would have to have been extraordinarily high in order to produce the numbers of people who occupied this region in the 14th and 15th centuries.

Because the fundamental problems associated with lots of people and not enough food had never been completely solved, at some point even the institutions associated with really big pueblos could not ensure the health, safety, and social stability of their members. In addition, beginning in the 1320s or 1330s, climatic cycles fluctuated enormously with short (five or ten years) intense periods of very high and very low rainfall. In spite of (or maybe because of) these fluctuations, some pueblos were able to develop ecological solutions to the problem of growing maize and other crops in an uncertain environment. La Bajada Pueblo (not to be confused with the La Bajada Archaic site discussed in Chapter 4) was situated at the base of a mesa located along the lower reaches of the Santa Fe River (figs. 62, 63). This location gave residents relatively easy access to three different types of farmland: floodplains near the river, garden plots at the base of the mesa where both rainwater and organic material would run off, and extensive dry farming plots on top of the mesa. The people at La Bajada structured their agricultural system around planting at different elevations, exploiting different soils, and relying on different water sources. During dry years when mesa top farming was unreliable, people focused on floodwater farming near the river and garden plots at the base of hills. During excessively wet years when floods limited planting on the floodplains, people focused on dry farm-

Fig. 62. La Bajada Pueblo. Photograph by Nels Nelson, courtesy American Museum of Natural History.

ing on the mesa top. In years without extremes both strategies may have worked well enough to accumulate some surplus.[19] The effectiveness of this strategy seems to be borne out by archaeological evidence that La Bajada was occupied for at least 200 years during a time when many pueblos were occupied only for a few generations. The use of mixed agricultural strategies was not unique to the Santa Fe district—pueblos north of the city in the Chama Valley and south of the city in the Galisteo Basin also adopted a variable mix of ways to successfully grow crops.[20]

Not every pueblo was situated as well as La Bajada to make natural ecology work for them. A different kind of solution to the insecurities of the 14th century was to get bigger, not by continuing to physically expand the already enormous pueblos but by binding several communities together into loose, temporary alliances. For example, looking at ceramic designs as ethnic identifiers, Judith Habicht-Mauche has found correlations between stylistic diversity and changes in cultural diversity among 14th-century groups living in the northern Rio Grande (fig. 64).[21] The essence of her research is about connections and, more specifically, the realization that for some pueblos emerging ethnic identification (or something like it) may have been more important than geographical proximity in establishing and maintaining connections with other selected pueblos. Specific ceramic designs are the markers from which the intra-pueblo connections can be inferred.[22]

The ways in which volumes of pottery were distributed among pueblos within particular areas may have reflected emergent ethnic differentiation and even more aggressive territorial control than we have seen during earlier periods. Habicht-Mauche uses the term "tribalization" in connection with the process of the production and distribution of glaze-painted pottery, and while Classic Period alliances were not "tribes" in any modern sense, these multi-pueblo associations undoubtedly broadened the concept of "community" to embrace wider areas and more people. Basically, we are looking at flexible, relatively informal but unstable forms of organization that operated above the level of individual pueblos. The difference between what Habicht-Mauche is referring to and the seeming control by Pindi and Agua Fria Schoolhouse of Santa Fe Black-on-white pottery that I discussed in Chapter 6 is that the scope of these 14th- and 15th-century exchange networks was more developed and involved several autonomous production centers (San Cristobal, San Marcos Pueblo, San Lazaro Pueblo, and so forth). Regardless of whether these expedient alliances were based on trade, shared language, or geography, they gave people more dependable access to resources (food, warriors, potential mates), and maybe that was enough of a reason for them to continue. Under no circumstances should these alliances be viewed as unified regional systems. There is no evidence of any kind of supervening political control like that which developed among the Mississippian chiefdoms operating in the southeastern United States at roughly this time period.[23] Even within each pueblo, there is no clear evidence of economic or socially elite groups of people, at least in terms of the number, quality, and overall distribution of household possessions. Most living rooms within Classic pueblos were about the same size, and archaeologists have not found evidence of larger and more elaborate dwellings, or of concentrations of fancy and exotic stuff,[24] or of privileged burials.[25] Not only can we not find a chief's house, but archaeologists have inferred that there was relative economic equality within these large towns.

On the other hand, just because we cannot find the chief's house does not mean there were no leaders and no hierarchies. Classic towns had grown to a point where

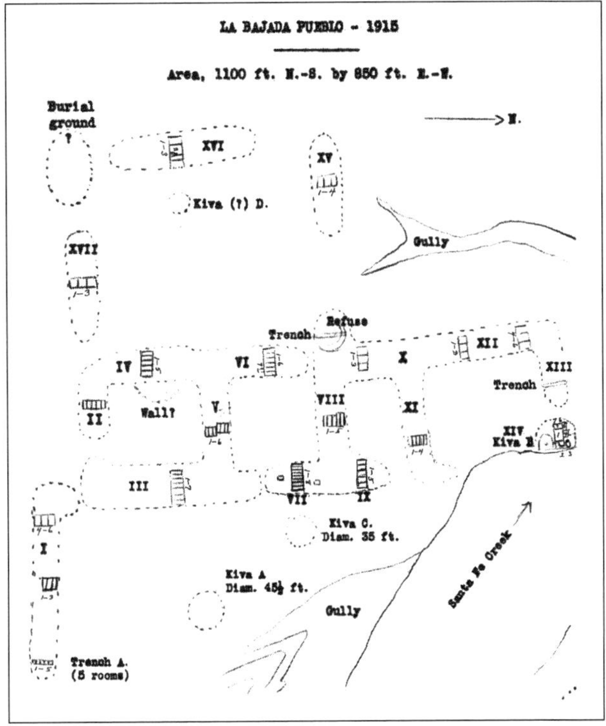

Fig. 63. La Bajada Pueblo. Illustration by Nels Nelson, courtesy American Museum of Natural History.

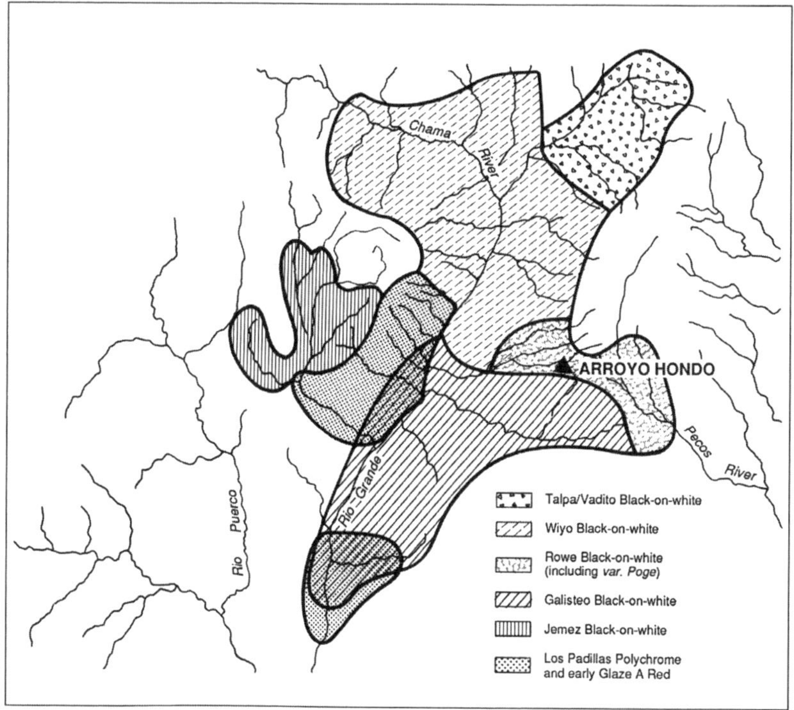

Fig. 64. Map illustrating ceramic distribution among Rio Grande pueblos. Illustration by Habicht-Mauche (1993), courtesy of School for Advanced Research.

management decisions had to be made above the level of individual families in ways that would keep the entire community together. There were simply too many people and the decisions too important to not have had some type of formal process capable of mediating among competing families. In the absence of clear hierarchies, it is likely that clans or moieties developed some kind of power sharing arrangements that mediated in part by rotating responsibility for seasonal agricultural activities and rituals.[26] This is not to imply that there were no internal or external disagreements: there is evidence of individual skeletal trauma as well as larger-scale conflict, such as the presence of burned and abandoned settlements and warrior-type iconography (fig. 65).[27]

Suppose this "bigger idea" of alliances mediated by the distribution of distinctive ceramics was not enough? Temporary alliances were notably unstable and at best could only offer localized ameliorations to broader environmental or political instability. Over the course of the 14th and 15th centuries, a belief system developed that in many ways connected the entire Ancestral Puebloan world, including the

Fig. 65. Rio Grande–style rock art showing warriors. Photograph by Jason S. Shapiro.

northern Rio Grande Valley. This is of course the katsina (or kachina) system. I have discussed the development of institutions that helped people become accepted members of new and growing communities. In one sense, the katsina system is just another, albeit a very large, example of those institutions. Many of the earlier integrating institutions included specialized and secret societies that initiated select members into sacred and esoteric knowledge. While I hesitate to use the word "democratic," the katsina system was open to more participants and was much more public in its ceremonialism. In addition to its inclusiveness, the katsina religion represented a new way of looking at the cosmos, and it became the most widespread cultural phenomena in the northern Southwest since the dissolution of the Chaco system in the 12th century.

The katsina system probably coalesced shortly before 1300, but it is still not entirely clear whether this ideology spread east-to-west across the northern Southwest from the Rio Grande Valley or west-to-east, from the Little Colorado River area in northeastern Arizona.[28] The recognition that elements of the katsina system remain strongest among the western Pueblos of Hopi and Zuni than among eastern Puebloan groups living in the Rio Grande Valley supports the latter scenario but, re-

Fig. 66. Cloud Dance, Santa Clara Pueblo. T. Harmon Parkhurst, 1925–1945(?). Photograph courtesy Museum of New Mexico.

gardless of its origin, by the end of the 14th century it had become the dominant ideology among the Ancestral Puebloans.[29] The development of the katsina system can be seen as a device for social integration and the amelioration of risk. Everyone participated in the katsina ceremonies either as dancers attempting to intercede with natural forces or as observers whose attendance legitimized and reified the efforts of the dancers. The world in which the Pueblo lived had changed and appeared "out of balance," and the elements of the katsina religion that focused on water and rain, or fertility and growth, operated as one more mechanism that societies could use to adapt to changes in both the physical and social environments.

Closely associated with the spread of katsina ceremonies was the appearance of new forms of iconography featuring costumed and masked dancers,[30] horned or plumed serpents, parrots,[31] butterflies, and stars. These shared symbols opened up a panoply of new possibilities. Suppose you had to move into a new area where the people were strangers and did not speak your language? If you followed the same ceremonial practices and understood their religious symbolism, you had at least some common ground on which to build a cooperative relationship. Among the western Puebloans, it is possible that the long-term stability of Pueblo society is due in part to the katsina system fostering and formalizing the concept of power sharing among the adherents. Katsina ceremonies involved the participation of large masses of people who could only be accommodated within the large open plazas that had come to characterize Classic Period settlements (fig. 66). By this time, kivas had become the exclusive domain of ceremonial groups rather than sites for the mixed kind of social, political, religious, and even residential functions they provided during earlier periods. The decreasing numbers of kivas constructed within settlements reflected this functional change.

The katsina system may not have had the same influence upon eastern Pueblos as it did among the western Pueblos, but there were other institutions, such as medicine societies, hunting and war *sodalities*, and *moiety* organizations that performed similar social, political, and ceremonial functions within the Rio Grande pueblos.[32] While none of these other institutions individually reached the magnitude of the katsina system, many of them operated at scales larger than individual pueblos. With specific reference to medicine societies, whose responsibilities involved overseeing the health of the community, it was not unusual for these societies to engage in a form of "cross training" in which initiates from "foreign" pueblos were trained in the pueblos where the societies originated. In addition, there appears to have been established mechanisms for the exchange of esoteric ritual knowledge and paraphernalia among various pueblos.[33] Some scholars have theorized that specialized societies and sodalities evolved in order to facilitate interaction among a diverse Rio Grande population that did not even speak the same language. The Northern and Southern Tewa, Northern and Southern Tiwa, Towa, Tano, and the Keresans are linguistically different.[34] If that many of these societies developed during the Classic Period, as has been hypothesized, they may represent another kind of large-scale networking system that helped to smooth out environmental and political uncertainties.

Archaeology operates at various levels, from individual actors to individual communities to regional patterns. As archaeologists, we try to explain how broad processes unfolded over time, and sometimes we can use a single well-researched site to illustrate those processes. Arroyo Hondo Pueblo (figs. 67, 68) is just such a site. What can Arroyo Hondo teach us about the Classic Period in Santa Fe? Located on a natural bench overlooking Arroyo Hondo Creek, this site is less than two miles downstream from Upper Arroyo Hondo Pueblo. Archaeological evidence has revealed that Arroyo Hondo had two separate and distinct occupations that spanned no more than 125 years. Beginning with the initial building phases around 1300 C.E., the pueblo

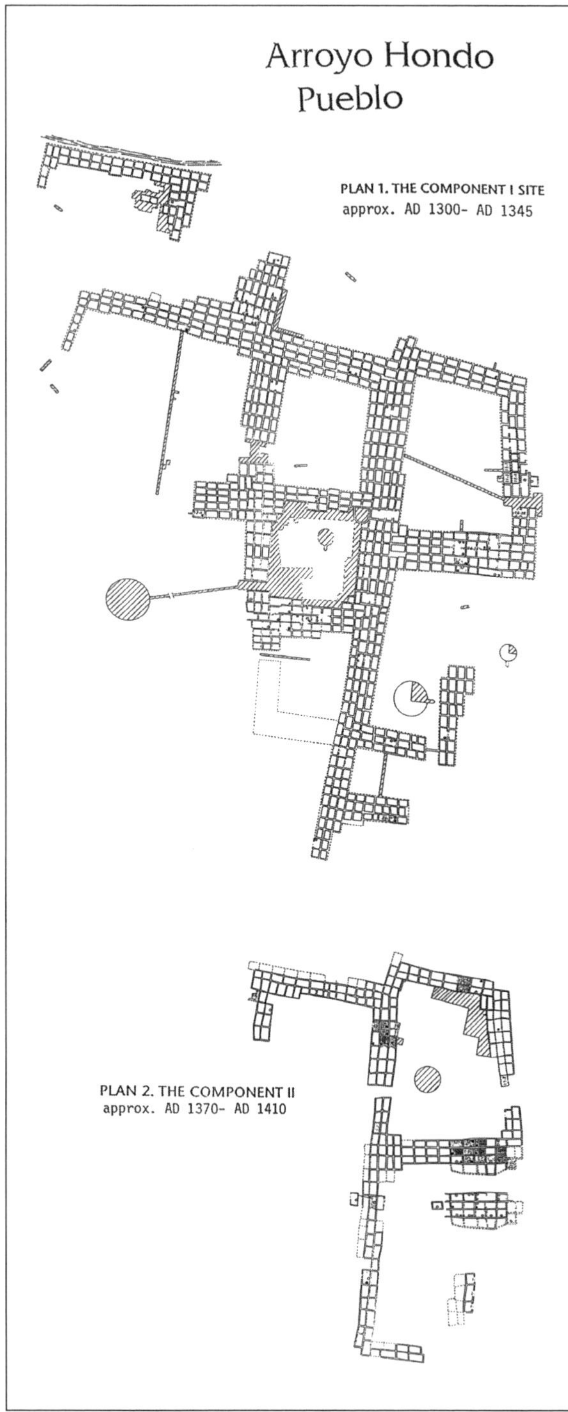

continued to expand. Within a few decades it had perhaps 1,000 rooms and was more than twenty times larger than the earlier and more modest Upper Arroyo Hondo Pueblo.

The enclosed plaza layout at Arroyo Hondo certainly suggests community-level planning, but it also suggests the existence of some "core group" who designed the settlement according to a sense of an expected (or proposed) population. In other words, pueblos such as Arroyo Hondo may look more planned and less eccentric than Coalition pueblos such as Pindi because the nature of decision-making may have been different. This does not mean these pueblos were always built in a single construction episode, but it implies some overriding and mutually acceptable idea about how things should look.[35]

Some archaeologists have associated the "enclosed plaza" form with the adoption of the katsina cult because of the historically observed associations between large plazas and large ceremonies.[36] Reflecting on the previous chapter's discussion about the evolution of local plaza-centered communities, it seems clear that the

Fig. 67. Illustration of Arroyo Hondo Pueblo showing components 1 and 2. Map courtesy School for Advanced Research.

Fig. 68. Aerial photograph of Arroyo Hondo Pueblo, ca. 1975. Photograph courtesy School for Advanced Research.

katsina system was not the reason for those plazas. Katsina ceremonialism did not appear in the middle northern Rio Grande until long after people had been building large enclosed plazas. On the other hand, as the process of settlement aggregation continued, people with different ethnicities or languages had to find ways to become accepted into larger communities. At Arroyo Hondo, it is notable that the plazas are not interconnected; rather, each plaza has its own external gateway (figs. 67, 69).[37] The implication is that plaza-roomblock sections did not blend seamlessly into one another but were discrete units within the larger settlement. In other words, the plaza-roomblock design allowed individual groups to maintain their own self-contained plaza-centered spaces yet still be an integral part of a larger community.[38]

A typical residential room at Arroyo Hondo was probably quite spartan, but readers should not immediately infer that ruled out the existence of art, music, and a complex spirituality rooted in the natural world (fig. 70). Among the innumerable pottery sherds and stone tools, archaeologists discovered bone, shell, and ceramic pendants and other kinds of jewelry and ornaments,[39] a variety of ceramic and carved

Fig. 69. Artist's reconstruction of Arroyo Hondo Pueblo Component I. Illustration by Dennis Holloway.

stone pipes, ceramic and carved stone animal effigies (probably associated with hunting), ceremonial stones, a prayer plume base,[40] and several bone whistles and other musical instruments.[41] Life at Arroyo Hondo was demanding but not without its pleasures.

Beyond its physical appearance, Arroyo Hondo may be atypical. Unlike many other contemporaneous pueblos, no unmistakable evidence of katsina ceremonialism was discovered at Arroyo Hondo, such as Rio Grande–style rock art, masks, painted murals, or obvious symbols on pottery. There was a great kiva or community structure located to the south of the pueblo on the easiest, flattest, least defensible, and presumably most common approach for visitors, but it had no obvious katsina connections. One wonders whether the Arroyo Hondonians deliberately opted out of the katsina system or were somehow excluded. Contemporary Americans may be obsessed with "networking," but one reason for Arroyo Hondo's ultimate failure may have been that its residents did not sufficiently connect to larger support systems.

Based upon estimates of the number of living rooms, family sizes, and the amount of food that the immediate area around the pueblo could provide, the maximum population for Arroyo Hondo has been calculated at between 600 and 2,700 people, an admittedly broad range.[42] Keeping in mind that pueblos were never 100 percent occupied, and using a combination of room occupation percentages, average numbers of rooms per family unit, and average numbers of persons per family, I estimate a somewhat smaller population of between 240 and 1,000 people living at Arroyo Hondo during the first half of the 14th century. In light of what we know about the overall health of the residents, the smaller numbers may be more realistic.[43] Although it would be nice to say that Arroyo Hondo thrived, "struggled" is probably more accurate—there is compelling evidence that the Arroyo Hondonians were not in robust health.

The mortuary data from Arroyo Hondo paints a picture of people under substantial nutritional stress, experiencing high infant mortality, and suffering from an incidence of anemia greater than most of the surrounding pueblos .[44] The most recent data indicates that a substantial subset of the population actually suffered from rickets.[45] Populations under stress typically exhibit decreased fertility, precisely the opposite condition of what would be necessary for high rates of natural increase.

Fig. 70. Interior, Room 36, Roomblock 16, ca. 1325. Illustration by R. W. Lang, courtesy of School for Advanced Research.

One of the challenges for archaeologists is to reconcile seemingly incompatible data. A preliminary analysis of the mortuary remains from El Pueblo de Santa Fe, just a few miles away, reveals a much healthier, more vigorous population with very little evidence of either the nutritional stress or physical trauma revealed at Arroyo Hondo.[46] Did the residents of El Pueblo de Santa Fe have access to more and better food, especially protein? Were the downtown residents connected to social or economic networks that provided them with both material support and protection that Arroyo Hondo did not have? I wish I could enlighten readers, but archaeologists have not yet answered the question why two contemporaneous settlements so close together should have such divergent demographic profiles.

For reasons that are not entirely clear but may be related to a drought, by the 1340s Arroyo Hondo could not support itself and the residents left. After a hiatus of perhaps twenty-five or thirty years, some people returned and built a new pueblo literally on top of the old one. Only 10 of the original 24 roomblocks were actually rebuilt, which resulted in a much smaller (200-room) pueblo. Clusters of tree-ring dates indicate relatively rapid room construction, particularly during the 1380s. In contrast to the larger, slower construction of the first occupation component, the

*Fig. 71. La Cieneguilla Pueblo.
Photograph by Nels Nelson,
courtesy American Museum of
Natural History.*

second component was built more quickly but was occupied for only a couple of generations. Archaeologists found evidence of extensive burning throughout the pueblo associated with tree-ring dates around 1410, supporting the idea of a major attack (shades of Burnt Corn and Los Alamos). The presence of several unburied bodies as well as twenty-five skulls without bodies also supports this assumption.[47] There may have been some minimal occupation after the fire, but the burned rooms were not reused and the last residents left around 1425. Conceivably, a pueblo as small as Arroyo Hondo's second occupation and located in a somewhat marginal agricultural zone simply could not sustain itself, and so became a target for larger pueblos in the area.[48] In any event, one enduring question has always been: "So, where did the remaining people go?" As the crow flies (or the dog trots) heading due west from Arroyo Hondo, it is not far to the pueblos of Cieneguilla (figs. 71, 72) and La Bajada. Either of these pueblos could have absorbed the relatively small population from Arroyo Hondo, and logic tells us that one or both settlements may have done just that. Logic, however, is not a substitute for evidence, and neither archaeology nor ethnography has provided any clear answers. None of the modern Rio Grande pueblos have claimed an ancestral relationship with Arroyo Hondo, and although I avoid applying words like *mysterious* or *enigmatic* to archaeological problems (they make the discipline sound too much like the History Channel), we simply do not know what happened to the refugees from Arroyo Hondo. Even though Arroyo Hondo failed as a long-lasting community, the sheer size of other Classic pueblos coupled with their apparent ability to field a critical mass of warriors may mean that it was the capacity to "look big" that was really important—an early manifestation of Cold War deterrence during a period of overall uncertainty and anxiety.

In the previous chapter, Figure 58 summarized the occupation data for a number of Coalition and Classic Period pueblos. In addition to Arroyo Hondo, all occupations at Pindi, Agua Fria Schoolhouse, and Chamisa Locita ended within the early part of the 15th century. The results of several excavations in the city of Santa Fe support the view that the downtown settlements were either completely or substantially unoccupied within a generation or two after 1400 C.E.[49] In other words, three of the 14th-century settlement nodes—east of the city, west of the city, and downtown—were essentially finished within a century. During the time between 1410–1430, a new style of glaze-painted pottery, glaze B (fig. 73), replaced the earlier glaze A and became the new "people's choice" for decorated pottery in the middle Rio Grande. Archaeologist Thomas Motsinger has connected this style change to what he sees as a movement away from large numbers of individual pottery producers towards a *village industry* level of glazeware production. In Motsinger's model, a small number of full-time craft specialists within selected pueblos came to control the pottery manufacturing process.[50]

The reasons for more specialization may relate to a perceived need to intensify the production of valuable, albeit standardized, trade pottery. The years around 1420 experienced some of the lowest levels of precipitation that archaeologists have been able to discern, and the local residents would have needed some way to alleviate food shortages.[51] People did not "consume" fancy pottery in the same way they consumed maize, but upscale glazeware may have been used to cement alliances and fa-

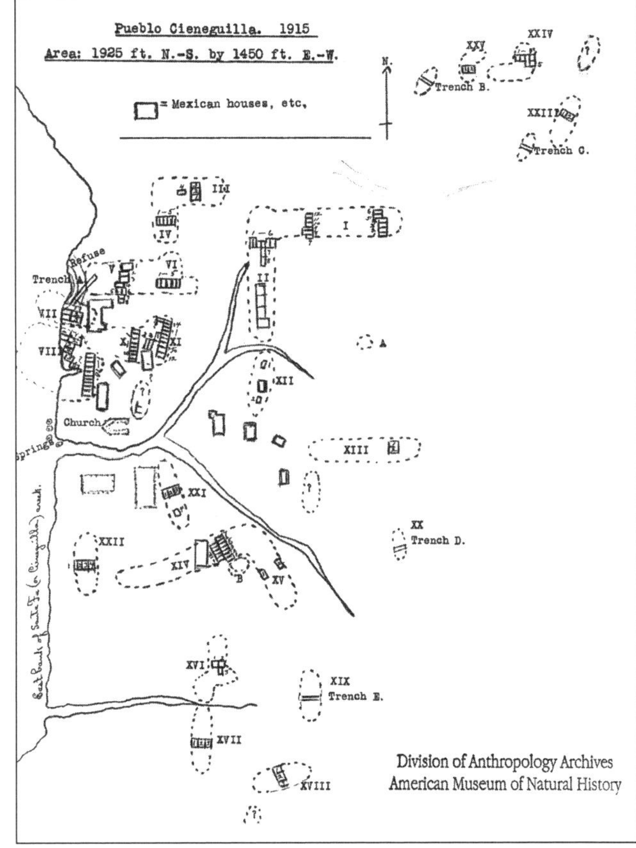

Fig. 72. La Cieneguilla Pueblo. Map by Nels Nelson, courtesy American Museum of Natural History.

Fig. 73. Example of Glaze B pottery, ca. 1425–1450. Museum of Indian Arts and Culture/ Laboratory of Anthropology (21217).

cilitate the redistribution of surplus food. During the early 15th century, there seems to have been a wholesale shift in settlements away from higher elevations in favor of lower elevations, and by now most readers can probably predict the "usual suspects" for this shift: the onset of cooler temperatures and shortened growing seasons, drought, population pressure on limited resources such as arable land, and conflict.[52] In one sense, I have come full circle from my initial discussions about Paleoindian and Archaic lifeways. If we substitute the term "settlement shifting" for the culturally loaded term "abandonment,"[53] then the idea of mobility, of being able to relocate when conditions were not conducive to group survival, appears to have been a constant theme throughout Ancient Puebloan history. Fifteenth-century Puebloan farmers may have had a more difficult time relocating to new areas than did small bands of Archaic foragers, but the conceptual strategy was essentially the same.

Even with all this settlement shifting, people continued to occupy areas north of Santa Fe in the Tesuque Basin, south of the city along the Santa Fe River near the Cienega escarpment (fig. 74), and, in particular, southeast of the city in the Galisteo Basin where several of the largest and most densely occupied Classic Period pueblos were built. Beyond the immediate vicinity of Santa Fe, large towns existed at Pecos, Taos, and the areas around Albuquerque. A number of these settlements, including several in the Galisteo Basin, remained occupied at the time of the Spanish entry into New Mexico. In my opinion, the roomblock-and-plaza form that evolved during the 14th century was more sustainable than the earlier Chacoan, Mesa Verdean, or even Coalition settlement forms. Either people had solved the problems of living in large groups or the external and internal stresses that continued to buffet these communities were insufficient to radically change the system.

*Fig. 74. La Cienega Pueblo and escarpment. Photograph by Nels Nelson,
courtesy American Museum of Natural History.*

If we cut away all the overlays of social and cultural elaboration and are willing
to indulge in some reductionism, we could say that the Classic Period was essentially
about the idea of "bigness" as an adaptive solution to the problems of environmental
productivity, population growth, and conflict. In a sense, bigness became the ultimate
survival strategy that packaged economic, social, political, and ideological ingredi-
ents in new and larger ways in order to ameliorate the inherent riskiness of life in
the northern Rio Grande. Bigger settlements were built, bigger associations of those
settlements were created, and finally even bigger ideological and ceremonial movements like the katsina system and medicine societies evolved. The ways in which
those "big" entities were organized and directed are still being studied by archaeologists, but if institutional continuity is one proxy measure of long-term cultural
success, then we know that at least until the 16th century when Europeans arrived in
the Rio Grande Valley, all three elements—large pueblos, multiple alliance systems,
and large-scale ceremonial systems—were still going strong.

*Fig. 75. Santa Fe Plaza showing monument. Photograph by Ben Wittick
(1835 – 1903), courtesy Museum of New Mexico. Neg number 15831.*

  Chapter 8

New People in the Neighborhood

EUROPEANS, ATHAPASKANS, AND UTES

There is a historical monument in the center of the plaza in Santa Fe that caused a certain amount of disquiet among some locals, primarily because of its references to soldiers who "fought with rebels" and fell "in battles with savage Indians" (fig. 75). After years of impassioned debate, the word "savage" was unofficially chiseled off the monument, illustrating how history is subject to reinterpretation by every generation.[1] Fewer people are aware of the words engraved on top of the same monument that read, "*In this plaza Gen. S. W. Kearny, U.S.A., proclaimed the peaceable annexation of New Mexico, Aug. 19, 1846.*" There is no doubt in my mind that when a resplendent General Kearny rode into Santa Fe on that fine August day, someone in the crowd muttered, "*Ay va el barrio,*" translation: "Well, there goes the neighborhood." The idea that as new people arrive things will change and probably not for the best is as new as today's headlines and as old as forever. This penultimate chapter is concerned with the new people who "discovered" Santa Fe in the 16th century.

I said at the outset of this book that I was not going to delve too far into the historical period, but the 16th century was a time of such cultural adjustment for Ancestral Puebloans in the northern Rio Grande that in order to complete the story some examination of that period is necessary. I have talked about people moving into and out of the Santa Fe area, connecting with one another through kinship, trade, political alliance, or ceremonial participation. With a few notable exceptions, such as various buffalo hunting groups living on the Great Plains,[2] the Ancestral

Puebloans in the northern middle Rio Grande interacted with other corn-growing, pottery-making, pueblo-dwelling people. In other words, their interactions were based on common cultural foundations. Beginning in the 16th century, people arrived in the northern Rio Grande with worldviews and cultural traits that were very different from the normative ideas upon which the Puebloans had learned to rely. And these new people planned to stay.

Before I discuss events that transpired in the mid-1500s, I need to take a half step back. Archaeologists have learned that the century 1450–1550 was one in which major cultural transformations were already unfolding across the entire Southwest. By 1450 or shortly thereafter, the large and complex community of Paquimé in the Casas Grandes Valley of northern Chihuahua had been abandoned,[3] most likely the victim of extreme climatic events, external warfare, or an internal revolt.[4] Similarly, by 1450 the Classic Hohokam culture centered in the Phoenix Basin had also collapsed, the probable result of flooded irrigation systems, environmental degradation, salinization,[5] the overuse of agricultural land, or, once again, warfare. Local population declines and movements accompanied these social and political collapses as people reorganized themselves into smaller and simpler societies or moved to different areas.

Conversely, within the northern Rio Grande Valley, the regions around Zuni, New Mexico, the Hopi mesas in Arizona, and the northern portion of the Mexican state of Sonora, there were fewer large-scale cultural changes. This is not to imply that all was peaceful and that nothing unsettling occurred. To the contrary, those areas also experienced the growth and abandonment of a number of large communities but maintained the fundamental systems of settlement. Within the middle northern Rio Grande, the basic cultural adaptations that had evolved in the 14th century persisted into the 16th century even as populations continued to shift within the region. I noted in the preceding chapter that by the 1420s, and certainly by 1450, there were no longer any permanent settlements within downtown Santa Fe, although Tewa people undoubtedly continued to visit and utilize the area for hunting or resource collecting. The 15th and early 16th centuries are often called the *Protohistoric Period* because one can see with hindsight how that period was intermediate between the events that played out during the Classic Period and those about to transpire in the looming Historical Period. Clearly, the Ancestral Puebloans could not have predicted the ways in which their world was about to be jolted by the arrival of new and unexpected people.

If you ask most people about new groups entering the Southwest during the 16th century, they will probably mention the Spanish *Entrada,* more accurately a series of *entradas,* or "entries," as first explorers and then colonists moved north from Mexico through the Rio Grande Valley. Less well known is that around the same time Europeans entered the Southwest from the south, the ancestors of non-Puebloan groups, including Navajo, Apache, and Ute, were entering from the north, east, and west.[6] In the long run, the impact of these groups upon Puebloan culture was far less than that of the Europeans, but they still caused changes in Puebloan economic, political, and social life. Some earlier scholars tried to connect the Pueblo abandonments of the Colorado Plateau during the 13th and 14th centuries to conflicts with these mobile hunters and gatherers. Those theories have not been supported by archaeological findings because even the earliest Navajo and Apache sites were occupied at least 150 years after the Ancestral Puebloans moved out of the Four Corners region.[7]

I opened Chapter 2 with a brief description of Adolph Bandelier and his contributions to local and regional archaeology. In addition to his scientific endeavors, Bandelier wrote *The Delight Makers,* an ethnographic novel about Pueblo life set in the northern Rio Grande just prior to the arrival of the Spanish.[8] The book is still worth reading. Woven into the struggles of a Keresan village in Frijoles Canyon (now part of Bandelier National Monument) is a subplot involving complex relationships between the Puebloan farmers and an aggressive and covetous band of Navajo. For my purposes, the significance of this work is that Bandelier unambiguously placed Navajo bands in the general vicinity of Santa Fe no later than the early 16th century. Although it is entirely possible that Navajos were visiting or even living in this district by the early 1500s, there is no unmistakable archaeological evidence that supports Bandelier's literary license. One question for this chapter, then, is "What is the earliest evidence for Athapaskan-speaking people (Navajo and Apache) living near Santa Fe in the northern Rio Grande?"

"Navajo" is a Pueblo term that literally means "Takers from the fields." Navajos call themselves the Diné, or "The People," and the actual time of their arrival in the Southwest is a matter of debate. At one time it was thought that both Navajo and Apache groups migrated into the Southwest around the time of the Pueblo Revolt of 1680. Some scholars place Navajos in the Southwest as early as 1400, but the weight of the evidence suggests that it is more likely they arrived during the last two decades of the 15th or the beginning of the 16th century.[9] Today, the best archaeological

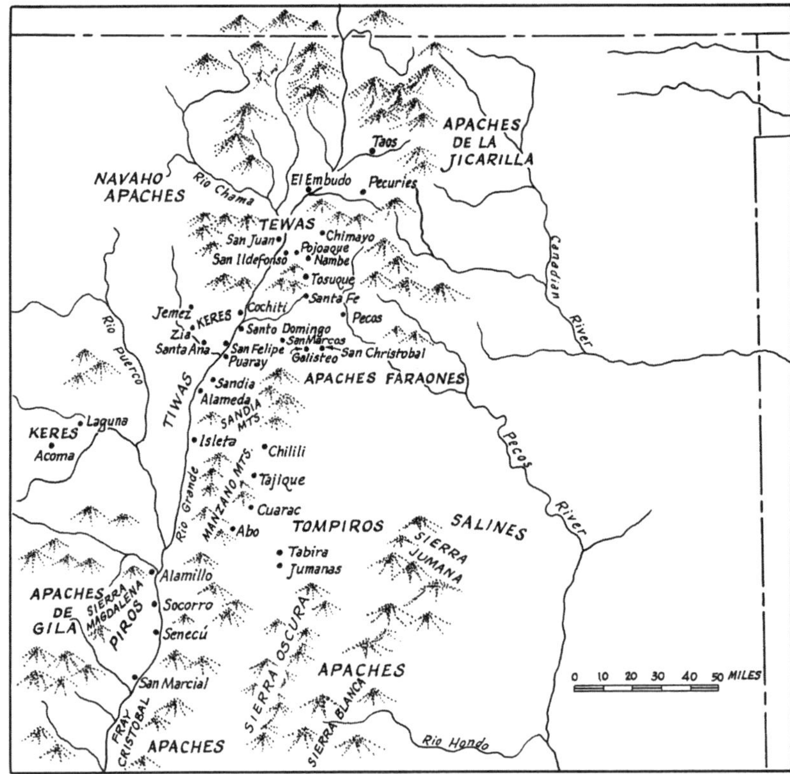

Fig. 76. Locations of Puebloan, Navajo, and Apache groups in New Mexico, 1600–1700. Map by Jack S. Forlies, in Kenner (1969), courtesy of University of Oklahoma Press.

evidence probably would place Navajos and Apaches on portions of the Colorado Plateau by the early 1500s.[10] The La Plata Mine excavations near Farmington, New Mexico, are among the earliest Navajo sites and have been dated to around 1500, although there may have been sporadic and seasonal entries prior to that time. In the 1620s, Fray Benavides attempted to Christianize people he called "Apaches de Navahu"[11] whose territory extended in a swath from the Chama Valley north of Santa Fe to northern Arizona,[12] but it is not entirely clear when this group first occupied the area.

Both Navajos and Apaches have linguistic and other cultural similarities with each other as well as with Athapaskan-speaking groups who still live in Alaska and western Canada. There have been suggestions that 13th-century volcanic eruptions

in Alaska caused popula-
tion displacements and may
have initiated movements of
Athapaskan-speaking people,
but there are still two basic theories regarding the
direction of entry of these
groups into the Southwest.
One approach holds that
Athapaskans gradually fil-
tered through the Rocky
Mountains and onto the
Great Plains by the 1400s

Fig. 77. *Teepee Rings at San Cristobal Pueblo. Photograph by Jason S. Shapiro.*

and eventually moved into the Southwest in an east-to-west direction. These nomadic hunters and gatherers settled in regions
that were not occupied or had been abandoned by the Puebloans,
such as the San Juan Basin in northwest New Mexico. Other areas such as the Upper
Chama Valley may have served as warmer wintering places from their usual locales
in the Rocky Mountains. A second possible route suggests that the Athapaskans
traveled along the western portions of the Rocky Mountains and entered the Southwest in a west-to-east direction. According to this premise, Athapaskan speakers
arrived in the Dinéteh region east of Bloomfield, New Mexico, as early as the mid-
1400s, but no indisputable examples of such early sites have been found. During
Coronado's expedition in 1541, he noted the presence of nomadic buffalo hunting
groups on the Great Plains that he called *Querechos* and *Teyas*. While there has been
speculation that these people may have been Navajo or Apache, neither their linguistic affiliations nor ethnicity is conclusively known.[13] We do know that by 1598
there were a substantial numbers of Athapaskan speakers in northern New Mexico
because when Juan de Oñate established the first permanent Spanish settlement in
New Mexico, he assigned a priest to minister to several identified ethnic groups,
including "Apaches." (fig. 76)[14]

One consistent problem associated with early Navajo archaeology is understanding what early Navajo sites are supposed to look like. As I noted when discussing
Paleoindian and Archaic groups, mobile bands of foragers leave relatively ephemeral
traces on the landscape. The diagnostic pottery associated with Navajos, namely

Dinéteh gray, did not appear until the 1600s, and teepee rings (fig. 77), while not uncommon, are difficult to assign to any particular cultural group. In some cases it is not archaeologically clear whether early non-Pueblo sites in the western San Juan Basin represent a Navajo or Ute presence. The difference is more than an academic exercise because the timing of each group's arrival helped to determine the nature of their relationships with the Ancestral Puebloans.

The question of when the first Athapaskans appeared in the Rio Grande Valley is an issue that has been fraught (and fought) with great emotion. Beginning with H. P. Mera in the 1930s and continuing through the 1960s and 1970s, a number of scholars have maintained that Navajos were present in areas north of Santa Fe by the early 1600s.[15] Almost forty years ago archaeologist James Gunnerson stated that by 1598 Apaches were living to the north and east of Picuris Pueblo in the Sangre de Cristo Mountains.[16] A review of early Spanish accounts and maps by archaeologist Curtis Schaafsma also supports the view that Navajo or Apache groups were living north of Santa Fe no later than 1600.[17] Schaafsma's position is not uniformly accepted, and some archaeologists and historians consider his proposed early Navajo Piedra Lumbre Phase in the Chama Valley (1640–1710) as a manifestation of Puebloan rather than Athapaskan culture. The architectural remains associated with these sites appear to reflect people living as pastoralists because corral-like structures and the remains of domestic sheep and goats are quite prominent. Although the Navajo began to acquire sheep in the 17th century, they apparently did so slowly.[18] What is more troublesome for the proponents of early Navajo settlement is the relative absence of Dinéteh-type (Navajo) ceramics, particularly because a number of Tewa and later Hispanic ceramics are present on these sites. These findings do not eliminate the potential for early 17th-century Athapaskans living in areas around the northern Rio Grande, but the documentation of the Piedra Lumbre Phase has probably raised as many questions as it has answered.

Overall, the archaeological and ethnohistoric evidence reveals a complex set of relationships between Navajos, Apaches, and Puebloans in terms of both time and space. "Raiding and trading" may be a simplistic shorthand view but the nature of their interactions radically changed over the course of the 16th, 17th, and 18th centuries. For example, from the Puebloans the Navajos learned farming, pottery, and weaving techniques and tailored them to their own needs, but there were also periods of conflict when Navajos and Apaches raided Pueblo settlements. Puebloans adapted to this new situation, and a growing body of evidence supports the existence of temporary alliances between various Puebloan and Athapaskan groups.[19] In other words, Rio Grande Puebloans expanded the concept of multi-pueblo alliances and used it as another way to buffer the uncertainties of a changed and more insecure social environment. In one of the more unique occurrences of the early historic period, a group of Taos Indians fled the Spanish in the 1650s and settled far to the east among a group of Plains Apaches. A few decades later, some Picuris Indians left their pueblo after the Pueblo Revolt of 1696 and settled among a group of Jicarilla Apaches until Spanish authorities convinced them to return. The El Cuartelejo site in Scott County, Kansas, may relate to both of those events and is evidence of the kinds of complications archaeologists face in trying to interpret past events and relationships on a much larger scale. The architecture at the El Quartelejo site looks Puebloan rather than Apachean, but the artifacts are more Apache-like in character.[20]

In addition to the Athapaskans, other groups entered the Southwest during the 16th century, such as the Numic-speaking people, including the ancestors of the historically identified Utes.[21] Called "Yutas" by the Spanish, the Ute refer to themselves as "Nuche". In all liklihood, these groups had their origins in the eastern California and Great Basin areas and were living in parts of Utah and western Colorado by the 1300s. It is not clear when these Numic-speaking groups first entered the Four Corners and northern San Juan Basin regions, but they probably arrived after the Navajos and appear not to have had a significant presence until the end of the 17th century.[22] The first Spanish account of the Ute may have been by Friar Geronimo Salmeron, who wrote about Oñate's 1604 expedition. Salmeron described a group of non-Puebloan peoples from the north whom he called "Quasuatos," a variation of "Yutas."

In 1776, Fray Francisco de Escalante described the area north of the San Juan River as being Ute territory, although, as with most of these early historical observations, it is not clear when the Utes initially arrived.[23] As with the early Navajos, recognizing the archaeological signatures of the earliest Numic occupations is difficult, so it is not possible to put a definite date on their entry into the Southwest let alone their first appearance along the Rio Grande. Some people have concluded that the Ute may have been living as far south as the La Plata River region north of Farmington, New Mexico, by the early 1500s. By the 16th century, some Utes had extended their territory as far to the east as the Front Range in Colorado and as far south as the Texas Panhandle.[24] The Muache, one of the easternmost Ute bands, occupied areas to the east of the Sangre de Cristo Mountains and as far south as Santa Fe.[25] As with the

Athapaskans, the Utes and Puebloans had periods of cooperation and conflict with each other, but this area of archaeological research is relatively undeveloped. A number of people believe that the highly defensive Navajo pueblito building phase in the Gobernador and Largo canyon areas during the early to mid-1700s was the result of Ute raiding, rather than conflicts with Puebloan groups moving into the canyons after the Revolt of 1680. There are historical records of Ute raiding against both Pueblo and Spanish settlements until well into the 18th century.

The movement of Europeans into the Southwest has been analyzed with such scholarly care that I hesitate to attempt a short summary. We have all heard the clichéd phrase of "God, Gold, and Glory" as the driving forces behind the Spanish *Entrada*, and although there is probably some truth behind every cliché, recent scholarship suggests that old explanation has obscured more individual motivations such as the desire for land, status, and social advancement. After more than 700 years of fighting a variety of Islamic groups, the Kingdom of Spain had only become united under a Catholic monarch in 1492. The *Reconquista* in Iberia was premised on papal decrees that asserted non-Christians (infidels, unbelievers, pagans) could lawfully be conquered and their lands confiscated by Christian armies in order to enforce the Christian version of a universal binding law, but it also broadened the concept of "land as wealth."[26] While it is true that the Spanish people believed in nationalism, Catholicism, and the legend of "Cibola,"[27] and while it is also true that barely twenty years had passed since Europeans had been exposed to the incredible wealth of the Aztecs and Incas, it may have been more modern ideas about social mobility and economic opportunity that drew people into the Southwest.[28]

Written history in the Southwest begins with Alvar Nunez Cabeza de Vaca because he was the first European to experience and write about this region. Cabeza de Vaca was part of the disastrous 1527 Narvaez expedition to Florida and, after being shipwrecked on the Texas coast, he and his three companions spent eight years being captured, enslaved, and traded among Indian groups. During their travels (and travails) the four came into contact with numerous Indian groups that probably included Jumanos in Texas and various O'odham groups in northern Mexico. However, there is no evidence they ever met any Rio Grande Puebloans, and they almost certainly never got within hundreds of miles of Santa Fe. The four survivors reached Mexico in 1536 and became celebrities, particularly after Cabeza de Vaca wrote an account of his travels that even today constitutes a fascinating ethnographic description of early 16th-century life in the Southwest.[29] De Vaca's

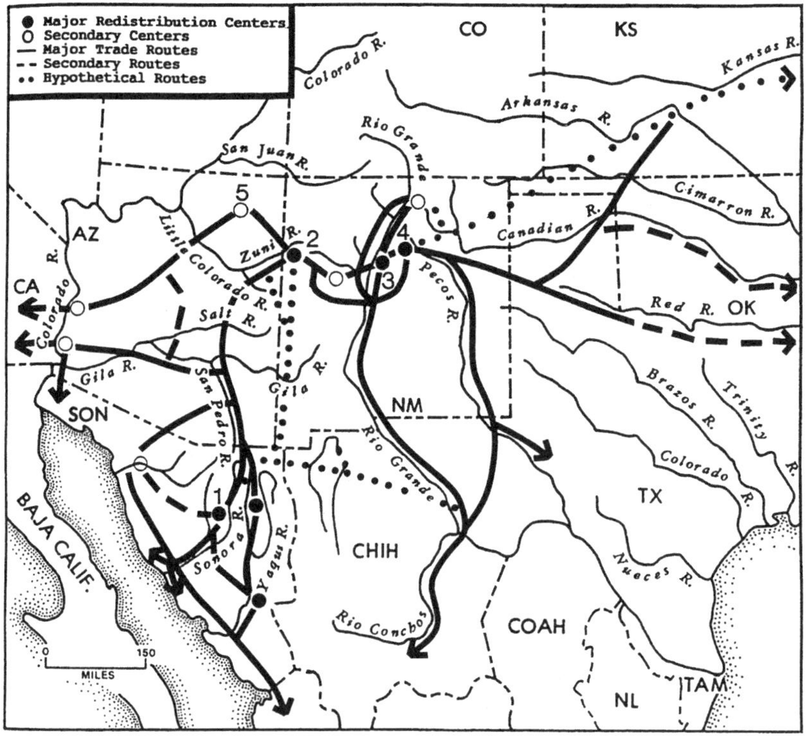

Fig. 78. Prehispanic trade routes and trails used by Spanish explorers. Map drawn by Shirley Cushing Flint, in Riley (1995).

account undoubtedly served as one of many impulses that led to Coronado's well-known expedition.

Francisco Vasquez de Coronado left Compostela on the west coast of Mexico on February 23, 1540. His expedition included more than 300 Spanish men-at-arms, numerous servants, as many as 400 black slaves, and at least 1,300 *Indios amigos,* or Mexican Indian allies.[30] The expedition traveled north through Arizona, fought battles at the Zuni pueblos, continued across New Mexico, and spent the winter of 1540–1541 camped near Bernalillo, New Mexico. From his camp, or more likely a series of camps, Coronado contacted and fought battles against several Rio Grande pueblos, including Kuaua, known today as Coronado State Monument.[31] Regardless of his predations around present-day Albuquerque, Coronado never reached Santa Fe because he traveled east through the Galisteo Basin, across the Pecos River, and then onto the Great Plains. Even if he had, there probably would not have been anyone living there to meet him, although he may have run into some Tewa-speaking people from the villages in the Tesuque Basin. Most people, including Coronado himself, considered the expedition a failure, but by any measure Coronado's actions irrevocably changed life in the Southwest in general and the northern Rio Grande in particular.[32]

Archaeologists and historians have examined the events of the contact period in increasing detail,[33] and one point to come out of that analysis is that many indigenous people felt the impacts of these interactions well before they ever met a European face-to-face. The same well-established trade routes and Indian paths that facilitated contact between different Indian groups also facilitated the spread of disease (fig. 78), and the introduction of horses, donkeys, and oxen only speeded up the process. As an illustration, perhaps an Indian in Mexico would come into contact with an ill European, and, lacking any natural resistance, the Indian would get sick or would carry the disease to his own or other communities. Pathogens for smallpox, typhus, measles, and other diseases were transmitted as people fled from epidemics, or in connection with contacts involving trade, bride exchange, or warfare. When these pathogens reached a sufficiently dense concentration of people, such as in 16th-century pueblos in the Rio Grande Valley, disease outbreaks occurred. The impacts were not limited to the immediate effects of morbidity and mortality but resulted in long-term negative consequences for the sizes, age compositions, and stability of Indian populations.[34] The implication of these indirect disease vectors is that by the time Coronado actually entered the Southwest in 1540, the demographics may have already been changed. Almost one hundred years after Coronado, a Spanish priest by the name of Juan de Prado described the smallpox epidemic of 1638. In referring only to the Pueblo population in New Mexico, Prado wrote: "The people that may be counted today in settlements will total 40,000 or a little less, for although there must have been more than 60,000 baptized, today those conversions are diminished to the extent on account of the very active prevalence of smallpox."[35]

Prado described a process that had already happened in the past and would occur again, and when one considers the effects of other factors such as warfare, starvation, and the problems caused by cultural dislocation, readers can begin to appreciate the enormous impacts upon local populations caused by the *Entrada*. Epidemic diseases are hardest on the very young and very old. The death of young cohorts in a population with already high infant mortality leaves a demographic hole that has its greatest impact as these cohorts enter their "productive years." Young adults and adults are important not only as food producers and warriors but also as community leaders and elders: if there are insufficient numbers of people to fill the necessary roles that exist under political and ceremonial systems, then the social fabric weakens and begins to unravel. When tribal elders or leaders in nonliterate societies with strong oral traditions die without passing on their esoteric knowledge, that knowledge is lost. In light of the large-scale deaths during and immediately after the contact period, it is both remarkable and admirable that contemporary Puebloans have retained so much traditional cultural knowledge.[36]

Following Coronado, a series of other expeditions (Chamuscado-Rodriguez in 1581, Espejo-Beltran in 1583, de Sosa in 1590, Bonilla-Humaña in 1593) continued the process of exploration.[37] The first permanent settlement was founded in 1598 by Juan de Oñate about 20 miles north of Santa Fe, near San Juan Pueblo, at a place the local Tewa people called *Oke ouinge* or *Yuqueyunque* and the Spanish called San Gabriel.[38] The difference between Oñate and the earlier expeditions was that he planned to stay and make a profit, and to that end he brought cattle, sheep, and goats as well as wheat, barley, peas, garbanzos, and a variety of other cultigens.[39] One thing to remember is that Indians in New Mexico and elsewhere were not passive recipients of European culture but were active participants in a complex process in which groups tried to take advantage of each other in order to advance their own interests. The idea of temporary political alliances was an old one among the Rio Grande Puebloans, and just as with their overtures to the Apaches, there were Puebloans willing to secure alliances with the Spanish in order to obtain exotic trade goods or weapons. Whether the local Puebloans were immediately aware of the implications of their dealings with the Spanish at the time is a question that may be debated for some time, but these alliances would prove to be a bad bargain for them—all the gifts, trade goods, and other benefits were essentially already paid for in terms of lost lands and people killed from war, disease, and social dislocation. Readers will recall that in Chapter 5 one of the direct effects of the transition from wild food collecting to agriculture was a restriction on mobility, because farmers could not move as freely as hunters and gatherers and still care for their crops. This is not to say that farmers were immobile because seasonal movements and settlement shifting remained a part of Puebloan life for 1,000 years. Beginning at the end of the 16th century, Puebloan farmers in the northern Rio Grande Valley found their mobility restricted in new and insidious ways as Spanish religious and political institutions began to amass and control large amounts of land. Although aggregation was a fact of life during the Classic Period, the Spanish mission and *encomienda* systems concentrated the Puebloan populations as a matter of official policy because the profitability of the New Mexico colony was premised in large measure on the control and exploitation of Puebloan labor on farms and ranches. On the other hand, the introduction of wheat, fruit trees, garden vegetables, and domesticated animals expanded the local economic base and served to mitigate environmental perturbations in ways that made periodic settlement shifting less of an economic necessity.[40] Ironically, as Puebloans had less freedom of movement, there was less need for them to actually move.

Oñate and his followers may have been the 16th-century equivalents of modern entrepreneurs seeking to squeeze maximum returns out of their investments, but a combination of factors burst their bubble, including their inability to find precious metals, an ongoing drought,[41] and Oñate's shortcomings as a leader. In 1606 Oñate was arrested and taken to Mexico City.[42] As a result of internal dissensions relating to Oñate's leadership, the need for a more defensible location, and the desire to be closer to larger Puebloan populations in order to facilitate missionization, a decision was made to relocate the San Gabriel settlement. I said in Chapter 1 that one of the reasons Santa Fe was attractive to Spanish colonists was the presence of the Santa Fe River. This perennial and dependable source of water would have been critically important to any group of people who were reliant on farming and pastoralism for their subsistence. It was not entirely the water, however, and just like the Paleoindians who found Santa Fe and its environs so attractive that they kept returning for thousands of years, it is doubtful that the Spanish would have been so persistent "if the returns had not been worth it."[43] By this time, Don Pedro de Peralta had been appointed as the third governor of the colony, and he arrived in New Mexico with some very explicit instructions:

> When he shall have arrived at said province, he shall inform himself of
> the condition of said settlements endeavoring before anything else the
> foundation and settlement of the Villa they claim and shall order the
> same to be made there so people may begin to live there with some
> cleanliness and stability, in which he shall allow the citizens select four
> councilmen and two ordinary alcaldes each year who shall try civil and
> criminal causes…but they shall have no jurisdiction over Indians, only
> the Governor or his Lieutenant shall have jurisdiction. . . .

The said ordinary alcaldes and councilmen of said Villa may mark
out for each resident two lots for house and garden and two suertes
for vegetable garden and two more for vineyard and for an olive grove
and four cavelarias of land, and for the irrigation thereof the necessary water obliging them to live thereon for ten years continuously
without absenting themselves. . . .

They will give the council power to elect a constable of justice
and a clerk with his approval. They shall mark out as belonging to
said Villa six Vecindades and one square of the streets for the purpose
of erecting Royal Buildings and other public buildings…until the
above mentioned Villa shall have been founded and inhabited nothing else shall be attended to.[44]

Don Pedro followed his instructions and, with the official founding of Santa
Fe in 1610, the portion of the story I wanted to tell is complete. Despite popular
mythologizing, the process of colonization was not a singular wave that crashed uniformly upon an ancient and immutable culture. Rather, developments were more
episodic as individual colonists and Indians negotiated relationships and learned
how to interact economically, socially, and politically. Obviously there is much more
that can be said about the events that transpired after 1610, but I will leave that part
of the story to other archaeologists, historical archaeologists, and historians.

Fig. 79. The Laboratory of Anthropology in Santa Fe. Photograph courtesy of Museum of New Mexico.

Epilogue

*M*useum Hill is less a hill than part of a *bajada*, a large sloping deposit of col-
luvial material washed down over eons from the 1.2 billion-year-old portions
of the Sangre de Cristo Mountains that rise above it. Museum Hill is, however,
where Santa Fe has aggregated much of its cultural heritage. Every year thousands of
people arrive to absorb myriad exhibits and events at the Museum of Indian Arts and
Culture, the Museum of International Folk Art, the Museum of Spanish Colonial
Art, and the Wheelwright Museum of the American Indian. Few of these visitors
notice the Pueblo Revival–style building on the southeast side of Milner Plaza (fig.
79). The Laboratory of Anthropology of the Museum of New Mexico ("the Lab")
was established in 1927 with money provided by the John D. Rockefeller Foundation.[1] More than 155,000 archaeological sites have been identified and recorded in
New Mexico, including several sites located directly on or in the immediate vicinity
of Museum Hill itself,[2] and all of those reports, together with associated maps, field
notes, and artifacts, are on file in the Lab. In fact, I have based much of this book on
materials the Laboratory of Anthropology has compiled and maintained.

I have drawn on many sources in order to present as clear a picture of the Ancient Puebloan cultures as possible, but for some periods the picture is hazy, almost
as if we were looking through layers of gauze. Despite our desire for certainty, an
honest inconclusiveness is often what we find. It is the height of folly to assume that
merely because archaeologists do not claim to know everything about the past, that

we do not know anything. One phrase that I have never heard any archaeologist utter is "More research is NOT needed." I began this book with a chapter about the local environment. The landscape in and around Santa Fe is heterogeneous, and there are some areas that are better suited for hunting or gathering, and others for growing crops. This patchwork of local settings helped to facilitate a somewhat more orderly process of cultural evolution than in other parts of the Southwest, where the irresistible forces of climatic change or agricultural expansion rapidly swept low-density subsistence foragers into new areas or new lifestyles. In Santa Fe, the enormous plant and animal diversity seemed to offer more options.

One theme that connects the people of Santa Fe to those throughout the Southwest is the idea that people acted in ways that allowed them to hedge their bets against the uncertainty of life in a risky and unpredictable place. "Unpredictability" might refer to the vagaries of rainfall or the length of the growing season as well as the appearance of needy, if not downright predatory, neighbors.

Over the past century, archaeologists have learned a great deal about 12,000 years of life in and around Santa Fe. We know that the Paleoindian Period was fundamentally different from the Archaic Period and the Archaic Period was fundamentally different from the Puebloan Periods. We have some idea about how these periods differed and why they differed, but rather than a video of seamless change over time, our picture of cultural progression is more like an old zoetrope machine in which individual images pass in front of our eyes one after the other so when the zoetrope wheel spins there is an illusion of movement.[3] The video may never be completed, but every year we add more pictures to the zoetrope so that the progression we see is ever smoother and more complete.

I have tried to emphasize that the transitional lines between cultural phases were fuzzy rather than sharp as people retained what was useful but expanded their knowledge and adapted as best they could to changing circumstances. Archaeologists need to draw lines in order to make sense out of the past, but it is unlikely that ancient indigenous people mentally separated and classified their behaviors in ways familiar to us. We talk about subsistence activities, settlement forms, technology, architecture, social organization, and ideology, but such separations would be meaningless if not absurd to indigenous people in terms of the integrated wholeness that describes how they lived. If one thing changed, such as a new technology like pottery or a new ideology like the katsina system, then many other things also changed. I mentioned in Chapter 3 the qualities of "opportunism, flexibility, and mobility" as being essential for late stone age hunting societies, and we have now come full circle because those were the very qualities that continued to sustain the sequential occupants of Santa Fe. Not only are the qualities the same, but some of the solutions to the fundamental problems of subsistence and survival also remained the same. Remember the transhumant lifestyles of Archaic foragers who moved their efforts and sometimes their base camps among different elevations in order to take advantage of seasonally available opportunities? Now think about Puebloan farmers who moved their fields and sometimes their entire settlements from upland to lowland elevations or vice versa in order to take advantage of changes in rainfall patterns and lengths of growing seasons. A similar analysis could be constructed around the larger concept of settlement shifting. Certainly agricultural societies were much more sedentary than hunting and gathering societies, but we have seen, beginning with the ever-mobile Paleoindians, how people in virtually every cultural period "repositioned" themselves as needed until we arrived at the Classic Period, which is virtually defined by the related processes of "abandonment and aggregation." In other words, the basic idea of *mobility*, of being willing or at least able to leave one place for another place, may be as close as we get to a universal theme in the story of ancient indigenous cultural evolution.

Readers will recall that I proposed to structure this book around two questions: "What's going on here?" and "So what?" I have tried to answer the first question by providing as much factual information as a curious reader might reasonably absorb, but I want to conclude this book by answering the second question in a larger context. For that purpose I want to return to the City of Santa Fe's Archaeological Ordinance that I discussed in Chapter 2. As much as any other factor, that ordinance has enabled the stories of Santa Fe's earliest inhabitants to be explained and understood because it has caused people to stop and consider what is literally lying under their feet before it is covered up by something else. The actual "digging," in terms of field surveys, excavation, and data analysis, accomplished by local archaeologists over the past two decades under the auspices of this ordinance is truly impressive, and this book owes a great deal to their efforts. Although there are many municipalities that have adopted analogous ordinances for the protection of cultural resources,[4] I take a certain amount of pride in the knowledge that our local ordinance has been extremely effective in accomplishing its goals.

In addition to the mechanical components of the ordinances that tell people what they have to do in order to receive clearance for their projects, there is a philosophical subtext that speaks very strongly to community values. Several years ago in a thoughtful essay with the unvarnished title of "Preserving the Archaeological Record in Santa Fe, Why Bother?"[5] David Cushman eloquently made the case for both the value and importance of archaeological ordinances to our collective commonweal. Certainly Cushman was not the first person to discuss the idea of Santa Fe's shared cultural heritage, but in my mind his essay provides the ultimate answer to the "So what?" question about the need, value, and importance of these laws and of this book.

> Indian, Hispanic, Anglo, the history of the Santa Fe area has been forged by the interaction of these people as well as others. The physical remains of this collective heritage are all around us. They not only remind us of who we are and where we have come from but they will continue to inform and educate our children and their children for years to come; that is, if we can preserve the record of the past for the future.[6]

Notes

Foreword

1   Emily Abbink's (2007) book *New Mexico's Palace of the Governors: History of an American Treasure* was drawn from a combination of archaeological and documentary studies focused on the Palace. Stephen Post's report on the archaeological studies that he has conducted at the Palace in the 1990s and more extensively from 2002 through 2006 will provide additional details about how people lived on the land and in the Palace for this period of 400 years.

2   John P. Harrington, Ethnogeography of the Tewa Indians, *29th Annual Report of the Bureau of American Ethnography for the Years 1909–1908* (1916:461) refers to old puddle adobe walls and an ancient burial ground located on the "backside" of the Palace of the Governors. In the extensive excavations conducted on the north side of the Palace by Steven Post in 2002 through 2006, no prehistoric components were found.

3   David W. Cushman, *Preserving Our Options: Public Archaeology in Santa Fe, New Mexico.* In *The Power to Preserve: Public Archaeology and Local Government,* ed. by David W. Cushman, *CRM* 21(10):20–22.

Introduction

1   The City of Santa Fe Archaeological Ordinance, SFCC Section 14-75-1 – 14-75-25 was passed in 1987. Copies of this ordinance may be obtained from the City of Santa Fe Planning Department. The Santa Fe County Special Districts – Archaeological, Historic, Cultural Sites and Landmarks, Santa Fe County Land Development Code Section 7.21 et seq. was adopted in 1988. Copies of this code may be obtained from the Santa Fe County Planning Department.

2   "Gray literature" refers to field reports, treatment plans, and other publications from government archaeologists and private consulting firms that are contracted by private parties, or local, state, and federal agencies to conduct cultural resource evaluation and treatment. These publications are typically kept on file by governmental agencies and are usually available, on request, as public documents.

3   In a perfect world, the archaeological record would contain a complete compilation of human cultural behavior, but in reality the record is incomplete. Not every human behavior is equally represented, and natural and human agents contribute to the destruction of both human and artifactual remains. Processes such as freezing and thawing, erosion, and the actions of animals and plants, as well as human activities associated with agriculture, land development, and even the practice of archaeology, can have similar negative impacts.

4   Bandelier and Hewett (1937:13).

5   Stuart and Gauthier (1984:44); Wendorf and Reed (1955).

6   Readers who are interested in traditional Puebloan histories and perspectives are referred to Suina (2002); Naranjo (1995); Sando (1992); Swentzell (1988, 1992); and Ortiz (1969). In addition, although he tells the stories of the White Mountain Apache in Arizona rather than Puebloan people in New Mexico, Basso (1995) provides excellent insights into the manner in which traditional accounts can be integrated with contemporary ethnographic studies. Finally, readers interested in more political articulations of the relationships between Indians and archaeologists may wish to consult Biolsi and Zimmerman, editors (1997).

7   The terminology conundrum of the Anasazi versus the Ancestral Puebloans is discussed in the brief article "What's in a Name?" *Archaeology Magazine,* July–August 2006:12.

Chapter 1 SETTING THE STAGE

1   http://www.city-data.com/city/Santa-Fe-New-Mexico.html

2   Elliott (1988:2).

3   Dickson (1979:5–6).

4   Dunmire and Tierney (1995:9). At least 120 species of wild plants have been collected and used for food or nonmedicinal purposes by Puebloans in New Mexico over the course of the past century (ibid., 54).

5   For an excellent summary of locally available wild plant and animal foods, see Wetterstrom (1986:11 – 32).

6   Kelley (1980:77).

7   Kantner (2004); Adams and Duff (2004); Cordell (1997, 1984); Plog (1997); Adler (1996); Gumerman (1994); Cordell and Gumerman (1989); Ortiz (1979); Wormington (1957); Kidder (1924).

8   Cordell (1997:33).

9   Hewett et al. (1913:13).

10   Krech examines this process in detail in *The Ecological Indian* (1999). Diamond approaches the same issues from a somewhat different perspective in *Collapse* (2005).

11   When describing local geology, most local archaeology reports rely upon Folks (1975) and Kelley (1980).

12   In this situation, "high quality" refers to rocks with high silica content such as chert and calcedony. Flaked stone tools are made by a process of literally flaking off smaller pieces from a larger piece of stone until the desired shape, size, and form of the tool are reached.

13   Lang (1989, 1993, 1995); Ambler and Viklund (1995).

14   Habicht-Mauche (1995:173).

15   Kelley (1980: 10).

16   The Little Ice Age was a 500-year period characterized by dramatic climatic shifts with very cold years interspersed with normal or even warm years. The most intense impacts occurred in Europe and eastern North America. Although climatologists and historians have marked the beginning of this period with the unusually intense rains in western Europe in 1315, significant climatic swings had already appeared in the Southwest in the 1200s. See generally, Fagan (2001).

17   Kelley (1980:39).

18   Ibid., 47.

19   "Short season" maize varieties historically grown in the Southwest can ripen in as little as sixty days. Muenchrath and Salvador (1995:311).

20   A study using tree-ring measurements to reconstruct annual precipitation levels at Arroyo Hondo Pueblo, New Mexico, for the years between 985 and 1970 C.E. found that in only forty-four individual years (0.045 percent) did the estimated precipitation levels approximately equal the mean level of 13.337 inches for all years. Rose et al. (1981:101–103).

21   D'Antonio (2004).

22   Lang and Scheick (1989:4).

23   Dunmire and Tierney (1995:11).

24   Kelley (1980:9).

25   Wissler (1914).

26   In addition to the references in note 7 above, readers seeking information concerning early Ancestral Puebloan developments should consult Paul F. Reed (2000); Powell and Smiley (2002); and Gumerman (1984).

27   "Hohokam" is an O'odham word meaning either "all used up," or "those who have gone."

28   For more information on the Hohokam, readers should consult Andrews and Bostwick (2000); more ambitious readers should consult Abbott (2000); Abbott (2003); and Downum (1998).

29   For more information on the Mogollon, readers should consult Whittlesey (1999).

Chapter 2 ARCHAEOLOGY AND ARCHAEOLOGISTS

1   Lange and Riley (1996:42).

2   Readers interested in more detailed descriptions of the early history of Southwest archaeology, including the Santa Fe region, should consult Snead (2001) and Fowler (2000).

3   Willey and Sabloff (1993:38).

4   Fowler (2000:177 – 179). Readers who wish to learn more about Adolph Bandelier should consult Lange and Riley's excellent biography (1996) or, for the more ambitious, Bandelier's own journals covering the years 1880 – 1892. (Lange and Riley 1966, 1970; Lange, Riley, and Lange 1975, 1984).

5   The Edgar L. Hewett Collection curated in the Museum of New Mexico's Fray Angelico Chávez History Library consists of eighteen bound volumes and almost 30 linear feet of Hewett's personal correspondence, excavation reports, notes, and articles that encompass his four-decade-long career.

6   Fowler (2003:307, 309 – 310).

7   The School of American Archaeology was founded in 1907. When it was incorporated in 1917 its name was changed to the School of American Research (SAR). In 2006, in order to more accurately reflect its evolving mission, SAR changed its name to the School for Advanced Research on the Human Experience.

8   One institution with which Hewett, despite his efforts, was not involved was the Laboratory of Anthropology ("the Lab") in Santa Fe. The Lab was created within the context of some serious tensions within the archaeological community. Jesse Nussbaum and Kenneth Chapman helped to steer Rockefeller Foundation money into the Lab as an institution that would be independent of Hewett, and prominent eastern anthropologists (and critics of Hewett) such as A.V. Kidder, Franz Boas, Clark Wissler, and Elsie Clews Parsons also supported formation of the Lab. Fowler (2000:366 – 369). In the 1930s, as part of a survey of archaeological sites on behalf of the Lab, Harry Mera developed the numbering system used to identify sites in New Mexico. Mera (1940). All registered sites have an "LA" number which stands for "Laboratory of Anthropology." Pindi Pueblo, discussed in Chapter 6, was assigned LA 1. Today there are approximately 155,000 sites with LA numbers.

9   Hewett allegedly named the Pajarito Plateau, which means "Little Bird" in the Tewa language.

10   Fowler (2003:311 – 312). In addition to his archaeological work, it was Hewett, together with a few others, such as Harry Mera and Jesse Nussbaum, who were instrumental in promulgating the architectural and design components known as "Santa Fe Style."

11   Fowler (2000:247).

12   A general summary of these projects is provided in Elliott (1988:51 – 53).

13   Nels Nelson did the first archaeological investigations at Arroyo Hondo in 1912 on behalf of the American Museum of Natural History. Nelson excavated numerous rooms and recovered innumerable artifacts, but his work did not provide a systematic picture of the site as a whole.

14   The Arroyo Hondo Collection, housed at the School of Advanced Research, includes more than 343,000 artifacts and samples, 20,000 pages of field and laboratory notes, and 16,000 color slides. Schwartz (1997).

15   One of the first such programs was the New Mexico State Highway Department's Salvage Archaeology Program that was begun in 1953.

16   Kidder (1927).

17   Wendorf (1954); Wendorf and Reed (1955).

18   There are many publications that discuss radiocarbon dating in more detail, and Bowman (1990) is a brief but good source.

19   Stone tools approximately 2.5 million years old have been recovered in Africa and the earliest pottery fragments approximately 10,000 years old have been recovered in Japan.

20   Turner, *Report of the American Historical Association for 1893*, 199 – 227.

21   The four surveys and their beginning years are: the Powell Survey (1869), the King Survey (1870), the Hayden Survey (1871), and the Wheeler Survey (1872). Each of these surveys was responsible for a different geographical area within the American West.

22   Edgar L. Hewett was instrumental in lobbying for the passage of the Act. Subsequent federal cultural resources protection laws include: the National Historic Preservation Act of 1966, the Archaeological Resources Protection

Act of 1979, and the Native American Graves Protection and Repatriation Act of 1990. There are in addition a myriad of state and local cultural preservation laws too numerous to list.

23   Hutt, Jones, McAllister (1992:19 – 21).

24   Douglas Schwartz, personal communication, October 3, 2006.

Chapter 3 THE FIRST SANTA FEANS

1   There is some historical evidence that Juan Martinez de Montoya may have founded Santa Fe as early as 1605 or 1606, but Peralta has nevertheless received recognition as the city's official founder. C. Snow (1992:4 – 8), Ivey (2003), Abbott (2007:22 – 23).

2   Bandelier (1882:90); Elliott (1988:51).

3   Tewa is one of the Kiowa-Tanoan languages spoken among contemporary Rio Grande Pueblos. Contemporary Tewa speakers include the pueblos of San Juan, Santa Clara, San Ildefonso, Nambe, Pojoaque, and Tesuque. Eggan (1979:224 – 235).

4   The issue of which species of megafauna were hunted is still unresolved. In a detailed analysis of 76 sites in which Paleoindians allegedly killed now-extinct large mammals, there were 14 sites (12 mammoths, 2 mastodons) that showed incontrovertible evidence of human killing or butchering. There were three additional sites with limited evidence of human predation on camels and horses. Grayson and Meltzer (2002:348). An expanded analysis that included extinct bison sites supports an inference of Paleoindian hunting of at least five megafaunal species (mammoths, mastodons, camels, horses, bison). Cannon and Meltzer (2004). See also Frison (1993).

5   Fagan (2004:68).

6   Kelly and Todd (1988:232). In this case "complex" implies "a greater diversity of species, a greater number of any given species, and larger individuals than have existed in North America." Ibid.

7   Partial skeletal remains of a mammoth dating to between 20,000 – 25,000 B.P. were discovered in connection with a highway project north of Santa Fe near

the town of Coyote, New Mexico. No cultural materials were found associated with the remains. Stephen S. Post, personal communication (August 3, 2006). This discovery demonstrates that the local region contained sufficient grasslands and surface water to support large Pleistocene herbivores.

8   The timing of some species extinctions has been subject to reevaluation. For example, initial reports from Rampart Cave, Arizona, concluded that Shasta ground sloths were extinct by 11,000. B.P. Phillips (1989). A recalculation of radiocarbon dates resulted in an earlier extinction date, possibly by 12,500 B.P., but well within the time frame associated with the First Americans. Although no ground sloth "kill sites" have been found in the Southwest, butchered sloth remains have been found in South America. Fiedel and Haynes (2004).

9   Anderson (1989) provides an extensive compendium of Pleistocene mammals, including their estimated extinction dates.

10   21 United States Code, sections 3001 – 3013.

11   See, e.g., Berger and Trinkaus (1995).

12   A flute is a longitudinal groove or channel on a projectile point created by the careful removal of thinning flakes. Fluting was ostensibly used to aid in hafting the point onto a shaft such as a dart or spear. Huckell and Judge (2006:151). Despite the widespread adoption of fluting, archaeologists have been unable to determine how the process functionally improved either the killing power of the projectiles or the ability to anchor them to shafts. Meltzer (1993:123). One recent book has suggested that fluting was developed in order to more effectively hold poisons used by Paleoindians in order to incapacitate large animals. Jones (2007:53–61).

13   *Bison occidentalis* was an extinct species of bison that evolved into the smaller, modern *Bison bison* approximately 5,000 years ago. Boldurian and Cotter (1999:2). The Logan County discovery is reported in Williston (1905).

14   For a detailed description of the Folsom discovery as well as a comprehensive synthesis of the most recent work at the Folsom site, readers should consult Meltzer (2006). For a longer and more explicit version of the discussion in the text, see Cordell (1997:69–71).

15   During the Pleistocene Period, several glacial advances occurred at varying intervals. The final advance, labeled the *Wisconsinin*, began around 70,000

years ago and ended around 15,000 years ago. At various times during the Wisconsinin advance, so much of the Earth's water was frozen into glaciers that the sea levels were substantially lower than they are today, and *Beringia*, a dry land mass more than 1,000 miles long and 500 miles wide, created a land bridge between Siberia and Alaska over which both animals and people could pass. Fagan (1998:177–181).

16   Dillehay (2000:295–321).

17   Arlington Springs woman represents the oldest human skeletal remains discovered in North America. Her partial skeletal remains were found on Santa Rosa Island off the coast of California and dated between 13,200 – 13,500 B.P. Despite her age, it is extraordinarily unlikely that Arlington Springs woman was the first American. Johnson et al. (2002).

18   The Solutrean Culture, defined by a particular style of finely fashioned stone tools, was present in portions of France and Iberia during the Upper Paleolithic Period between around 18,000 to 24,000 years ago. Scarre, ed. (2005:161 – 162, 166).

19   Kennewick Man is the name given to an almost complete male skeleton that was discovered in 1996 eroding out of the bank of the Columbia River near Kennewick, Washington. It has been the subject of a legal dispute between a group of scientists who wish to study these unique remains and several Indian tribes claiming reburial rights under the terms of the Native American Graves Protection and Repatriation Act of 1990. Readers desiring more detailed information are referred to Brunning (2006); Thomas (2001); and Chatters (2001).

20   The purported pre-Clovis deposits in Sandia Cave, New Mexico, excavated and dated by Professor Frank Hibben of the University of New Mexico, have remained controversial since their initial reporting. See Hibben (1941). Questions concerning the context of the "Sandia Man" artifacts as well as the authenticity of the artifacts themselves have caused this author to forego discussion of this troublesome site. For additional information, interested readers should consult Preston (1995) and Boldurian and Cotter (1999:120–122). For a review of pre-Clovis sites in the Southwest, see Huckell and Judge (2006:149 – 151).

21   A maximum population of 50,000 people for all of North America has been suggested for the Clovis era of around 12,900 B.P. Fiedel and Haynes (2004:126).

22   One of a very limited number of recovered Paleoindian artifacts made from perishable materials is a net woven from juniper bark cordage found near Cody, Wyoming. See Frison, Andrews, Adovasio, Carlisle, and Edgar (1986).

23   Cordell (1997:80).

24   Boldurian and Cotter (1999:113).

25   Grayson and Meltzer (2002).

26   Burch (1972, 1991).

27   Boldurian and Cotter (1999:114). For a contrary view, see Waguespack and Surovell (2003:333), who statistically analyzed the faunal remains from a number of Clovis sites and concluded that Clovis people were indeed big game hunting specialists.

28   Roosa (1956a, b).

29   Judge's survey encompassed an area of roughly 3,000 square miles in which he located 59 Paleoindian sites and over 1,500 Paleoindian artifacts. Plog (1997:42), Judge (1973).

30   Lang (1997:38). One of the largest Folsom campsites in the Rio Grande Valley was discovered at Rio Rancho, New Mexico. Huckell and Kilby (2002).

31   Judge (1973).

32   The Caja del Rio site, LA 112527, was never scientifically excavated but was illegally collected during the 1970s and 1980s by an individual named Ed Hyde. Although Mr. Hyde maintained his own records and artifact descriptions and surrendered the artifacts to the U.S. Department of the Interior on whose land they were found, the actual context and provenience of these materials has been irrevocably lost. Williams et al. (1996). In addition to the projectile points and tools, the site also has what appears to be a number of [undated] rock alignments which one local archaeologist hypothesizes may relate to some kind of offertory or sacred site designation. Stephen Post, personal communication, December 14, 2006.

33   Scarre, ed. (2005:442–444).

34   Williams et al. (1996). The distribution of high-quality lithic materials may have moved eastward as well as westward because several obsidian artifacts have been discovered at Paleoindian sites as far east as Oklahoma. The poten-

tial sources for the obsidian at those sites includes Idaho and Utah as well as New Mexico. Baugh and Nelson (1987).

35   David Meltzer has estimated that the band responsible for the Folsom bison kill may have easily inhabited a territory of 90,000 square kilometers or approximately 35,000 square miles, an area slightly less than 1/3 the size of New Mexico. Meltzer (2006:304).

36   Acklen (1997).

37   A biface is a tool that has been extensively flaked over both of its major surfaces. Conversely a uniface is a tool that has had all the flaking undertaken on only one of the two major sides. Kooyman (2000:48).

38   Warren (1974); Lang (1995:19–20).

39   For example, site LA 132212 was an artifact scatter located on the floodplain between the Santa Fe River and the Arroyo de Los Chamisos that was investigated by archaeologist Stephen Post (1991). Among Post's discoveries was an Eden Point (ca. 6,500–7,000 B.C.E.) that may have been collected and curated by later Puebloan people using the same area. Elliott (1988:12) lists several isolated Paleoindian occurrences, as do Scheick and Viklund (1991).

40   Futch and McIntosh (1999). Both Folsom- and Midland-style projectiles and tools were recovered from LA 127340. Materials on file at the Archaeological Records Management Section (ARMS), Laboratory of Anthropology, Santa Fe.

41   Honea (1971); Lang (1977).

42   Lang (1997:775).

43   Scheick and Viklund (1991).

44   Doleman (1996).

45   Meltzer (1999:410). Amick (1996) has suggested a similar idea in connection with Folsom people living on the Great Plains. Readers interested in the capacity of hunting and gathering bands to sustain themselves through the winter based solely on the hunting of large game animals such as mule deer, elk, and bighorn sheep should consult Osborn (1993).

46   Flannery (2005:61).

47   Wormington (1957).

48   Cordell (1997:96).

Chapter 4   SEASONAL VISITORS

1   For the most comprehensive treatment of how "the idea of Santa Fe" evolved I recommend Chris Wilson's excellent study, *The Myth of Santa Fe: Creating a Modern Regional Tradition* (1997).

2   Bousman et al. (2002:987).

3   Chapin (2005:656); Post (2000).

4   Kelley (1980:10).

5   Fire-cracked rock is an indicator of places where people made fires for cooking or simply to keep warm. Hearths were often lined with rocks whose internal structure and mineral composition caused them to change colors and break into fragments because of the stresses of repeated heating and cooling.

6   In my efforts to distinguish cultural periods, I have, of necessity, made some very general statements. In actuality, features such as hearths, scatters of fire-cracked rock, and grinding stones have been found in connection with several Paleoindian sites, including, for example, some in the San Pedro Valley in southern Arizona. These findings tend to blur the "bright lines" that differentiate cultural periods, but my point is that at least in the northern middle Rio Grande such features are normally associated with Archaic occupations.

7   Kantner (2004:56).

8   Irwin-Williams (1967, 1973, 1979). Some archaeologists assign the Jay Phase to the end of the Paleoindian Period rather than to the beginning of the Archaic (Judge 1973), and other archaeologists question the efficacy of the Jay Phase itself (Chapin 2005). Most archaeologists have simply noted the problems of classifying Jay points with one or the other periods without resolving the dispute (Cordell 1997:108).

9   Chapin (2005:658).

10   Chapin (2005:144–145).

11   Cultural deposits at the Wilson-Leonard site in central Texas span almost 13,500 years of occupation and offer clues regarding the Paleoindian-Archaic transition. The deposits reveal a gradual change from more Paleoindian-like assemblages of artifacts to more Archaic-like assemblages. The most important

finding is that while a number of similar artifacts are found in each distinctive stratigraphic deposit, the percentages of artifact types change over time in such a way as to suggest a gradual shift away from technology directed towards the hunting of large animals towards technology associated with hunting smaller animals and plant processing. Bousman et al. (2002:980).

12   Figure 29 illustrates the most common types of Archaic projectiles found in the Santa Fe area, but at least one San Augustin-Gypsum Cave–style point has been recovered. The small (3 cm), triangular dart point was unexpectedly recovered from a cultural deposit dating to 5260–5040 B.C.E. and is a type generally associated with early Archaic occupations on the Colorado Plaeau and southern New Mexico. Its presence suggests that our understanding of population movements during the early Archaic Period throughout the intermountain area is still incomplete. Post (2000:29); Stephen Post (Personal communication, December 12, 2006).

13   McBrinn (2005).

14   Bradley (1991:395), quoted in Kooyman (2000:120).

15   Chapin (2005:652).

16   A mano is a hand stone used for grinding. A metate is a flat or trough-shaped grinding stone upon which seeds or grain are placed to be worked on with a mano.

17   Elliott (1988:14).

18   Elliott (1988:15).

19   One of the earliest Archaic Period sites near Santa Fe is located north of the city along State Route 599 near the Tano Road interchange. LA 61315 has several components, including a campsite that has been dated to 5260–5040 B.C.E. associated with the late Jay or very early Bajada Period. Post (2000:29).

20   Site numbers LA 9500 and LA 9500. Materials on file at ARMS Site Records, Laboratory of Anthropology, Santa Fe.

21   A resharpened San Jose projectile point was recovered in the area of Las Campanas, west of the city, suggesting the possibility of occupation or use of that area during the middle Archaic. Post (1992:88).

22   Scheick (2006: 170–172).

23   Miller and Wendorf (1958).

24   Scheick and Viklund (1991); Lakatos et al. (2001); Post (2004, 1998); Moore (personal communication, December 14, 2006).

25   Post (2004:71).

26   Lang (1995).

27   As an illustration, LA 61315 is a multicomponent site that includes a Late Bajada Phase base camp as well as a much later En Medio phase residential camp. These components were separated by at least 2,400 years, a time span that suggests variable suitability of this locale for long-term camps. Post (2000). Archaeologists can infer that a particular site was a base camp by looking to see whether the assemblage of artifacts reflects a more general range of activities rather than specific and limited activities such as hunting or plant processing in which only limited and specific types of artifacts are found. Post (1994:47, referring to LA 84787).

28   Schmader et al. (1994). See also Hannaford (1986).

29   Schmader et al. (1994:4).

30   Site numbers: LA 54744, LA 54749, LA 54751, and LA 54752. Schmader (1994).

31   Schmader et al. (1994:97).

32   Schmader et al. (1994:56, 65, 77). For a more extensive summary of potentially edible plant remains, readers are directed to McBride's "Macrobotanical Analysis" of the subject sites. (Appendix B in Schmader et al. 1994).

33   Schmader et al. (1994:75).

34   Excavations of several Late Archaic features at LA 61282, only a few miles from Schmader's sites, failed to produce any evidence of cultigens. Post (2004).

35   For example, in a survey of 435 acres in the Dos Griegos subdivision located about ten miles southeast of Santa Fe, the discovery of several Late Archaic sites and isolated occurrences echo the kinds of multiple resource subsistence patterns seen in Tierra Contenta and areas to the north of the city. Lang (1992). See also Post (1994, 2000, 2004).

36   Lang (1977:16).

37   Scheick (1999:4), citing Lang (1977, 1986, 1995); Vierra (2005:22–25). The

most comprehensive treatment of usable wild plants in the Middle Rio Grande Valley is Dunmire and Tierney (1995).

38   Dunmire and Tierney (1995:163,192, 210).

39   Scheick and Viklund (1991a).

40   Schmader (1994); Hannaford (1986); Post (1992, 2000); Lang (1997).

41   Dickson (1979); Post (1994, 1996); Lang (1995); Scheick and Viklund (1991b).

42   Wendorf and Miller (1959); Lang (1989).

43   Stuart and Gauthier ([1984] 1996:47).

44   Dunmire and Tierney (1995:vii, 9).

45   The "forager-collector" dichotomy is a somewhat artificial but still useful way to distinguish among different types of hunter-gatherers. "Foragers" move constantly across the landscape searching for food. In other words, the people move to the food. "Collectors" rely more upon known and predictable food sources and send out small groups to collect food and bring it back to a base camp. In other words, the food moves to the people. See generally, Sutton and Anderson (2004:125–132).

46   Chapin (2005:171).

47   No Archaic Period burials have been discovered in northern New Mexico. Stephen Post (personal communication, July 12, 2006). Several Late Archaic or Early Agricultural burials were encountered in connection with a highway project between Silver City and Lordsburg in southern New Mexico. The burials dated to between 895 B.C.E. and 160 C.E. and all individuals had been interred in a flexed position, laying on their sides. One was under a large rock cairn composed of "milling stones." Three burials were discovered in a large bell-shaped storage pit and included shell beads. Christopher Turnbow (personal communication, October 10, 2006). Archaic Period burials have been encountered in Arizona, Carpenter et al. (2005:26); Colorado, Nelson (2001:75); the northern plains, Wendt (2004); and Texas (Bousman et al. (2002:984).

48   Studies of semi-sedentary hunter-gatherer populations living in the Great Basin, an arid region encompassing Nevada, Utah, and parts of California, Oregon, Idaho, and Arizona, have estimated population densities that vary

between one person per 30 square miles (1:30) to one person per two square miles (1:2). The numbers vary according to local productivity with the highest densities associated with the most biologically productive areas such as the Owens Valley in Nevada (Sutton 2004:168). Other researchers have estimated the population density of the Great Basin as one person per ten square miles (1:10) Krech (1999:93–99; 264 n. 37). Using these numbers as reference points gives a potential Archaic population of between 40 and 600 persons for the study area of 1200 square miles identified in Chapter 1 (1200/30=40; 1200/10=120; 1200/2=600). It occurs to me that 600 people is probably too high a number for such a circumscribed area, but these admittedly rough estimates are offered to let the reader see that Archaic populations were relatively small, and that even varying the population densities would not involve large numbers of people.

Chapter 5   SANTA FE HORTICULTURAL SOCIETIES

1   In a broad-ranging study, Yesner (1994:166) concluded, "evidence for episodic seasonal population stress appears to be widespread among hunter-gatherers in arctic, temperate, and arid regions where any degree of resource seasonality existed." The Southwest was clearly an area of "resource seasonality."

2   Piñon trees produce nut masts every three to seven years that are sufficient to support hunter-gatherer bands. The mast periodicities are dependent upon tree species, location, and climate. Wills (1995:221).

3   For a broad overview of the worldwide beginnings of agriculture, see Scarre (2005), Chapters 5–7, 9–11.

4   See, e.g., Price and Gebauer (1995).

5   Richerson et al. (2001:387).

6   Weaver (1993:13–24); Pearsall (1995).

7   Matson (2005: 279).

8   It occurs to me that I should offer a few comments about domesticated animals. European colonists introduced all of the well-known domesticated animals we see in the Southwest today. The only domesticated animals in the

New World prior to 1492 C.E. were dogs, turkeys, honey bees in Mexico, and guinea pigs and llamas in South America. Although their potential uses seem limited, some of these indigenous animals not only provided food products but the raw materials for blankets, cordage, and other tools. For example, turkey feather blankets are lightweight, warm and highly durable, as are dog hair blankets. Dogs were first domesticated in the Old World more than 10,000 years ago and probably accompanied the Paleoindians in their large-scale movements. The earliest undisputed evidence of dog domestication in the Americas comes from Archaic Period dog burials. Carpenter et al. (2005:27); Ezzo and Steiner (2000:291); and Morey and Wiant (1992:224).

9   See, e.g., Matson (2005: 279–281). Hill (2002:465, 470–471) marshals linguistic evidence to support the theory that maize cultivation was brought to the Colorado Plateau as early as the first millennium B.C.E. by a group of Uto-Aztecan speakers who originated in Mexico. Hill believes that these Uto-Aztecans came into contact with an indigenous group of Kiowa-Tanoan speakers, who after having been taught about maize cultivation, evolved into the Fremont culture of the eastern Great Basin, a portion of whom became the Tanoan speakers (Tewa, Tiwa, Towa) who were living in the Rio Grande Valley by the 13th century.

10   Renfrew and Bahn (2004:459–460).

11   Marsha Ogilvie's research suggests that gender-specific-changes in labor organization had already begun to occur during the Late Archaic Period. In a comparison of the physical structure of Late Archaic male and female femurs, Ogilvie found that male femurs tended to approximate the structures associated with mobile foraging populations, whereas female femurs tended to approximate the structures associated with early agricultural populations leading to an inference of sex-based divisions of labor. Ogilvie (2005).

12   LeBlanc (1999:149–152).

13   Wills (1995,1988) has interpreted the spread of horticulture in upland areas in southern New Mexico based on the idea that the initial adoption of agriculture resulted from the need to monitor animals and wild foods such as nut masts. In Wills's estimation, planting small plots of maize and squash almost became a form of "resource caching" that ensured the existence of food reserves in foraging areas and enabled small-scale cultivators to go out on longer forag-

ing trips. Wills suggests that the development of agriculture supplemented long-standing food-collecting systems and allowed mobile bands to do what they already knew how to do a little bit better, namely continue to hunt and gather. While Wills's theory helps to explain the development of agriculture in the Mogollon Highlands, it does not explain what happened around Santa Fe, where the close proximity of several ecozones made small-scale maize cultivation unnecessary as a supplementary food source and where populations of Late Archaic combination "forager-farmers" are not evident.

14   Vierra and Ford (2007:119). Some of the earliest examples of domesticates in the Southwest were discovered in Bat Cave, near the Plains of St. Augustin in south-central New Mexico and are dated 2284–2039 B.C.E. for maize, 1377–1952 B.C.E. for squash, and 389–400 B.C.E. for beans. Wills (1995:218).

15   Scheick (2005a:13); Lang (1995:23).

16   The features have been radiocarbon dated to between 400–600 C.E. Three of the features were bell-shaped and one was a large basin-shaped pit. This grouping may represent the earliest agriculturally related features in Santa Fe. Post et al. (2006:5).

17   Lang (1995:23); Akins, Post, and Wilson (2003).

18   Readers will recall the Pecos Classification discussed in Chapter 2, and while most archaeologists working in the Rio Grande refer to the Developmental Period, some archaeologists refer to Basketmaker II or Basketmaker III sites around Santa Fe. Use of such dual terminology is neither "right nor wrong," but the chronological periods of the Pecos and Rio Grande systems overlap and can cause some confusion, which is why only the Rio Grande system is used in this book.

19   Cordell (1989:18).

20   Schmader et al. (1994: 29).

21   Wendorf (1954); Wendorf and Reed (1955).

22   Wiseman (1995:238). The earliest forms of pottery found in the Santa Fe area are delineated as Lino Gray or Lino Black-on-gray, Whitemound Black-on-white, and an early from of Red Mesa Black-on-white. Dickson (1979:11).

23   Elliott (1988); Cordell (1989); Stuart and Gauthier (1996); Dickson (1979).

24 Dickson (1979); Lang (1992); Doleman (1996). Excavations at El Pueblo de Santa Fe in the downtown area have uncovered purported agricultural features dating to 400–600 C.E. Post et al. (2006). An additional Developmental Period site not far from downtown is LA 618, a pit house and associated structures located on a terrace above the Santa Fe River. Materials on file at ARMS, laboratory of Anthropology. For a summary of early Developmental sites in the Santa Fe area, see Scheick (2005a:8–10).

25 There are three descriptive terms for early agricultural settlements that are used interchangeably but which have different meanings based on size. *Farmsteads* are individual homesteads or farm enterprises, typically represented during the Developmental Period by one or perhaps two pit houses and a few small surface structures. *Hamlets* are clusters of between two and eight farmsteads, and for our purpose would be characterized by several pit houses and associated surface structures. *Villages* are clusters of dwellings that are larger than hamlets and may be characterized by a dozen or more pit houses and numerous surface structures. Roberts (1996:16–18). Irrespective of size, all three forms are social communities with a complex range of inter- and intra-settlement relationships.

26 Scheick (2005b:9).

27 Lang (1988). Additional support for Plains-Puebloan interaction is provided by the existence of pueblo-like villages dating to between 1200–1500 C.E. and located in the vicinity of the Alibates quarries in the Texas Panhandle. Identified as the Panhandle Aspect of the Antelope Creek Phase of the Plains Village Culture, these Buffalo-hunting horticulturalists maintained a vigorous trade with southwestern Puebloans as evidenced by discoveries of Puebloan pottery, turquoise beads, and obsidian tools and jewelry. Green (1986); Derrick (2004).

28 What is the big deal about corn? For one thing, on a per unit weight basis corn has more caloric value than any other grain. Muenchrath and Salvador (1995). Aside from its nutritive content, corn is subject to manipulation to take account of different growing zones, and can be dried or parched for long-term storage. On the other hand, it is lacking in iron, calcium, and the amino acid lysine so that a diet based almost completely on corn will lead to anemia. Ethnographic evidence of corn consumption by small-scale corn growers reveals an average daily consumption of between .6 – .8 kilograms. At an average

caloric value of approximately 3.48 cal/gm, those amounts would provide between approximately 2100 – 2800 calories per day. Based on these figures one can also estimate the amount of person days of corn stored by calculating all of the available storage (pits, baskets, other containers)(225 kg/cu. meter) in a particular settlement. For a discussion of the connections between beliefs and agricultural practices, see Bohrer (1995:361).

29   Polyak and Asmerom (2001:150); Eric Blinman (personal communication, December 14, 2006).

30   Forenbaher and Miracle (2005).

31   This general assertion is supported by the observation that the earliest pottery in the northern Rio Grande Valley reflects both Ancestral Puebloan and Mogollon traditions. Cordell (1997:197). Readers should be aware, however, that the phrase "reflects…traditions" is not necessarily to be equated with "made by" because local groups often copied and reinterpreted imported styles.

32   Boggess (2006:11 – 12); Vierra and Ford (2007).

33   Wiseman (1995:241, 246).

34   According to one report LA 166 was one of the largest Developmental Period pueblos in the Rio Grande drainage, but Dickson reported it consisting of only 50 – 75 rooms and seven kivas. Dickson (1979:88). Additional materials on file at ARMS, Laboratory of Anthropology, Santa Fe.

35   Wiseman (1995:247). Archaeologists do not dispute the local presence of small pit house hamlets prior to 900 C.E., but the open question is whether Early-to-Middle Developmental pit house communities represented completely sedentary village life, or were part-time, perhaps the seasonal abodes of still semi-mobile groups. Many of these pit house communities have an air of impermanence, and it is likely that many of these structures were used intermittently during the year.

36   Post (2004:69).

37   Both clans and moieties are kinship-based social categories with clans being more prominent among western Puebloans and moieties being more prominent among eastern Puebloans. A clan is a form of social organization in which members claim common descent but do not specify how they are related. The

purported common ancestor may be fictional. Webster et al. (1993:579). A moiety is a division of a society into two distinct social categories or groups, often on the basis of kinship. Thomas (1989:660). Some moieties, such as those operating within the historic eastern pueblos are involved primarily with the ceremonial organization of the community. Fowles (2005).

38   Levy (1992).

39   Hegmon (1996:237, 240).

40   Fagan (2004:213-228).

41   Kantner (2004:69).

42   Rose et al. (1981:104).

43   Stubbs (1954:45).

44   It was during this period that some of the most impressive Puebloan achievements in architecture, social, and political organization occurred in the San Juan Basin, specifically, in and around Chaco Canyon. The published materials about Chaco Canyon constitute an archaeological history as voluminous and monumental as the Chacoan great houses themselves. Readers who desire an introduction to the subject of Chaco Canyon should begin with Reed (2004) and Vivian and Hilpert (2002). Those readers wishing a more detailed approach should consider Lekson, ed. (2005), Mathien (2005), Sebastian (1992), and Vivian (1990). Each of those volumes contains a vast number of additional references that readers may pursue.

45   LA 114, materials on file at ARMS, Laboratory of Anthropology, Santa Fe.

46   Stubbs and Stallings (1953:14−15).

47   Dickson (1979:124-125).

48   Post et al. (2006).

49   Elliot (1988:17).

50   Acklen et al. (1994:31, 36). The actual pottery distribution suggests an occupation beginning around 1000 C.E. and ending as late as 1200 C.E. For additional information, see LA 111 and 114 materials on file at ARMS, Laboratory of Anthropology, Museum of New Mexico, Santa Fe.

51 Of the 75 pottery sherds collected in this limited study, the majority consisted of undecorated plainware or corrugated ware. Of the 21 decorated sherds, 11 were identified as Red Mesa Black-on-White. Acklen et al. (1994:30–31).

52 LA 46300, materials on file at ARMS, Laboratory of Anthropology, Santa Fe. Wiseman (1989).

53 Comedian George Carlin's sketch about stuff (Carlin 2001) is a humorous but not inaccurate metaphor for how the linked processes of agriculture, pottery production, and sedentary living changed the relationship between people and their material possessions during the Developmental Period.

54 For example, LA 15969, a small site with a midden, wall alignment, and rubble mound suggesting surface habitation. Materials on file at ARMS, Laboratory of Anthropology, Santa Fe. Wiseman (1978).

55 Wiseman (1989:78–83).

56 D. H. Snow (1989:2).

57 Scheick (2005b)

58 Ibid., 6.

59 LA 143460. Materials on file at ARMS, Laboratory of Anthropology, Santa Fe. These presumed abandonment dates were based on an archaeomagnetic sample from the hearth. Scheick (2005a:239). Several earlier dates were associated with maize kernals and carbonized twigs suggesting a period of contemporaneous occupation with both the KP and Diker sites (Scheick 2007:140)

60 Ibid., 247. Post (1993:43).

Chapter 6 IT TAKES AN EVOLVING VILLAGE

1 Lentz (2005); Lentz, Barbour, Post (2006); Post et al. (2006).

2 LA 111. Materials on file at ARMS, Laboratory of Anthropology, Santa Fe. Acklen et al. (1994).

3 LA 191. Materials on file at ARMS, Laboratory of Anthropology, Santa Fe.

4 LA 76. Materials on file at ARMS, Laboratory of Anthropology, Santa Fe.

5   LA 8. Materials on file at ARMS, Laboratory of Anthropology, Santa Fe. See Elliott (1988:56–57).

6   Among these early Coalition communities were LA 1 (Pindi), LA 2 (Agua Fria Schoolhouse), LA 109, LA 114 (Arroyo Negro), LA 117, LA 118, and LA 119. Winters (2006:13). The presence of similar ceramic assemblages at all of these settlements supports an inference they were occupied at approximately the same time. Lakatos, Post, and Murrell (2001:11).

7   Cherie Scheick (personal communication, August 17, 2006).

8   Post (1994:15).

9   Elliott (1988:19).

10   Shapiro (2005:22).

11   Dickson (1975:169).

12   Cameron (1995); Lekson and Cameron (1995); Crown, Orcutt, and Kohler (1996); Cordell, Van West, Dean, and Muenchrath (2007). The Gallina people lived along mesa tops, steep hillsides, and at the heads of relatively inaccessible valleys, primarily in the area between the Chama and San Juan Rivers on the west slopes and foothills of the Jemez Mountains. For more information, see Ellis (1988).

13   Stuart and Gauthier (1996 [1984]:51).

14   For some time archaeologists have noted design similarities between Mesa Verde pottery and the pottery produced in the northern Middle Rio Grande. Roney (1995). The discovery of a complete Mesa Verde-style container in the 2006 excavations at El Pueblo de Santa Fe strengthens the possibility of local connections with western Puebloan groups, but archaeologists have not yet concluded whether the container was made locally or imported. Linda Cordell, Stephen Lentz (personal communication, September 7, 2006).

15   Habicht-Mauche (1993:86, quoting Cordell, 1979:144; 1984:333).

16   In addition to architectural similarities, at least one pottery type collected at Pinnacle Ruin (Magdalena Black-on-white) is suggestive of Mesa Verde designs. Lekson (2004). For an earlier discovery purportedly involving Mesa Verde-style pottery and architecture in the Rio Puerco Valley in central New Mexico, see Davis and Winkler (1959). A keyhole-style kiva, stylistically remi-

niscent of Mesa Verdean kivas, was excavated at the Saltbush Pueblo site in Bandelier National Monument. D. H. Snow (1974).

17   Cordell (1995:207).

18   Crown, Orcutt, and Kohler (1996:193); Stuart and Gauthier (1996:51).

19   Scheick (2005a:18).

20   Ibid., 188.

21   Rose, Dean, and Robinson (1981:104).

22   Dickson (1979:69). One study concluded that the 19th-century farmers of San Juan Pueblo, located north of Santa Fe at the confluence of the Chama and Rio Grande Rivers, never produced more than a single month's food surplus. Ford (1968:116), quoted in Wetterstrom (1986:104). One study may not be determinative of the "surplus question," but it certainly offers food for thought.

23   Maxwell and Anschuetz (1992).

24   Jones et al. (1999).

25   Lang and Scheick (1989:196). "Successful" in this case is no doubt a euphemism for continued growth and expansion.

26   Wiseman (1995:238).

27   Eric Blinman (personal communication, December 14, 2006).

28   Post (1999).

29   Habicht-Mauche (1993, 1995).

30   Ibid.

31   Post (1994, 1999); Post and Lakatos (1995); Scheick and Viklund (1991).

32   Post and Lakatos (1995:145–147).

33   Post (1999:40).

34   Assuming such control ever existed it may not have lasted more than a few decades in the 13th century because excavations at Agua Fria Schoolhouse revealed that by the early 14th century the amount of Santa Fe Black-on-white pottery was substantially diminished, and the frequency of two new varieties, Galisteo Black-on-white and Wiyo Black-on-white, had substantially increased. Lang and Scheick (1989:192).

35 Dickson (1979:69); Post (1994:59) (for a brief discussion relating to constraints on land use and resources); Adler et al. (1996:422)("Ancestral Pueblo communities may have reacted…by reducing the availability of lands to migrants . . ."). For a different perspective, archaeologists who excavated a portion of Agua Fria Schoolhouse in 1988 offer a rough picture of how far pottery could move across the Southwest. They discovered a Klagetoh Black-on-white jar that originated in the Little Colorado River area of eastern Arizona and western New Mexico. Assuming for the sake of argument that an itinerant pottery peddler walked in a straight line, that region is more than 190 miles from Santa Fe. Lang and Scheick (1989:192). If (and it is still a big "if") the Mesa Verde–style jar previously described in note 14 was a genuine import and not a locally made "knock off" copy, the case for long-distance trade networks is strengthened.

36 LA 15969. Materials on file at ARMS, Laboratory of Anthropology, Santa Fe.

37 Shapiro (2005).

38 McNutt (1969) found a D-shaped kiva at the 11th-12th century Tesuque By-Pass site north of Santa Fe. Whether this architectural form was imported from areas to the west or developed independently in the northern Rio Grande is an open question, but D-shaped kivas have been found from sites in northern Arizona all the way to Arrowhead Ruin, 18 miles east of Santa Fe. W. Morgan (1994:229).

39 Stubbs and Stallings (1953:24–47); Munro (2006:463, 467).

40 Scheick (2005a).

41 Creamer (1993:85); Lang and Harris (1984:101–105). Despite the indisputable presence of turkey remains at Arroyo Hondo Pueblo, these birds may not have accounted for more than 2 percent of the food supply, (Wetterstrom 1986:84–85), an observation that may underscore the breeding of turkeys for non-food purposes.

42 Stubbs and Stallings (1953:143).

43 This feature of "paired settlements," often separated by a river or stream, appears to have developed locally during the late Coalition and early Classic Periods.

44 Lang and Scheick (1989:196); Scheick (personal communication, August 18, 2007).

45 Dickson (1979:31).

46 Chamisa Locita (LA 4) is located a few miles south and slightly west of Los Alamos and was a much larger settlement. From an analysis of pottery sequences and a few tree-ring dates it looks as if this site was occupied for only a short period in the late 13th and early to middle 14th centuries. It may have had as many as 280 to 300 rooms, making it one of the larger Late Coalition-Early Classic periods settlements southeast of Santa Fe. For comparison purposes, Los Alamos had perhaps 70 rooms. Dickson (1979:117–120).

47 Scheick (2005a:21).

48 Snead (2006).

49 Additional groups of Coalition Period settlements were located in the Galisteo Basin several miles to the east of Los Alamos Pueblo and Chamisa Locita, including Manzanares (LA 1104/10607) and the Lamy Junction sites (LA 27, 362-368, 31774–31779). These sites were outside the bounds of the middle northern Rio Grande as I defined it in Chapter 1, and so they were not included in this analysis. See generally, Snead (2005:10).

50 Lentz (2005); Lentz, Barbour, Post (2006); Post et al. (2006). Additional materials on LA 1051 are on file at ARMS, Laboratory of Anthropology, Santa Fe. Ethnographer John Harrington reported in 1916 that local Tewa Indians indicated that if there had been a village downtown it would have been a Tano village because they did not know of any Tewa villages in that area. The Tano Indians are generally associated with a number of villages south of Santa Fe, including several large Classic period pueblos in the Galisteo Basin. Elliott (1988:51).

51 See generally, Bandelier (1882); Harrington (1916); Mera (1934); Peckham (1977); and Deyloff (1997, 1998).

52 Lentz, Barbour, and Post (2006:8).

53 Ibid., 10.

54 LA 16. Materials on file at ARMS, Laboratory of Anthropology, Santa Fe.

55 Cuyumongue (LA 38) is located on a terrace above the Rio Tesuque about a mile south of the present Tesuque Pueblo. Wilmeth (1956:4). See also additional materials for LA 38 on file at ARMS, Laboratory of Anthropology, Santa Fe.

56 Dickson (1979:81). The occupation dates based on an earlier tree-ring study are given as 1193–1268 C.E. Smiley et al. (1953).

57 Ibid., 82.

58 Snead (2006, 2005). It should be noted that the beginning occupation date for Burnt Corn is based upon a single tree-ring sample with a cutting date of 1272 C.E. collected by Bertha Dutton in 1962 (Snead 2006:9) and that a more accurate date for the beginning of Burnt Corn may be closer to 1292 C.E. (Snead 2007).

59 Snead (2006, 2005). Nels Nelson's 1915 field notes for Alamo Pueblo (a.k.a. Los Alamos) make numerous references to rooms that contained "charred wood" and "burnt adobe." Evidence of burned and destroyed Coalition Period villages is not limited to areas around Santa Fe as several sites in the Chama Valley, including the Palisade Ruin (LA 3505) and the Leafwater site (LA 300), also were burned. James Moore (personal communication, December 19, 2006). See also Peckham (1981).

Chapter 7 BIG BOX ZONING

1 See, e.g., "Examining the Big Box Effect." *Santa Fe New Mexican*, July 11, 2006, page 1.

2 For example, Ponsipa'akeri and Pose'uinge in the Chama River area had at least 2,000 rooms. Pueblos Blanco and San Lazaro located in the Galisteo Basin had at least 1,400 rooms. Adams and Duff, editors (2004:157 – 182). San Marcos Pueblo had at least 2,600 rooms. Lightfoot (1996:132).

3 Crown, Orcutt, and Kohler (1996:201).

4 Adler et al (1996:383) define "an aggregated site as a tight cluster of 50 or more contemporaneous surface and subsurface structures." Based upon this definition, the process of aggregation already was well developed during the Late Coalition Period but the scope and scale of aggregation became much greater during the Classic Period.

5 Dickson (1979); Scheick (1999:13).

6 For example, LA 61282 is a small Classic Period site identified by pottery sherds located along the Santa Fe River just over three miles from Cieneguilla Pueblo. Post (2004). Similarly, the residents of Arroyo Hondo may have developed agricultural fields as much as three miles away from the pueblo (Wetterstrom 1986:105) and may have also established temporary foraging camps at a similar distance (Post 1998:20).

7   At least one Classic Period hunting camp has been discovered at an altitude of approximately 8,000 feet in the Sangre de Cristo Mountains. Lang (1997:44).

8   Adler et al. (1996).

9   Welker (1997).

10   Ibid., 194.

11   Roomblocks arranged at right angles to one another.

12   Wendorf and Reed (1955).

13   Elliott (1988:20).

14   Habicht-Mauche 1995:181.

15   Staley (1990:150, 232–233).

16   E. Reed (1956: 15–16).

17   Ladder style roomblocks were built with an initial construction of two long parallel walls that formed the outside walls of a roomblock. Individual rooms were then created through the addition of shorter cross walls.

18   Shapiro (2005).

19   Herhahn (1995:81-82).

20   Lightfoot (1993).

21   Habicht-Mauche (1993, 1995)

22   Creamer (2000:114) takes a somewhat contrary view and does not find evidence of emerging ethnic groups. In her view, political interactions among Classic Rio Grande pueblos were essentially "local and situational."

23   For an excellent description of this period in eastern North America, see Milner (2004:124 – 176). In addition, Neitzel, ed. (1999) has collected a number of outstanding essays describing and comparing late pre-Hispanic societies in the Southwest and Southeast regions.

24   This is not too say that exotic materials such as foreign pottery, macaws, and non-local minerals were not regularly traded, only that there does not appear to be any evidence of elite hoarding of exotic items such as has been hypothesized for Chaco Canyon, Paquimé, and other complex polities.

25   Palkovich (1980).

26   Fowles (2005); see also Plog (1997:18 – 21).

27   Archaeologists have interpreted the concept of "warfare" expansively to extend beyond physical conflict and include threats, coercion, and the ability and willingness to resort to violence. See generally, LeBlanc (1999). Early

Spanish accounts described Puebloan warfare and noted the use of bows and arrows, wood javelins, fending sticks, clubs, lances, and shields. Wilmeth (1956: 205–209). More compelling evidence includes the Riana Ruin located on the Chama River which was burned and in which a charred skeleton was found sprawled in one of the burned rooms, (Hibben 1937:48–49); the burned kiva at Te'ewi (LA 252) also located in the Chama Valley, in which the burned remains of 24 young men were discovered, Wendorf (1953:46); and the burned pueblo of Poshu'ouinge in which a skeleton was discovered sprawled in a plaza, Jeançon (1923:5–6). For a contrary, albeit not entirely convincing view, see Spielmann (2004:137, 143) who opines that the maintenance of long-distance trade networks that facilitated the movement of significant quantities of goods across the Pueblo world "indicates that endemic warfare did not characterize this [Classic] period."

28   For an east-to-west view of the diffusion of the katsina system, see Schaafsma and Schaafsma (1974); for a west-to-east view of this diffusion, see Adams (1991).

29   In point of fact, the katsina system is exceedingly weak among contemporary Rio Grande Pueblos in which the primary organizational structure is the moiety system. Some pueblos such as Taos have no ceremonies or iconography that even looks like a katsina. Eric Blinman (personal communication).

30   In August 1992, two helmet-style, gypsum plaster katsina masks representing badgers or bears were discovered at San Lazaro Pueblo, located in the Galisteo Basin. These masks are the only artifacts of this nature ever discovered in the Southwest. Ware and Blinman (2000:381).

31   Two macaw burials were discovered at Arroyo Hondo Pueblo (Creamer 1993), and at least one such burial has been discovered at El Pueblo de Santa Fe. Lentz, Post, and Barbour (2006). Macaw burials are significant because these birds were used for ceremonial rather than dietary purposes and were highly valued because of their extraordinary multi-colored plumage. Macaws are not native to the northern Southwest but were imported, possibly from as far away as Casas Grandes in Chihuahua, Mexico, via either long distance trading networks, or more likely via some kind of down the line "hand-to-hand" system involving intermediate traders.

32   Ware and Blinman (2000). A sodality is a social group that is organized

around specific interests or goals and whose members are not necessarily connected via kinship. Webster, Evans, Sanders (1993:582).

33 Ware and Blinman (2000:383, 393).

34 Ibid., 397.

35 For details about the architecture and construction of Arroyo Hondo, see Creamer (1993).

36 Adams (1991).

37 Creamer (1993:68).

38 Shapiro (2005).

39 Palkovich (1980:159–164); Lang and Harris (1984:247–253).

40 Habicht-Mauche (1993:182–185, 209). "A prayer plume base or *tiponi,* would be pushed into the sand of an altar or shrine and prayer feathers can be inserted into a tiny hole on the top along the edge." Ibid., 200.

41 Lang and Harris (1984:207–211). A review of the nature and uses of Ancestral Puebloan musical instruments is provided in Hoover (2004/2005).

42 Creamer (1993:152–154).

43 Although it is sometimes difficult to agree on these numbers, room occupation percentages of between 30–60 percent appear to be reasonable. Applying these percentages to Arroyo Hondo's estimated 1,000 rooms during its Component I occupation, together with average number of rooms per family (3–5), and average number of persons per family (4–5) provides an approximate population of at least 240 but no more than 1,000 people. Lightfoot (1993:135).

44 Palkovich (1980).

45 Palkovich (2006).

46 In fact El Pueblo de Santa Fe, together with pueblos north of Santa Fe in the Pojoaque/Tesuque/Nambe area, appears to have contained one of the healthier Puebloan populations during the 14th and 15th centuries. Nancy Akins (personal communication, December 20, 2006); Post et al. (2006). On the other hand, Martin (1995) found serious health problems among the Puebloans at San Cristobal (Galisteo Basin), the Salinas pueblos south of Albuquerque, and Hawikuh, near Zuni, New Mexico. Merbs (1989) found similar health problems in a comparison of skeletal remains from Arroyo Hondo, Grasshopper Pueblo on the Little Colorado River in Arizona, and Sundown, an 11th-century Sinagua settlement in Arizona.

47 Palkovich (1980), LeBlanc (1999). Most of the evidence for warfare in
the Rio Grande is circumstantial and includes burned settlements, some
unburied bodies, and warrior rock-art imagery. The Classic Period may have
been anxiety-ridden, but incontrovertible evidence of large-scale warfare is
limited. For example, of the 111 sets of skeletal remains from Arroyo Hondo,
one male suffered from an embedded projectile point and a second male
showed evidence of a healed fracture. Palkovich (1980:168).

48 Ceramic seriation evidence shows that at some point the Component II
residents ceased importing glazed pottery from the Galisteo Basin. This
change might be reflective of a breach with the large pueblos immediately to
the south of Arroyo Hondo that ultimately resulted in political or economic
isolation, or even a final battle. Habicht-Mauche (1991:181). Pecos Pueblo
also ceased trading for Galisteo glazes during the 14th century and historical
accounts confirm ongoing hostile relations between Pecos and Galisteo
communities. Spielmann (2004:142).

49 Peckham and Snow (1982).

50 Motsinger (1997:101).

51 Rose et al. (1981:104).

52 For example, see Hewett et al. (1913); Kidder (1924).

53 Many contemporary Puebloan people and some archaeologists question the
term "abandonment" because it implies irrevocably severed connections with
ancestral settlements. Even when ancestral settlements remained unoccupied,
people continued to visit them for religious and other purposes. "Settlement
shifting" is a more accurate description of the concept being discussed
because it incorporates the idea of movement as an adaptive response to
changed circumstances without necessarily implying a final intention to
permanently desert a particular place.

Chapter 8 NEW PEOPLE IN THE NEIGHBORHOOD

1 Lewis Henry Morgan developed a classification scheme to explain the process
of cultural evolution in which all societies passed through a series of stages that
he called "barbarism," "savagery," and "civilization." Each stage was marked
by a particular set of technological attributes, such as bows and arrows being

associated with savagery and writing being associated with civilization. Morgan (1965) [1877]. At the time the monument was commissioned, "savagery" did not have the racist associations it does today.

2   Archaeological evidence indicates that after 1450 C.E. a strong east-west trading network developed between eastern Puebloans and Plains Caddo people that was based in part on obsidian, which was highly valued by Plains groups for projectiles and tools. Baugh and Nelson (1987).

3   Dean and Ravesloot (1993:96–98).

4   Whalen and Minnis (2001:200–204).

5   Salinization occurs when farmers in arid areas irrigate their crops with water that is naturally high in dissolved mineral salts, such as the Salt River that flows through the Phoenix Basin in Arizona. Over time, the continuous deposition of mineral salts caused by evaporation from irrigation canals results in soil that will no longer support most crops.

6   Whiteley (2004:144,150).

7   Brugge (1992:341). Archaeologist Richard Wilshusen excavated a Navajo-type forked stick hogan site on Frances Mesa just south of the San Juan River (LA 55979) that has been dated to 1541 C.E. Richard Wilshusen (personal communication, December 21, 2006).

8   Bandelier (1971) [1890].

9   Towner and Dean (1996:13–14).

10   Towner, ed. (1996).

11   *Apaches de Navahu* is a term that has been variously identified as a place name for an area of cornfields in the Chama Valley, Towner and Dean (1996:5), or as a Tewa term meaning "Apaches of the fields." Linda Cordell (personal communication recounting a conversation with Alfonso Ortiz).

12   Brown (1996:55).

13   Casteñeda et al. (1990:59–60); Hammond and Rey (1940:185). For additional background information about Pueblo-Navajo interactions, see Brooks (2002:83–88).

14   Forbes (1960).

15   Mera (1934); Hester (1962); Schaafsma (1981).

16   Gunnerson (1969:23).

17   Schaafsma (1992, 2002a).

18   Carillo (1992:325).

19   Brugge (1969); Gunnerson and Gunnerson (1970); Schaafsma (2002b:198).

20   Williston and Martin (1900); Martin (1909); Opler (1982).

21   Numic languages constitute the northern branch of the Uto-Aztecan language family. They are primarily associated with groups that traditionally occupied the Great Basin, although Hopi, a Puebloan language, is closely related. Miller (1986:98–99).

22   Schaafsma (1996:31–33).

23   Warner (1995:11).

24   Nelson (2001:117).

25   Callaway, Janetski, and Stewart (1986:339).

26   Williams (1990).

27   The legend of the seven golden cities of Cibola was based on a story that at the time of the Moorish invasion of Spain in 714 C.E., seven bishops fled and established themselves in a rich kingdom "somewhere to the west." An Aztec origin myth that spoke about seven caves somewhere far to the north of the Valley of Mexico also helped to sustain the legend of Cibola. Casteñada et al. (1990:xi–xii).

28   Flint (2005:203, 212–213).

29   Cabeza de Vaca (1990 [1542]).

30   Flint (2005:208–209).

31   Hordes (1992) and Vierra (1992) offer fascinating companion pieces to one another as they compare the ways in which an historian and an archaeologist examine Coronado's presumed campsite discovered in Bernalillo, New Mexico.

32   For a much more complete version of Coronado's expedition, readers should consult Hammond and Rey (1940).

33   See, for example, Thomas, ed. (1989, 1990, 1991).

34   Lycett (1989:115).

35   Ramenofsky (1987) citing Hackett (1923–1937:3, 107–108).

36   Some of the reasons for this cultural persistence are recounted in Suina (2002:212).

37   Readers who are interested in additional details about these expeditions should consult Hammond and Rey (1966). It is possible that members from the advance party of Castano de Sosa's 1590 expedition passed through or near Santa Fe, making them the first Europeans to do so. Hammond and Rey (1966:37, 280, note 40).

38   Ford (1987); Ellis (1989).

39   C. Snow (1999:18).

40   Ford (1987:73, 86–87).

41   D. Snow (1999:47).

42   Simmons (1991:177–178). This is admittedly an all too brief description of the founding of the New Mexico colony, and readers looking for more details should consult Hammond and Rey (1953) or, for a shorter version, Simmons (1991).

43   C. Snow (1999:18).

44   Chaves (1990 [1929]).

Epilogue

1   The building housing the Lab was designed by John Gaw Meem, built in 1930, and is on the National Register of Historic Places.

2   Post (1993); Procter (2006).

3   A zoetrope is a device that produces an illusion of movement from a rapid succession of static pictures. It consists of a cylinder with slits cut vertically in the sides. Beneath the slits, on the inner surface of the cylinder, is a band with individual frames from a sequence of drawings or photographs. As the cylinder spins and the user looks through the slits at the pictures on the opposite side

of the cylinder's interior, the viewer gets the impression of constant movement. Welling (1978:155).

4   For example: City of Alexandria, VA, Zoning Ordinance, Section 11-411, Archaeological Protection; City of Durango, CO, City Code 10-5-16, Archaeological Ordinance; County of Monterey, CA, Zoning Ordinance, Title 21, Section 21.66.050 Standards for Archaeological Resource Areas; City of Scottsdale, AZ, Ch. 46, City Code, Protection of Archaeological Resources.

5   Cushman (1999).

6   Ibid., 27.

❧

Glossary

ABSOLUTE DATING: A variety of techniques used for the dating of cultural remains that provide a specific age of the materials and not just a determination that something is "older" or "younger" than something else. Radiocarbon dating and tree-ring dating are among the best-known absolute dating techniques.

ADOBE: Earth, mixed with water and sometimes straw or other binding material, and used for the construction of structures or other features (i.e., hearths). ,

ALLUVIUM: Natural sedimentary deposits created by the effects of water or wind.

ANCESTRAL PUEBLOAN/ANASAZI: The cultural group defined by archaeologists based on particular forms of pottery, architecture, and lifestyle, who occupied the northern Southwest, including the Colorado Plateau and Rio Grande Valley.

ARCHAEOLOGY: the discipline that systematically studies ancient human behavior and past cultures based on their material remains.

ARCHAEOLOGICAL CULTURE: The sum total of the material assemblages produced by related cultures in a region. The material "lifestyle" referred to as archaeological culture may be different from an ethnographic definition of culture. For example, if two ethnic groups share the same material culture there may be one archaeological culture and two ethnographic cultures.

ARCHAEOLOGICAL RECORD: The collective material remains and modified landscapes of past cultures.

ARCHAEOLOGICAL RESOURCE: Any place or object that provides evidence of past human occupation or behavior.

ARCHAEOMAGNETISM: A dating technique based upon two discoveries: that the direction and intensity of the Earth's magnetic field is constantly changing, and that clay contains magnetized minerals. The orientation of magnetized minerals fixed into position in baked objects such as ovens, kilns, and hearths can be "read" by a magnetometer and correlated with known locations of the magnetic north pole at particular points in time.

ARCHAIC PERIOD: The cultural period that lasted from approximately 6000 B.C.E. until approximately 400/600 C.E. Lifeways during this period were characterized by small band mobility and hunting, gathering, and foraging.

ARMS: Archaeological Records Management Section of the New Mexico Historic Preservation Division. This section is located in the Laboratory of Anthropology, Santa Fe, New Mexico.

ARTIFACT: Any object either altered, modified, or used in any way by humans for some purpose. The archaeological context may be sufficient to prove cultural use of an otherwise equivocal object.

ARTIFACT TYPES: A collection or grouping of artifacts classified according to function based upon a range of relevant attributes.

ASSEMBLAGE. The sum total of the range of objects identified with a particular society. This term is synonymous with material culture.

ATHAPASKAN: Language group that includes languages spoken by Navajos and Apaches.

ATLATL: An Aztec word for a spear thrower; a type of hand-held device used to propel a spear with greater force and accuracy.

ATTRIBUTES: The characteristics or components of artifacts. Attributes may relate to an object's function or its appearance and style.

BAJADA: A foothill slope.

BIFACE: A flaked stone artifact with evidence of having been modified on two faces that intersect along a common edge such as an arrowhead.

CERAMICS: Containers and other artifacts made of clay and temper, and then fired. Synonymous with pottery.

CHERT: A fine-grained type of rock containing high amounts of silica used in the production of flaked-stone tools.

CHRONOLOGY: The process of arranging events in a temporal sequence from earliest to latest or youngest to oldest along some kind of scale.

CLAN: A social group claiming descent from a common ancestor, who may have been a real or fictional person or may not have even been human.

CLASSIC PERIOD: A cultural period in the northern Rio Grande that archaeologists have defined between 1325–1600 C.E. that was characterized by very large adobe and masonry pueblos (500–2500 rooms) and the production of glaze-painted pottery.

CLOVIS: A cultural manifestation in North America that existed approximately 12,000–13,000 years ago and characterized by exquisitely made fluted projectile points and other stone tools.

COALITION PERIOD: A cultural period in the northern Rio Grande that archaeologists have defined as occurring between 1175/1200–1300/1325 C.E. that was characterized by medium-sized pueblos (50–200 rooms) and the production of carbon-painted pottery.

COMPONENT: An occupation sequence by a particular group of people at a particular point in time. Each occupation episode constitutes a separate component. A site may include a single component, or if there were several occupation episodes, may have multiple components.

CONTEXT: The spatial distribution of artifacts (in three-dimensional space) on a site. The context may be the result of human arrangements and patterns, natural stratification processes, or a combination of cultural and natural processes.

CULTURE: The collective knowledge and behavior of a group of people, including their internal rules defining relationships, forms of social organization, and beliefs.

DENDROCHRONOLOGY: See tree-ring dating.

DEVELOPMENTAL PERIOD: A cultural period in the northern Rio Grande that extended between approximately 400/600–1175/1225 C.E. and was characterized by the initial appearance in this region of agriculture, pottery, and pit house villages.

DIAGNOSTIC: Any distinctive attribute or other characteristic of an artifact that allows for the dating or assignment of cultural affiliation.

DIFFUSION: The process by which material objects, technical innovations, or ideas are spread from one group of people to another.

DOMESTICATION: The growth and breeding of human-selected plant or animal species.

FAUNA: Animals.

FLORA: Plants.

FEATURES: Small, localized human use areas characterized by non-portable elements that are too large, bulky, or otherwise impossible to remove from archaeological sites, such as hearths, pits, walls, rock carvings, or structures.

FIRE-CRACKED ROCK: An indicator of places where people made fires for cooking or simply to keep warm. Hearths were often lined with rocks whose internal structure and mineral composition caused them to change colors and break into fragments because of the stresses of repeated heating and cooling.

FLAKE: A small piece of rock removed from a larger core by either the process of percussion or pressure.

GROUND STONE: Tools made of stone that are formed by grinding and polishing, as opposed to chipping and flaking.

HAFTING: The procedure for securing stone or bone projectile points onto a shaft.

HEARTH: A thermal feature made of rocks or adobe.

ICONOGRAPHY: A set of symbols and images associated with a particular activity, often with ceremonial or religious connotations.

IDEOLOGY: A belief system that encompasses ideas about the structure and origin of the universe or cosmos together with the place of people within that structure.

INDUSTRY: All of the tools of a particular material found within the context of a particular site, for example, the stone tool industry or the bone tool industry.

ISOLATED OCCURRENCE: A single artifact, not directly associated with other artifacts, features, or sites.

JACAL: A method of construction in which upright poles are placed close together and interlaced with smaller branches, then plastered with adobe or mud.

KATSINA: In Pueblo religion, a supernatural being personified by masked dancers. In addition, these katsinas are often depicted as carved wooden figures.

KERESAN: A linguistic and cultural group of Puebloans who entered the Rio Grande Valley by the 13th century. Contemporary Keresan-speaking Pueblos include: Cochiti, Santo Domingo, San Felipe, Santa Ana, and Zia. Although not within the Rio Grande Valley, Acoma and Laguna Pueblos are also Keresan speaking.

KINSHIP: The persons to whom you are related. Kinship systems are universally recognized among all societies and are bilateral (because everyone has a father and mother).

KIVA: A ceremonial chamber used by Ancestral Puebloans. Kivas may have different shapes (round, square, rectangular) and be constructed either below ground or as an integrated element in an aboveground roomblock.

LA NUMBER: A numerical identification assigned to all registered archaeological sites in New Mexico. "LA" stands for the Laboratory of Anthropology of the Museum of New Mexico.

LINEAGE: A social group claiming descent from a common, identifiable ancestor.

LITHICS: Tools, partial tools, and the remnant debris associated with the manufacture of tools made out of stone.

MANO: A grinding stone. Manos may be one-handed or two-handed.

MATERIAL CULTURE: The full range of tools, clothing, and other physical objects associated with a particular cultural group.

METATE: A grinding platform used in conjunction with manos.

MIDDEN: A trash pit, dump, or refuse pile.

MOIETY: A social organizational system consisting of two groups of clans (kinship groups sharing a common ancestor) into which a tribe is separated. Rio Grande pueblos are organized around moiety systems.

MORPHOLOGY: The physical structure or form of something.

PALEOINDIAN PERIOD: A cultural period that began with the initial peopling of the Americas (probably somewhere between 15,000 and 20,000 years ago) and lasted until approximately 7,500 and 8,000 years ago, characterized by small, mobile bands of people whose remnant material culture consisted of a variety of types of stone tools.

PLAINWARE: Undecorated pottery.

PUEBLO: A village consisting of a series of attached or detached buildings made out of adobe or masonry.

RADIOCARBON DATING: A type of absolute dating based on the principle that living things continuously incorporate an unstable form of carbon ($C14$) into their tissues until they die. At that point the proportions of the stable and unstable forms of carbon change at a specific, measurable rate that allows organic materials to be dated.

RELATIVE DATING: The chronological ordering of a series of objects or events earlier to later without a precise idea as to the actual amount of time that has passed.

RIO GRANDE GLAZE PAINT WARE: A sequence of pottery types decorated with a lead glaze-based paint. There were six different glaze paint types produced between approximately 1325–1700 C.E.

ROCK ART: Carved, pecked, or painted symbols, designs, or pictures on rock panels.

ROOMBLOCK: A distinct set of rooms within a structure or pueblo in which each room shares at least one common wall with one other room.

SHERD: Literally a piece of broken pottery; sometimes referred to as potsherd.

SITE: A geographical location with tangible, physical evidence of human activity that has survived to the present and is recognizable with current technology. Sites generally contain two basic classes of things of interest to archaeologists: 1) artifacts and 2) features.

SODALITY: A social group constructed around a set of common interests or goals such as medicine and curing, or warfare. The memberships of these groups are usually not based upon kinship.

STRATIGRAPHY: The process of analyzing sedimentary deposits that includes cultural materials in order to determine an orderly sequence of occupation or land use. Under normal circumstances the shallowest deposits are the youngest; the deepest deposits are the oldest.

SURVEY: A method of archaeological data collection in which archaeologists crisscross a geographic area on foot, in order to identify artifacts, features, and structures that are described and recorded on maps.

TEMPER: Material added to a mix of clay and water in order to improve the firing qualities of ceramics and prevent cracking.

TEWA: One of three extant Tano language groups in the Rio Grande Valley. Current Tewa speakers include members of the Pueblos of Tesuque. Pojoaque, Nambe, Santa Clara, San Ildefonso, and San Juan.

TIWA: One of three extant Tano language groups in the Rio Grande Valley. Current Tiwa speakers include members of the Pueblos of Taos, Picuris, Sandia, and Isleta.

TOWA: One of three extant Tano language groups in the Rio Grande Valley. Current Towa speakers include members of the Pueblo of Jemez.

TRANSHUMANCE: Seasonal migrations between lowland and upland areas.

TREE-RING DATING: A dating technique officially referred to as "dendrochronology" in which the tree-ring pattern of a particular specimen is matched against a master tree-ring sequence in order to determine the age (in calendar years) of the specimen.

References

Abbink, Emily
2007 *New Mexico's Palace of the Governors: History of an American Treasure.* Santa Fe: Museum of New Mexico Press

Abbott, Alysia, David Eck, and Cordelia T. Snow
2007 *Report of 2% Archaeological Testing and Archival Research: The First National Bank of Santa Fe Parking Lot 114 West Palace Avenue and 115 West San Francisco, in the National Register of Historic Places Santa Fe Historic District, the State of New Mexico Register of Cultural Properties and the Downtown Historic Archaeological Review District, Santa Fe, New Mexico.* Abboteck, Inc. PAS Report 0611/NMCRIS 102829, ARC Case AR-06-07, report on file, City of Santa Fe, Division of Planning.

Abbott, David R.
2000 *Ceramics and Community Organization Among the Hohokam.* University of Arizona Press, Tucson.

Abbott, David R., ed.
2003 *Centuries of Decline During the Hohokam Classic Period at Pueblo Grande.* University of Arizona Press, Tucson.

Acklen, John C.
1997 *OLE,* vol. 1, *Context,* TRC Mariah Associates, Albuquerque, New Mexico. Published by Public Service Company of New Mexico.

Acklen, John C., John A. Evaskovich, and Christopher A. Turnbow
1994 *Results of Archaeological Investigations of Old Fort Marcy, Santa Fe County,*

New Mexico. Prepared for the City of Santa Fe Planning and Land Use Department, Mariah Associates, Inc., Albuquerque.

Adams, E. Charles
1991 *The Origins and Development of the Pueblo Katsina Cult.* University of Arizona Press. Tucson.

Adams, E. Charles, and Andrew I. Duff, eds.
2004 *The Protohistoric Pueblo World A.D. 1275–1600.* University of Arizona Press, Tucson.

Adler, Michael, ed.
1996 *The Prehistoric Pueblo World, A.D. 1150–1350.* University of Arizona Press, Tucson.

Adler, Michael, Todd Van Pool, and Robert D. Leonard
1996 "Ancestral Pueblo Population Aggregation and Abandonment in the North American Southwest." *Journal of World Prehistory* 10 (3): 375–438.

Akins, Nancy J., Stephen C. Post, and C. Dean Wilson,
2003 "Life at the Edge: Early Developmental Period Mobility and Seasonality in the Northern Middle Rio Grande." In *Anasazi Archaeology at the Millennium: Proceedings of the Sixth Occasional Anasazi Symposium,* pp. 145–154. Center for Desert Archaeology, Tucson.

Ambler, Bridget M. and Lonyta Viklund
2005 "Chert Procurement and Processing at Los Cerros Colorados, Santa Fe County, New Mexico." Southwest Archaeological Consultants Research Series 356B, Santa Fe, NM.

Amick, Daniel
1996 "Regional Patterns of Folsom Mobility and Land Use in the American Southwest." *World Archaeology* 27:411–426.

Anderson, Elaine
1989 "Who's Who in the Pleistocene: A Mammalian Bestiary." In *Quaternary Extinctions: A Prehistoric Revolution,* edited by Paul S. Martin and Richard G. Klein, University of Arizona Press, Tucson.

Andrews, John P. and Todd W. Bostwick
2000 *Desert Farmers at the River's Edge: The Hohokam and Pueblo Grande.* City of Phoenix Parks, Recreation, and Library Department, Phoenix.

Bandelier, Adolph F.
1882 *Final Report of Investigation of Among the Indians of Southwestern United States, Carried Out Mainly Between 1880–1885,* 2 vols. Papers of the Archaeological Institute of America, American Series IV, University Press, Cambridge, England.

1890 *The Delight Makers.* Reprint, Harcourt Brace and Company, San Diego, 1971.

Bandelier, Adolph F. and Edgar L. Hewett
1937 *Indians of the Rio Grande Valley.* University of New Mexico Press, Albuquerque.

Basso, Keith H.
1996 *Wisdom Sits in Places: Landscape and Language Among the Western Apache.* University of New Mexico Press, Albuquerque.

Baugh, Timothy G., and Fred W. Nelson, Jr.
1987 "New Mexico Obsidian Sources and Exchange on the Southern Plains." *Journal of Field Archaeology* 14:313–329.

Berger, Thomas, and Eric Trinkaus
1995 "Patterns of Trauma Among Neanderthals." *Journal of Archaeological Science* 22:841–852.

Biolsi, Thomas, and Larry J. Zimmerman, eds.
1997 *Indians and Anthropologists: Vine Deloria Jr. and the Critique of Anthropology.* University of Arizona Press, Tucson.

Boggess, Douglas H. M.
2006 Cultural Resource Survey Of 19.74 Acres for the Proposed Vista Grande Subdivision, Santa Fe County, New Mexico. Reported submitted by Lone Mountain Archaeological Services to the City of Santa Fe Archaeological Review Committee, Manuscript on file, City of Santa Fe Planning Division, NMCRIS No. 98843.

Bohrer, Vorsila L.
1995 "The Where, When, and Why of Corn Guardians." In *Soil, Water, Biology, and Belief in Prehistoric and Traditional Southwestern Agriculture,* edited by H. Wolcott Toll, pp. 77–84, New Mexico Archaeological Council, Special Publication 2, Albuquerque.

Boldurian, Anthony T. O., and John L. Cotter
1999 *Clovis Revisited: A New Perspective on Paleoindian Adaptations from Blackwater Draw, New Mexico.* University Museum, University of Pennsylvania, Philadelphia.

Bousman, C. Britt, Michael B. Collins, Paul Goldberg, Thomas Stafford, Jan Guy, Barry W. Baker, D. Gentry Steele, Marvin Kay, Anne Kerr, Glen Freudlund, Phil Dering, Vance Holliday, Diane Wilson, Wolf Gose, Susan Dial, Paul Takac, Robin Balinsky, Marilyn Masson, and Joseph F. Powell
2002 "The Paleoindian-Archaic Transition in North America: New Evidence from Texas." *Antiquity* 76:980–990.

Bowman, Sheridan
1990 *Radiocarbon Dating.* University of California Press, Berkeley.

Bradley, Bruce A.
1991 "Flaked Stone Technology in the Northern High Plains." In *Prehistoric Hunters of the High Plains*, edited by George C. Frison, pp. 369–395, Academic Press, San Diego.

Brooks, James F.
2002 *Captives and Cousins: Slavery, Kinship, and Community in the Southwest Borderlands.* University of North Carolina Press, Chapel Hill.

Brown, Gary M.
1996 "The Protohistoric Transition in the San Juan Region." In *The Archaeology of Navajo Origins,* edited by Ronald H. Towner, pp. 47–71, University of Utah Press, Salt Lake City.

Brugge, David M.
1992 "Discussion of Athapaskan Research." In *Current Research on the Late Prehistory and Early History of New Mexico*, edited by Bradley J. Vierra, pp. 337–352, New Mexico Archaeological Council Special Publication No. 1, Albuquerque.

1969 "Pueblo Factionalism and External Relations." *Ethnohistory* 16(2):191–200.

Brunning, Susan
2006 "Complex Legal Legacies: The Native American Graves Protection and Repatriation Act, Scientific Study, and Kennewick Man." *American Antiquity* 71(3):501–521.

Burch, Ernest Jr.
1991 "Herd Following Reconsidered." *Current Anthropology* 12 (2):439–445.

1972 "The Caribou/Wild Reindeer as a Human Resource. *American Antiquity* 37(3):339–368.

Cabeza de Vaca, Alvar Nunez de
1542 *Cabeza de Vaca's Adventures in the Unknown Interior of America.* Reprint: Cyclone Covey trans. and ed. University of New Mexico Press, Albuquerque, 1990.

Callaway, Donald D., Joel Janetski, and Omer C. Stewart
1986 "Ute." In *Handbook of North American Indians, Volume 11, Great Basin*, edited by Warren L. D'azevedo, pp. 336–367, Smithsonian Institution, Washington, D.C.

Cameron, Catherine M.
1995 "Migration and the Movement of Southwestern Peoples." *Journal of Anthropological Archaeology* 14(2):104–124.

Cannon, M. D., and D. J. Meltzer
2004 "Early Paleoindian Foraging: Examining the Faunal Evidence for Large Mammal Specialization and Regional Variability in Prey Choice." *Quaternary Science Reviews,* 23:1955–1987.

Carlin, George
1981 *A Place for My Stuff.* Reissue, Atlantic Recording Corporation, A Division of Time Warner, Inc., New York. 2001.

Carillo, Charles M.
1992 "Where Were the Sheep: The Piedra Lumbre Phase Revisited." In *Current Research on the Late Prehistory and Early History of New Mexico*, edited by Bradley J. Vierra, pp. 323–326, New Mexico Archaeological Council Special Publication No. 1, Albuquerque.

Carpenter, John P., Guadalupe Sanchez, and Maria Elisa Villalpando C.
2005 "The Late Archaic/Early Agricultural Period in Sonora, Mexico." In *The Late Archaic: Across the Borderlands*, edited by Bradley Vierra, pp. 13–40, University of Texas Press, Austin.

Castañeda, Pedro de, et al.
1596 *The Journey of Coronado.* Reprint, Dover Publications, Inc., New York, 1990.

Chapin, Nicholas, M.
2005 "Archaic Period in Northern New Mexico." Ph.D. diss., University of New Mexico, Albuquerque.

Chatters, James
2001 *Ancient Encounters: Kennewick Man and the First Americans.* Simon and Schuster, New York.

Chaves, Irene L.
1929 "Instructions to Peralta By Vice Roy (translation)." *New Mexico Historical Review* 4(2):179–180. Reprinted in *Santa Fe Historic Plaza Study I*, edited by Linda Tigges, City Planning Department, Santa Fe, NM, 1990.

Cordell, Linda S.
1997 *Archaeology of the Southwest.* 2nd ed. Academic Press, Inc., New York.

1995 "Tracing Migration Pathways from the Receiving End." *Journal of Anthropological Archaeology* 14(2):203–211.

1989 "Durango to Durango: An Overview of the Southwest Heartland." In *Columbian Consequences, Vol. 1*, edited by David Hurst Thomas, pp. 17–40. Smithsonian Institution Press, Washington, D. C.

1984 *Prehistory of the Southwest.* Academic Press, Inc., San Diego.

1979 *A Cultural Resources Overview of the Middle Rio Grande Valley, New Mexico.* United States Department of Agriculture, Forest Service and Bureau of Land Management, Albuquerque and Santa Fe. U.S. Government Printing Office, Washington, D. C.

Cordell, Linda S. and George J. Gumerman, eds.
1989 *Dynamics of Southwest Prehistory.* Smithsonian Institution Press, Washington, D.C.

Cordell, Linda S., Carla R. Van West, Jeffrey S. Dean, and Deborah A. Muenchrath
2007 "Climate Change, Social Networks, and Ancestral Pueblo Migrations." *Kiva* 72(4): 391–417.

Creamer, Winifred

2000 "Regional Interactions and Regional Systems in the Protohistoric Rio Grande." In *The Archaeology of Regional Interaction: Religion, Warfare, and Exchange Across the American Southwest and Beyond*, edited by Michelle Hegmon, pp. 99–118, University Press of Colorado, Boulder.

1993 *The Architecture of Arroyo Hondo Pueblo, New Mexico*. School of American Research Press, Santa Fe, NM.

Crown, Patricia L., Janet D. Orcutt, and Timothy A. Kohler

1996 "Pueblo Cultures in Transition: The Northern Rio Grande." In *The Prehistoric Pueblo World A.D. 1150–1350*, edited by Michael A. Adler, pp. 188–204, The University of Arizona Press, Tucson.

Cummings, Linda Scott

1995 "Agriculture and the Mesa Verde Area Anasazi Diet: Description and Nutritional Analysis." In *Soil, Water, Biology and Belief in Prehistoric and Traditional Southwestern Agriculture*, edited by H. Wolcott Toll, pp.335–352, New Mexico Archaeological Council, Special Publication No. 2, Albuquerque.

Cushman, David W.

1999 "Preserving the Archaeological Record in Santa Fe, Why Bother?" In *Archaeology in Your Backyard: Proceedings of a City of Santa Fe Symposium*, edited by Charles Haecker, pp. 25–28, City of Santa Fe Planning Division, Santa Fe, NM.

D'Antonio, John

2004 "Managing New Mexico's Water in Times of Drought." Paper delivered at the 2004 New Mexico Drought Summit, September 27–28, 2004, UNM Continuing Education, Albuquerque.

Darwin, Charles

1859 *The Origin of Species by Means of Natural Selection*. Reprint: J. W. Burrow, ed. Penguin Classics, New York, 1985.

Davis, Emma Lou, and James H. Winkler

1959 "A Late Mesa Verde Site in the Rio Grande Valley." *El Palacio* 66 (3): 92–100.

Dean, Jeffrey S., and John C. Ravesloot
1993 "The Chronology of Cultural Interaction in the Gran Chichimeca." In *Culture and Contact: Charles C. DiPeso's Gran Chichimeca,* edited by Anne I. Woosley and John C. Ravesloot, pp. 83–104, Amerind Foundation, Dragoon, AZ and University of New Mexico Press, Albuquerque.

Derrick, Randall
2004 "The Antelope Creek Phase: Advanced Pre-Columbian Civilization of the Texas Panhandle." *Handbook of Texas Online,* http://www.tsha.utexas.edu/handbook/online/articles/AA/bba7.html .

Deyloff, Glenda
1997 *Preliminary Results of Archaeological Monitoring of a Backhoe Trench in the Santa Fe City Hall Parking Lot, LA 1051.* Southwest Archaeological Consultants Research Series 421, Santa Fe, NM.

1998 *Results of Archaeological Sewer Line Excavations Monitoring in the Santa Fe City Hall Parking Lot.* Southwest Archaeological Consultants Research Series 421b, Santa Fe, NM.

Diamond, Jared
2005 *Collapse: How Societies Choose to Fail or Succeed.* Viking Press, New York.

1997 *Guns, Germs, and Steel.* W.W. Norton & Company, Inc., New York.

Dickson, D. Bruce, Jr.
1979 *The Arroyo Hondo New Mexico Site Survey.* School of American Research Press, Santa Fe, NM.

1975 "Settlement Pattern Stability and Change in the Middle Northern Rio Grande Region, New Mexico: A Test of Some Hypotheses." *American Antiquity* 40(2):159–171.

Dillehay, Thomas
2000 *The Settlement of the Americas: A New Prehistory.* Basic Books, New York.

Doleman, William H.
1996 *Archaeological Survey of the Southern Caja del Rio: Class III Inventory of a Portion of the Camel Tracks Training Area, Santa Fe County, New Mexico.* University of New Mexico Office of Contract Archaeology, Report No. 185–548, University of New Mexico, Albuquerque.

Downey, Roger
2000 *Riddle of the Bones: Politics, Science, Race and the Story of Kennewick Man.* Copernicus, New York.

Downum, Christian E., ed.
1998 *Archaeology of the Pueblo Grande Platform Mound and Surrounding Features. Volume 4 The Pueblo Grande Platform Mound Compound.* City of Phoenix Parks, Recreation, and Library Department, Phoenix.

Dunmire, William W. and Gail D. Tierney
1995 *Wild Plants of the Pueblo Province: Exploring Ancient and Enduring Uses.* Museum of New Mexico Press, Santa Fe, N.M.

Eggan, Fred
1979 "Pueblos: Introduction." *Handbook of North American Indians, Volume 9, Southwest,* edited by Alfonso Ortiz, pp. 224–235. Smithsonian Institution, Washington, D.C.

Elliott, Michael
1988 *The Archaeology of Santa Fe: A Background Report.* Jemez Mountains Research Center Report No. 87–13, prepared for the City of Santa Fe Planning Department, Santa Fe, NM.

Ellis, Florence Hawley
1988 *From Drought to Drought: Gallina Culture Patterns. Volume 2, Canjilon Mountains, Hunting and Gathering Sites.* Sunstone Press, Santa Fe, NM.

1989 *San Gabriel Del Yungue As Seen By An Archaeologist.* Sunstone Press, Santa Fe, NM.

Ezzo, Joseph A., and Mary C. Steiner
2000 "A Late Archaic Period Dog Burial from the Tucson Basin, Arizona." *Kiva* 66(2): 291–305.

Fagan, Brian M.
2004 *The Long Summer.* Basic Books, New York.
2001 *The Little Ice Age.* Basic Books, New York.

1998 *Peopling of the Earth: An Introduction to World Prehistory,* 9th ed. Longman, New York.

Ferguson, William M. and Arthur H. Rohn
1991 *Anasazi Ruins of the Southwest in Color.* University of New Mexico Press, Albuquerque.

Fiedel, Stuart, and Gary Haynes
2004 "A Premature Burial: Comments on Grayson and Meltzer's 'Requiem for Overkill.'" *Journal of Anthropological Science,* 31:121–131.

Flannery, Tim
2005 *The Weather Makers.* Atlantic Monthly Press, New York.

Flint, Richard,
2005 "What They Never Told You about the Coronado Expedition." *Kiva,* 71(2):203–217.

Folks, James J.
1975 *Soil Survey of Santa Fe Area, New Mexico: Santa Fe County and Part of Rio Arriba County.* USDA Soil Conservation Service and New Mexico Experimental Station, Las Cruces.

Forbes, J. D.
1960 *Apache, Navajo, and Spaniard.* University of Oklahoma Press, Norman.

Ford, Richard I.
1968 "An Ecological Analysis Involving the Population of San Juan Pueblo, New Mexico." Ph. D. diss., University of Michigan, Ann Arbor.

1987 "The New Pueblo Economy." In *When Cultures Meet: Remembering San Gabriel Del Yunge Oweenge, Papers from the October 20, 1984 Conference held at San Juan Pueblo, New Mexico.* Sunstone Press, Santa Fe, NM.

Forenbaher, Staso, and Preston T. Miracle
2005 "The Spread of Farming in the Eastern Adriatic." *Antiquity* 79(305):214–228.

Fowler, Don D.
2000 *A Laboratory for Anthropology: Science and Romanticism in the American Southwest, 1846–1930.* University of New Mexico Press, Albuquerque.

2003 "E. L. Hewett, J. F. Zimmerman, and the Beginnings of Anthropology at the University of New Mexico, 1927–1946." *Journal of Anthropological Research* 59(3):305–327.

Fowles, Severin M.
2005 "Historical Contingency and the Prehistoric Foundations of Moiety Organization among the Eastern Pueblos." *Journal of Anthropological Research* 61(1):25–52.

Frison, George C.
1993 "North American High Plains Paleo-Indian Hunting Strategies and Weaponry Assemblages." In *Kostenki to Clovis: Upper Paleolithic Paleo-Indian Adaptations*, edited by Olga Soffer and N. D. Praslov, pp. 237–249, Plenum Press, New York.

Frison, George C., R. L. Andrews, James M. Adovasio, R. C. Carlisle, and R. Edgar
1986. "A Late Paleoindian Trapping Net from Northern Wyoming." *American Antiquity* 51:352–261.

Futch, T.G. and Thomas McIntosh
1999 "An Archaeological Assessment and Cultural Properties Inventory of El Guiche Gravel Mine for Espanola Transit Mix. El Guiche, Rio Arriba County, New Mexico." Manuscript on file at ARMS, Laboratory of Anthropology, Santa Fe, NM.

Grayson, Donald K., and David J. Meltzer
2002 "Clovis Hunting and Large Mammal Extinction: A Critical Review of the Evidence. "*Journal of World Prehistory* 16(4):313–360.

Green, E. F.
1986 *Report on Archaeological Salvage in the Sanford Reservoir Area*. Panhandle Archaeological Society Publication No. 4.

Gumerman, George J.
1984 *The View from Black Mesa: The Changing Face of Archaeology*. University of Arizona Press, Tucson.

Gunnerson, James H.
1969 "Apache Archaeology in Northeastern New Mexico." *American Antiquity* 34(1):23–39.

Gunnerson, James H., and Dolores A. Gunnerson
1970 "Evidence of Apaches at Pecos." *El Palacio* 76(3):1–6.

Habicht-Mauche, Judith A.

1995 "Changing Patterns of Pottery Manufacture and Trade in the Northern Rio Grande Region." In *Ceramic Production in the American Southwest*, edited by B. J. Mills and P. L. Crown, pp. 167–199, University of Arizona Press, Tucson.

1993 *The Pottery from Arroyo Hondo Pueblo, New Mexico: Tribalization and Trade in the Northern Rio Grande.* School of American Research Press, Santa Fe.

Hackett, C.W., ed.

1923–1937 "Historical Documents Relating to New Mexico, Nuevo Vizcaya, and Approaches Thereto, to 1773." In *Adolph A. Bandelier and Fanny R. Bandelier Collections,* vols. 1 and 2, Carnegie Institution of Washington 330. Washington, D.C.

Hammond, George P., and Agapito Rey

1940 *Narratives of the Coronado Expedition.* University of New Mexico Press, Albuquerque.

1953 *Don Juan de Oñate, Colonizer of New Mexico* (2 vols). University of New Mexico Press, Albuquerque.

1966 *The Rediscovery of New Mexico 1580–1594.* University of New Mexico Press, Albuquerque.

Hannaford, Charles A.

1986 *Tierra Contenta Subdivision for Bellamah Community Development and the Historic Preservation Division.* Laboratory of Anthropology, note 356, Santa Fe, NM.

Harrington, John P.

1916 "The Ethnogeography of the Tewa Indians." In *Twenty -ninth Annual Report of the Bureau of American Ethnology for the Years 1907–1908.* Government Printing Office, Washington, D.C.

Hegmon, Michelle

1996 "Variability in Food Production, Strategies of Storage and Sharing and the Pit house-to-Pueblo Transition in the Northern Southwest." In *Evolving Complexity and Environmental Risk in the Prehistoric Southwest*, edited by J. A. Tainter and B. B. Tainter, pp. 223 – 250. Santa Fe Institute Studies in the Science of Complexity, Addison-Wesley, Reading, Pennsylvania.

Herhahn, Cynthia L.

1995 "14th Century Dry Farming Features in the Northern Rio Grande Valley, New Mexico." In *Soil, Water, Biology, and Belief in Prehistoric and Traditional Southwestern Agriculture*, edited by H. Wolcott Toll, pp. 77 – 84. New Mexico Archaeological Council, Special Publication 2, Albuquerque.

Hester, James J.

1962 "Early Navajo Migrations and Acculturations in the Southwest." Museum of New Mexico Papers in Anthropology No. 9, Santa Fe.

Hewett, Edgar Lee, Junius Henderson, and Wilfred William Robbins

1913 *The Physiography of the Rio Grande Valley, New Mexico, In Relation to Pueblo Culture*. Bureau of American Ethnology Bulletin 54, Smithsonian Institution, Government Printing Office, Washington, D.C.

Hibben, Frank

1941 "Evidences of Early Occupation in Sandia Cave, New Mexico, and Other Sites in the Sandia-Manzano Region." Smithsonian Miscellaneous Collections Vol. 99(23). Publication 3636, Washington, D.C.

1937 *Excavation of the Riana Ruin and Chama Valley Survey*. University of New Mexico Bulletin, Anthropological Series 2(1). University of New Mexico, Albuquerque.

Hill, Jane H.

2002 "Toward a Linguistic Prehistory of the Southwest: 'Azteco-Tanoan' and the Arrival of Maize Cultivation: *Journal of Anthropological Research* 58:457 – 475.

Honea, Kurt

1970 *La Balsa, A Quemado Phase Component Site of the Early Rio Grande Complex in the Galisteo Basin, New Mexico*. Manuscript on file in ARMS, Laboratory of Anthropology, Museum of New Mexico, Santa Fe.

Hoover, Joanne Sheehy

2005 "Making Prehistoric Music." *American Archaeology* (Winter 2004/2005): 12 – 19.

Hordes, Stanley M.

1992 "A Sixteenth-century Spanish Campsite in the Tiguex Province: A Historian's Perspective." In *Current Research on the Late Prehistory and Early His-*

tory of New Mexico, edited by Bradley J. Vierra, pp. 155–164. New Mexico Archaeological Council Special Publication No. 1, Albuquerque.

Huckell, Bruce B. and W. James Judge
2006 "Paleo-Indian: Plains and Southwest." In *Handbook of North American Indians, Southwest, Vol. 3*, edited by Douglas H. Ubelaker, pp. 148–170. Smithsonian Institution, Washington, D.C.

Huckell, Bruce B., and J. David Kilby
2002 "Folsom Point Production at the Rio Rancho Site, New Mexico." In *Folsom Technology and Lifeways*, edited by John E. Clark and Michael B. Collins, University of Tulsa, Department of Anthropology, Lithic Technology Special Publication 4, Tulsa.

Hutt, Sherry, Ellwood W. Jones, and Martin J. McAllister
1992 *Archaeological Resource Protection*. The Preservation Press, National Trust for Historic Preservation, Washington, D.C.

Irwin-Williams, Cynthia
1967 "Picosa: The Elementary Southwestern Culture." *American Antiquity* 32(4):441–457.

1973 "The Oshara Tradition: Origins of Anasazi Culture." *Contributions in Anthropology* 5(1), Eastern New Mexico University, Portales.

1979 "Post-Pleistocene Archaeology. 7000–2000 B.C." In *Handbook of North American Indians, Southwest, Vol. 9*, edited by Alfonso Ortiz, pp. 31–42, Smithsonian Institution, Washington, D.C.

Ivey, James
2003 "An Uncertain Founding: Santa Fe." *Common Place: An Interactive Journal of Early American Life* 3(4), <www.common-place.org>.

Jeançon, J. A.
1923 *Excavations in the Chama Valley, New Mexico*. Bureau of American Ethnography Bulletin 81, Government Printing Office, Washington, D.C.

Johnson, J. R., T. W. Stafford, Jr., H. O. Ajie, and D. P. Morris
2002 "Arlington Springs Revisited." In *Proceedings of the Fifth California Islands Symposium*, edited by D. R. Brown, K. C. Mitchell, and H. W. Chaney, pp. 541–545, Santa Barbara Museum of Natural History, California.

Jones, David E.
2007 *Poison Arrows: North American Indian Hunting and Warfare.* University of Texas Press, Austin.

Jones, Terry L., Gary M. Brown, L. Mark Rabb, Janet L. McVickar, W. Geoffrey Spaulding, Douglas J. Kennett, Andrew York, and Phillip L. Walker
1999 "Environmental Imperatives Reconsidered: Demographic Crises in Western North America during the Medieval Climatic Anomaly." *Current Anthropology* 40(2):137–169.

Judge, W. James
1973 *Paleoindian Occupation of the Central Rio Grande Valley in New Mexico.* University of New Mexico Press, Albuquerque.

Kantner, John
2004 *Ancient Puebloan Southwest.* Cambridge University Press, Cambridge, England.

Kelley, N. Edmund
1980 *The Contemporary Ecology of Arroyo Hondo, New Mexico.* School of American Research Press, Santa Fe, NM.

Kelly, Robert L., and Lawrence C. Todd
1988 "Coming into the Country: Early Paleoindian Hunting and Mobility." *American Antiquity* 53(2):231–244.

Kidder, Alfred V.
1924 *An Introduction to the Study of Southwest Archaeology with a Preliminary Account of the Excavations at Pecos.* Phillips Academy of Archaeology, Andover, Massachusetts, and Yale University Press.

1927 "Southwestern Archaeology Conference." *El Palacio,* 23:554–561.

Kooyman, Brian P.
2000 *Understanding Stone Tools and Archaeological Sites.* University of Calgary Press, Alberta, and University of New Mexico Press, Albuquerque.

Krech, Shepard III
1999 *The Ecological Indian.* W.W. Norton and Co., New York.

Lakatos, Steven A., Stephen S. Post, and Jesse B. Murrell
2001 *Data Recovery Results from Two Archaeological Sites Along North Ridgetop*

Road, Santa Fe County, New Mexico. Archaeology Notes 290, Office of Archaeological Studies, Museum of New Mexico, Santa Fe.

Lang, Richard W.

1977 *Archaeological Survey of the Upper San Cristobal Arroyo Drainage, Galisteo Basin, Santa Fe County, New Mexico.* Contract Archaeology Program Report 37, School of American Research, Santa Fe, NM.

1986 *Pinkauwa: A Specialized Basketmaker II Hunting Site on Galisteo Creek, Santa Fe County, New Mexico.* Manuscript, Wheelwright Museum of the American Indian, Santa Fe, NM.

1988 "The First Six Millennia: Early Foragers of the Upper Pecos." In *Pecos, Gateway to Pueblos and Plains: The Anthology,* edited by John V. Bezy and Joseph P. Sanchez, pp. 20–25, Southwest Parks and Monuments Association, Tucson.

1989 *A Cultural Resources Sample Survey of Upper Tesuque Creek, Raven's Ridge, and the Lake Peal Divide of the Santa Fe Range, Sangre de Cristo Mountains, New Mexico.* Southwest Archaeological Consultants Research Series 229, Santa Fe, NM.

1992 *Archaeological Excavations at Dos Griegos, Upper Canada de Los Alamos, Santa Fe County, New Mexico: Archaic Through Pueblo V.* Southwest Archaeological Consultants Research Series 283, Santa Fe, NM.

1993 *The Sierra del Norte Sites: Processing and Use of Flint Quarries of the Lower Santa Fe Range, New Mexico.* Southwest Archaeological Consultants, Research Series 241b, Santa Fe, NM.

1995 *Flint Procurement and Other Limited Activity Sites of the Upper Tesuque Valley, New Mexico: A Sampling from the Bishop's Lodge Locality.* Southwest Archaeological Consultants Research Series 284b, Santa Fe, NM.

1997 *The Archaeological Landscape of Las Campanas: Archaic and Pueblo Use of the Piedmont Slopes Northwest of Santa Fe, Santa Fe County, New Mexico.* Parts I and II, Southwest Archaeological Consultants Research Series 317, Santa Fe, NM.

Lang, Richard W., and Arthur H. Harris
1984 *The Faunal Remains from Arroyo Hondo, New Mexico: A Study in Short-Term Subsistence Change.* School of American Research Press, Santa Fe, NM.

Lang, Richard W., and Cherie Scheick
1989 *Limited Excavations at LA 2, the Agua Fria Schoolhouse Site, Agua Fria Village, Santa Fe County, New Mexico.* Southwest Archaeological Consultants Research Series 216, Santa Fe, NM.

Lange, Charles H., and Carroll L. Riley
1996 *Bandelier: The Life and Adventures of Adolph Bandelier.* University of Utah Press, Salt Lake City.

Lange, Charles H., and Carroll L. Riley, eds.
1966 *The Southwestern Journals of Adolph Bandelier, 1880–1882.* University of New Mexico Press, Albuquerque.

1970 *The Southwestern Journals of Adolph Bandelier, 1883–1884.* University of New Mexico Press, Albuquerque.

Lange, Charles H., Carroll L. Riley, and Elizabeth M. Lange, eds.
1975 *The Southwestern Journals of Adolph Bandelier, 1885–1888.* University of New Mexico Press, Albuquerque.

1984 *The Southwestern Journals of Adolph Bandelier, 1888–1890.* University of New Mexico Press, Albuquerque.

LeBlanc, Stephen
1999 *Prehistoric Warfare in the American Southwest.* The University of Utah Press, Salt Lake City.

Lekson, Stephen H.
2004 "Pinnacle Ruin." In *Archaeology Southwest* 18(2):6–7, Center for Desert Archaeology, Tucson.

Lekson, Stephen H., ed.
2005 *The Archaeology of Chaco Canyon.* School of American Research Press, Santa Fe.

Lekson, Steven H., and Catherine M. Cameron
1995 "The Abandonment of Chaco Canyon, the Mesa Verde Regions, and the Reorganization of the Pueblo World." *Journal of Anthropological Archaeology* 14 (2):184–202.

Lentz, Stephen C.
2005 *El Pueblo de Santa Fe (LA 1051): Archaeological Testing of the Proposed Santa Fe Civic Center.* Archaeology Notes 355. Office of Archaeological Studies, Museum of New Mexico, Santa Fe, NM.

Lentz, Stephen C., Matthew Barbour, Stephen S. Post
2006 *Second Interim Report on the Data Recovery Program at LA 1051, El Pueblo de Santa Fe.* NMCRIS Activity No. 90579, MNM # 41.776, Office of Archaeological Studies, Santa Fe, NM.

Levy, Jerrold
1992 *Orayvi Revisited: Social Stratification in an Egalitarian Society.* School of American Research Press, Santa Fe, N.M.

Lightfoot, Dale
1993 "The Cultural Ecology of Puebloan Pebble Mulch Gardens." *Human Ecology* 21(2):115–143.

Lycett, Mark T.
1989 "Spanish Contact and Pueblo Organization: Long-term Implications of European Colonial Expansion in the Rio Grande Valley, New Mexico." In *Columbian Consequences, Volume I Archaeological and Historical Perspectives on the Spanish Borderlands West,* edited by David Hurst Thomas, pp. 115–125. Smithsonian Institution Press, Washington, D.C.

Martin, Deborah L.
1995, "Patterns of Diet and Disease—Health Profiles for the Prehistoric Southwest." In *Themes in Southwest Prehistory,* edited by George J. Gumerman, pp. 87–108. School of American Research Press, Santa Fe, NM.

Martin, H. T.
1909 *Further Notes on the Pueblo Ruins of Scott County.* Kansas University Science Bulletin, Vol. V, No. 2, pp. 22.

Mathien, Frances Joan
2005 *Culture and Ecology of Chaco Canyon and the San Juan Basin.* National Park Service, U.S. Department of the Interior, Santa Fe, NM.

Matson, R. G.
2005 "Many Perspectives But A Consistent Pattern: Comments on Contributions." In *The Late Archaic: Across the Borderlands*, edited by Bradley Vierra, pp. 279–299. University of Texas Press, Austin.
Maxwell, Timothy D. and Kurt F. Anschuetz
1992 "The Southwestern Ethnographic Record and Prehistoric Agricultural Diversity." In *Gardens in Prehistory: The Archaeology of Settlement Agriculture in Greater Mesoamerica*, edited by T. W. Killion, pp. 35–68. University of Alabama Press, Tuscaloosa.

McBrinn, Maxine
2005 *Social Identity Among Mobile Hunters and Gatherers in the American Southwest*. Arizona State Museum Archaeology Series 197, Arizona State Museum, Tucson.

McNutt, Charles
1969 *Early Puebloan Occupation at Tesuque By-Pass Site and in the Upper Rio Grande Valley*. Anthropological Papers No. 40. Museum of Anthropology, University of Michigan, Ann Arbor.

Meltzer, David J.
2006 *Folsom: New Archaeological Investigations of a Classic Paleoindian Bison Kill*. University of California Press, Berkeley.

1999 "Human Responses to Middle Holocene (Altithermal) Climates on the North American Great Plains." *Quaternary Research* 52:404–416.

1993 *Search for the First Americans*. St. Remy Press and Smithsonian Institution, Washington, D.C.

Mera, H. P.
1934 "A Survey of the Biscuit Area in Northern New Mexico." *Laboratory of Anthropology Technical Series, Bulletin No. 6*, Santa Fe, NM.

1940 "Population Changes in the Rio Grande Glaze-Paint Area." *Laboratory of Anthropology Archaeological Survey, Technical Series, Bulletin No. 9*, Santa Fe, NM.

Merbs, C. F.
1989 "Patterns of Health and Sickness in the Pre-Contact Southwest." In *Columbian Consequences Volume 1, Archaeological and Historical Perspectives on the Spanish Borderlands West*, edited by David Hurst Thomas, pp.41–55, Smithso-

nian Institution Press, Washington, DC.

Miller, John P., and Fred Wendorf
1958 "Alluvial Chronology of the Tesuque Valley, New Mexico." *The Journal of Geology* 66(2):117–194.

Miller, Wick C.
1986 "Numic Languages." In *Handbook of North American Indians, Volume 11, Great Basin*, edited by Warren L. D'azevedo, pp. 98–106. Smithsonian Institution, Washington, D.C.

Milner, George R.
2004 *The Moundbuilders: Ancient Peoples of Eastern North America*. Thames and Hudson, London.

Morey Darcy F. and Michael D. Wiant
1992 "Early Holocene Dog Burials from the North American Midwest." *Current Anthropology* 33(2):224–229.

Morgan, Lewis Henry
1877 *Ancient Society*. Reprint, The Belknap Press of Harvard University Press, Cambridge, MA.

Morgan, William N.
1994 *Ancient Architecture of the Southwest*. University of Texas Press, Austin.

Motsinger, Thomas H.
1997 "Tracking Protohistoric Glazeware Specialization in the Upper Rio Grande Valley, New Mexico." *Kiva* 63(2):101–116.

Muenchrath, Deborah A., and Ricardo J. Salvador
1995 "Maize Productivity and Agroecology: Effects of Environment and Agricultural Practices on the Biology of Maize." In *Soil, Water, Biology, and Belief in Prehistoric and Traditional Southwestern Agriculture*, edited by H. Wolcott Toll, pp. 303–334. New Mexico Archaeological Council, Special Publication 2, Albuquerque.

Munro, Natalie D.
2006 "The Role of the Turkey in the Southwest." In *Handbook of North American Indians, Volume 3, Environment, Origin, and Population*, edited by Douglas H. Ubelaker, pp. 463–470. Smithsonian Institution, Washington, D.C.

Naranjo, Tessie
1995 "Thoughts on Migration from Santa Clara Pueblo." *Journal of Anthropological Archaeology* 14(2):247–250.

Neitzel, Jill E., ed.
1999 *Great Towns and Regional Polities in the Prehistoric American Southwest and Southeast.* Amerind Foundation and University of New Mexico Press, Dragoon and Albuquerque.

Nelson, Sarah M.
2001 *Denver: An Archaeological History.* University of Pennsylvania Press, Philadelphia.

Ogilvie, Marsha D.
2005 "A Biological Reconstruction of Mobility Patterns in Late Archaic Populations." In *The Late Archaic: Across the Borderlands*, edited by Bradley Vierra, pp. 84–112, University of Texas Press, Austin.

Opler, Morris E.
1982 "The Scott County Pueblo Site in Historical, Archaeological, and Ethnological Perspective." In *Pathways to Plains Prehistory: Anthropological Perspectives on Plains Natives and Their Pasts*, edited by Don C. Wycoff and Jack L. Hofman, Oklahoma Anthropological Society Memoir 3.

Ortiz, Alfonso
1969 *The Tewa World: Space, Time, Being and Becoming in a Pueblo Society.* University of Chicago Press, Chicago.

Ortiz, Alfonso, editor
1979 *Handbook of North American Indians, Volume 9, Southwest.* Smithsonian Institution, Washington, D.C.

Osborn, Alan J.
1993 "Snowblind in the Desert Southwest: Moisture Islands, Ungulate Ecology, and Alternative Prehistoric Overwintering Strategies." *Journal of Anthropological Research* 49(2):135–164.

Palkovich, Ann M.
2006 "Rickets, Community Dynamics and Gender Relations at Arroyo Hondo, a 14th Century Ancestral Pueblo: Reanalysis and New Insights." Unpublished manuscript in possession of the author.

1980 *The Arroyo Hondo Skeletal and Mortuary Remains.* School of American Research Press, Santa Fe, NM.

Pearsall, Deborah M.
1995 "Domestication and Agriculture in the New World Tropics." In *Last Hunters, First Farmers*, edited by T. Douglas Price and Anne Birgitte Gebauer, pp. 157–192, School of American Research Press, Santa Fe, NM.

Peckham, Stewart L.
1977 "Field Notes for the Fine Arts Museum Excavation." Materials on file at ARMS, Laboratory of Anthropology, Museum of New Mexico, Santa Fe, NM.

1981 "The Palisade Ruin." In *Collected Papers in Honor of Eric Kellerman Reed*, edited by A. H. Schroeder, pp. 113–147, Papers of the Archaeological Society of New Mexico, Vol. 6, Santa Fe, NM.

Peckham, Stewart L., and David H. Snow
1982 "Clues to Santa Fe's Past: Excavating the Fine Arts Site." *El Palacio* 88(2): 38–41.

Phillips, Arthur M. III
1989 "Shasta Ground Sloth Extinction." In *Quaternary Extinctions: A Prehistoric Revolution*, edited by Paul S. Martin and Richard G. Klein, University of Arizona Press, Tucson.

Plog, Stephen
1997 *Ancient Peoples of the American Southwest.* Thames and Hudson, London.

Polyak, Victor, J., and Yemane Asmerom
2001 "Late Holocene Climate and Cultural Changes in the Southwestern United States." *Science* 294:148–151.

Post, Stephen S.
1991 *An Archaeological Survey of 6 Acres for the Santa Maria de la Paz Catholic Community, along Richards Avenue, Santa Fe County, New Mexico.* Report 23, Stephen A. Post, consulting archaeologist, Santa Fe, NM.

1992 *Archaeological Survey and Testing at Las Campanas, Santa Fe County, New Mexico.* Archaeology Notes 108, Office of Archaeological Studies, Museum of New Mexico, Santa Fe.

1993 *An Archaeological Inventory of the Museum of New Mexico Hill Complex, along Camino Lejo in Santa Fe, New Mexico.* Archaeology Notes 134, Office of Archaeological Studies, Museum of New Mexico, Santa Fe, NM.

1994 *Archaeological Testing and Treatment Plan for a Late Archaic Period Site and Three Coalition-Early Classic Period Sites, Estates V and Other Areas, Las Campanas de Santa Fe, Santa Fe County, New Mexico.* Archaeology Notes 140, Office of Archaeological Studies, Museum of New Mexico, Santa Fe.

1996 *Las Campanas de Santa Fe Sunset Golf Course, and Estates IV, Estates V, and Estates VII Excavations: Small Sites in the Piñon-Juniper Piedmont North of the Santa Fe River, Santa Fe County, New Mexico.* Office of Archaeological Studies, Archaeology Notes 193, Museum of New Mexico, Santa Fe.

1998 *Excavations at Rancho Viejo de Santa Fe Ancient Patterns of Mobility and Land Use.* Archaeology Notes 252, Office of Archaeological Studies, Museum of New Mexico, Santa Fe.

1999 "Santa Fe Black-on-White: The People's Choice in Thirteenth Century Santa Fe." In *Archaeology in Your Backyard: Proceedings of a City of Santa Fe Symposium*, edited by Charles Haecker, pp. 35–40, City of Santa Fe Planning Division, Santa Fe, NM.

2000 *Archaic Seasonal Camps and Pueblo Foraging in the Piedmont: Excavation of Two Small Sites, LA 61315 and LA 61321 Along the Northwest Santa Fe Relief Route (State Road 599)*, Phase 3, Santa Fe, New Mexico. Office of Archaeological Studies, Museum of New Mexico, Santa Fe, NM.

2002 *The Rufina Meadows Project: Excavations in Lower Agua Fria, Santa Fe, New Mexico.* Report No. 103. On file at the Archeological Records Management Section, Santa Fe, NM.

2004 *Excavation of LA 61282, The Airport Road Site: Late Archaic and Classic Period Occupation Near the Santa Fe River, Santa Fe, New Mexico.* Archaeology Notes 274, Office of Archaeological Studies, Museum of New Mexico, Santa Fe.

Post, Stephen S., Stephen C. Lentz, Mathew Barbour, Susan Moga, Nancy J. Akins, and Eric Blinman, Ph.D.
2006 "Third Interim Report on the Data Recovery Program at LA 1051, El Pueblo De Santa Fe." Museum of New Mexico, Office of Archaeological Stud-

ies, submitted to the New Mexico Historic Preservation Division, NMCRIS Activity No. 90579, MNM # 41.776, Santa Fe, NM.

Post, Stephen S., and Stephen A. Lakatos
1995 "Santa Fe Black-on-White Pottery Firing Features of the Northern Rio Grande Valley, New Mexico." In *Of Pots and Rocks, Papers in Honor of A. Helen Warren,* Archaeological Society of New Mexico, Vol. 21, pp. 141–153, Rio Rancho.

Powell, Shirley and Francis E. Smiley, eds.
2002 *Prehistoric Culture Change on the Colorado Plateau: Ten Thousand Years on Black Mesa.* University of Arizona Press, Tucson.

Preston, Douglas
1995 "The Mystery of Sandia Cave." *New Yorker* 71(16):66–83.

Price, T. Douglas, and Anne Birgitte Gebauer, eds.
1995 *Last Hunters, First Farmers.* School of American Research Press, Santa Fe.

Procter, Rebecca
2006 *Proposed Recreational Trails for the Santa Fe Botanical Garden: Cultural Resources Survey and Evaluation in Santa Fe, New Mexico.* NMCRIS #99581. Report Prepared for the Santa Fe Botanical Garden and Submitted to the Archaeological Review Committee for the City of Santa Fe in Case No. AR-10-06.

Ramenofsky, Ann F.
1987 *Vectors of Death: The Archaeology of European Contact.* University of New Mexico Press, Albuquerque.

Reed, Erik K.
1956 "Types of Village Plan Layouts in the Southwest." In *Prehistoric Settlement Patterns in the New World,* edited by G. R. Willey, pp. 11–17, Johnson Reprint, New York.

Reed, Paul
2004 *The Puebloan Society of Chaco Canyon.* Greenwood Press, Westport, CT.

Reed, Paul F., ed.
2000 *Foundations of Anasazi Culture: The Basketmaker-Pueblo Transition.* University of Utah Press, Salt Lake City.

Renfrew, Colin, and Paul Bahn
2004 *Archaeology: Theory, Methods, Practice.* 4th ed. Thames and Hudson, New York.

Richerson P. J., R. Boyd, and R. L. Bettinger
2001 "Was Agriculture Impossible During the Pleistocene but Mandatory During the Holocene? A Climate Change Hypothesis." *American Antiquity* 66(3):387–411.

Riley, Carroll L.
1995 *Rio del Norte: People of the Upper Rio Grande from Earliest Times to the Pueblo Revolt.* University of Utah Press, Salt Lake City.

Roberts, Brian K.
1996 *Landscapes of Settlement: Prehistory to the Present.* Routledge, London.

Roney, John G.
1995 "Mesa Verde Manifestations South of the San Juan River." *Journal of Anthropological Archaeology* 14:170–183.

Roosa, William B.
1956a "A Preliminary Report on the Lucy Site." *El Palacio* 63(2):36–49.

1956b "The Lucy Site in Central New Mexico." *American Antiquity* 21(3):310.

Rose, Martin R., Jeffrey S. Dean, and William J. Robinson
1981 *The Past Climate of Arroyo Hondo, New Mexico Reconstructed from Tree-rings.* School of American Research Press, Santa Fe, NM.

Sando, Joe
1992 *Pueblo Nations Eight Centuries of Pueblo Indian History.* Clear Light Publishers, Santa Fe.

Scarre, Chris, editor
2005 *The Human Past: World Prehistory and the Development of Human Societies.* Thames and Hudson Ltd., New York.

Schaafsma, Curtis F.
1981 "Early Apacheans in the Southwest: A Review." In *The Protohistoric Period in the North American Southwest, A.D. 1450–1700,* edited by David R. Wilcox and W. Bruce Masse, pp. 291–320, Arizona State University Anthropological Research Papers 24, Tempe.

1992 "A Review of the Documentary Evidence for a Seventeenth Century Navaho Occupation in the Chama Valley." *Current Research on the Late Prehistory and Early History of New Mexico*, edited by B. J. Vierra, pp. 313–321, New Mexico Archaeological Council Special Archaeological Publication No. 1, Albuquerque.

1996 "Ethnic Identity and Protohistoric Sites in Northwest New Mexico." In *The Archaeology of Navajo Origins*, edited by Ron Towner, pp. 19–46, University of Utah Press, Salt Lake City.

2002a. *Apaches De Navajo: Seventeenth Century Navajos in the Chama Valley, New Mexico.* University of Utah Press, Salt Lake City.

2002b. "Pueblo and Apachean Alliance Formation in the Seventeenth Century." In *Archaeologies of the Pueblo Revolt: Identity, Meaning and Renewal in the Pueblo World*, edited by Robert Preucel, pp. 198–211, University of New Mexico Press, Albuquerque.

Schaafsma, Polly, and Curtis F. Schaafsma
1974 "Evidence for the Origin of the Pueblo Kachina Cult as Suggested by Southwestern Rock Art." *American Antiquity* 39(4):535–545.

Scheick, Cherie L.
2006 "The Late Developmental and Early Coalition of the Northern Middle Rio Grande–Time or Process?" *Kiva* 73(2):131–154

2005a *Coalition Period Remains Under the West Alcove, U.S. Federal Courthouse, Santa Fe, New Mexico.* Prepared for Steve Kline, AIA, New Mexico Service Center, U.S. General Service Administration, Fort Worth, Texas, NMCRIS No. 87632, Southwest Archaeological Consultants Research Series 477C, Santa Fe.

2005b "The Late Developmental and Early Coalition: Time or Process." Paper presented at the 2005 Pecos Conference, August 11–14, 2005, White Rock, New Mexico.

1999 "When Land and Water Were A Plenty: A View of Santa Fe's Early History as a Master Plan." In *Archaeology in Your Backyard: Proceedings of a City of Santa Fe Symposium*, edited by Charles Haecker, pp. 1–16, City of Santa Fe Planning Division, Santa Fe, NM.

Scheick, Cherie, ed.
2006 *A Study of Pre-Columbian and Historic Uses of the Santa Fe National Forest: Competition and Alliance in the Northern Middle Rio Grande.* The Archaeological and Historical Cultural Resources. U.S. Department of Agriculture, Forest Service, Southwestern Region, Report No. 18.

Scheick, Cherie, and Lonyta Viklund
1991a *A Cultural Resources Survey of Bishop's Lodge.* Southwest Archaeological Consultants Research Series 271, Santa Fe, NM.

1991b *Cultural Resources of Piedmont Slopes Northwest of Santa Fe: Estates III, the West Golf Courses and Adjacent Properties.* Southwest Archaeological Consultants Research Series 278, Santa Fe, NM.

Schmader, Matthew F., C. Wayne Oakes, and Timothy Binzen
1994 *Archaic Occupation of the Santa Fe Area: Results of the Tierra Contenta Archaeology Project.* Rio Grande Consultants, Albuquerque.

Schwartz, Douglas
1997 *A Model of Internet Access to Humanities Collections and Data from the Fourteenth-Century Pueblo at Arroyo Hondo, New Mexico.* A Proposal to the National Endowment for the Humanities, Division of Preservation and Access, the National Heritage Preservation Program. Application on file, School of Advanced Research, Santa Fe, NM.

Sebastian, Lynne
1992 *The Chaco Anasazi: Sociopolitical Evolution in the Prehistoric Southwest.* Cambridge University Press, Cambridge, England.

Shapiro, Jason S.
2005 *A Space Syntax Analysis of Arroyo Hondo Pueblo : Community Formation in the Northern Rio Grande.* School of American Research Press, Santa Fe, NM.

Simmons, Marc
1991 *The Last Conquistador: Juan de Oñate and the Settling of the Far Southwest.* University of Oklahoma Press, Norman.

Smiley, Terah I., Stanley A. Stubbs, and Brian Bannister
1953 "A Foundation for the Dating of Some Late Archaeological Sites in the Rio Grande Area, New Mexico. Based on Studies on Tree-ring Methods and Pottery Analyscs." *University of Arizona Bulletin,* V. 24(3), *Laboratory of Tree-Ring Research Bulletin* No. 6. Tucson.

Snead, James E.

2007 "The Tano Origins Project 2001–2006." Paper presented at the 2007 Pecos Conference, August 9–12, 2007, Pecos, New Mexico.

2006 "Ancestral Pueblo Warfare and Migration in the Galisteo Basin, New Mexico." *Report of the Tano Origins Project, 2005 Season.* Submitted to the National Science Foundation, BCS #352702, NMCRIS #99578.

2005 "Ancestral Pueblo Warfare and Migration in the Galisteo Basin, New Mexico." *Report of the Tano Origins Project, 2004 Season.* Submitted to the National Science Foundation, BCS #352702, NMCRIS #88274.

2001 *Ruins and Rivals: The Making of Southwest Archaeology.* University of Arizona Press, Tucson.

Snow, Cordelia

1992 *An Archaeological Reconnaissance at 210 Canyon Road, Santa Fe, New Mexico.* Prepared for Mark Hogan and Richard Yates, Architects, Manuscript on file, City of Santa Fe Planning Division, Santa Fe.

1999 "(Re)Placing Historic Archaeology in New Mexico in Context." In *Archaeology in Your Backyard: Proceedings of a City of Santa Fe Symposium*, edited by Charles Haecker, pp. 17–24, City of Santa Fe Planning Division, Santa Fe, NM.

Snow, David H.

1974 "The Excavation of Saltbush Pueblo, Bandelier National Monument, New Mexico, 1971." *Laboratory of Anthropology Notes 97*, Santa Fe.

1989 "Survey and Testing: 334 Otero Street, Santa Fe, New Mexico, for Monroe and Associates." Manuscript on file, City of Santa Fe Planning Office and Cross Cultural Research Systems, Santa Fe, NM.

1999 "… The Pigs Running Loose in this Villa…." In *Archaeology in Your Backyard: Proceedings of a City of Santa Fe Symposium*, edited by Charles Haecker, pp. 45–52, City of Santa Fe Planning Division, Santa Fe, NM.

Spielmann, Katherine A.

2004 "Clusters Revisited." In *The Protohistoric Pueblo World A.D. 1275–1600*, Charles E. Adams and Andrew I. Duff, eds., pp. 137–143, University of Arizona Press, Tucson.

Staley, Barbara D.
1990 "Production of Rio Grande Glazewares: Refining the Concepts of Standardization and Specialization." In *Economy and Polity in Late Rio Grande Prehistory*, Steadman Upham and Barbara D. Staley, eds., University Museum, New Mexico State University, Occasional Papers, No. 16, Las Cruces.

Stuart, D. E., and R. P. Gauthier
1984 *Prehistoric New Mexico Background for Survey*. Reprint: Thomas Merlan, ed. University of New Mexico Press, Albuquerque, 1996.

Stubbs, Stanley A.
1954 "Summary Report on an Early Pueblo Site In The Tesuque Valley, New Mexico." *El Palacio* 71(2):43–45.

Stubbs, Stanley A., and W. S. Stallings, Jr.
1953 *The Excavation of Pindi Pueblo, New Mexico*. School of American Research Monograph 18, Santa Fe.

Suina, Joseph H.
2002 "The Persistence of the Corn Mothers." In *Archaeologies of the Pueblo Revolt: Identity, Meaning and Renewal in the Pueblo World*, edited by Robert Preucel, pp. 212–216. University of New Mexico Press, Albuquerque.

Sutton, Mark
2004 *An Introduction to Native North America*. 2d ed. Pearson, Boston.

Sutton, Mark, and E. N. Anderson
2004 *Introduction to Cultural Ecology*. Alta Mira Press, Walnut Creek, CA.

Swentzell, R.
1992 "Pueblo Space, Form and Mythology." In *Pueblo Style and Regional Architecture*, edited by N. Markovich, W. F. E. Preiser, and F. Sturm, pp. 23–30. Van Nostrand Reinhold, New York.

1988 "Bupingeh: The Pueblo Plaza." *El Palacio* 94(2):14–19.

Thomas, David Hurst
1989 *Archaeology*. 2d ed. Holt, Rinehart, and Winston, Fort Worth.

2001 *Skull Wars: Kennewick Man, Archaeology, and the Battle for Native American Identity*. Basic Books, New York.

Thomas, David Hurst, ed.
1989 *Columbian Consequences Volume 1, Archaeological and Historical Perspectives on the Spanish Borderlands West.* Smithsonian Institution Press, Washington, D.C.

1990 *Columbian Consequences Volume 2, Archaeological and Historical Perspectives on the Spanish Borderlands East.* Smithsonian Institution Press, Washington, D.C.

1991 *Columbian Consequences Volume 3, Archaeological and Historical Perspectives on the Spanish Borderlands in Pan-American Perspective.* Smithsonian Institution Press, Washington, D.C.

Towner, Ronald H., and Jeffrey S. Dean
1996 "Questions and Problems in Pre-Fort Sumner Navajo Archaeology." In *The Archaeology of Navajo Origins,* ed. Ronald H. Towner, pp. 3–18, University of Utah Press, Salt Lake City.

Towner, Ronald H., ed.
1996 *The Archaeology of Navajo Origins.* University of Utah Press, Salt Lake City.

Turner, Frederick Jackson
1893 "The Significance of the Frontier in American History." *Report of the American Historical Association for 1893,* pp.199–227.

Vierra, Bradley J.
1992 "A Sixteenth-century Spanish Campsite in the Tiguex Province: An Archaeologist's Perspective." In *Current Research on the Late Prehistory and Early History of New Mexico,* edited by Bradley J. Vierra, pp. 165–174, New Mexico Archaeological Council Special Publication No. 1, Albuquerque.

2005 "Ancient Foragers of the High Desert Country." In *The Peopling of Bandelier: New Insights from the Archaeology of the Pajarito Plateau,* edited by Robert P. Powers, pp. 19–25, School of American Research Press, Santa Fe.

Vierra, Bradley J., and Richard I. Ford
2007 "Foragers and Farmers in the Northern Rio Grande Valley, New Mexico." *Kiva* 73(2): 117–130.

Vivian, R. Gwinn
1990 *The Chacoan Prehistory of the San Juan Basin.* Academic Press, Inc., San Diego.

Vivian, R. Gwinn, and Bruce Hilpert
2002 *The Chaco Handbook — An Encyclopedic Guide*. University of Utah Press, Salt Lake City.

Waguespack, Nicole M., and Todd A. Surovell
2003 "Clovis Hunting Strategies, or How to Make Out on Plentiful Resources." *American Antiquity* 68(2):333–352.

Ware, John A., and Eric Blinman
2000 "Cultural Collapse and Reorganization: Origins and Spread of Pueblo Ritual Sodalities." In *The Archaeology of Regional Interaction: Religion, Warfare, and Exchange Across the American Southwest and Beyond*, edited by Michelle Hegmon, pp. 381–409, University Press of Colorado, Boulder.

Warner, Ted J., ed.
1995 *The Dominguez-Escalante Journal*. Translated by Fray Angelico Chavez, University of Utah Press, Salt Lake City.

Warren, A. H.
1974 "The Ancient Mineral Industries of Cerro Pedernal, Rio Arriba County, New Mexico." In *New Mexico Geological Society Guidebook, 25th Field Conference, Ghost Ranch, Central Northern New Mexico*, pp. 87–93. New Mexico Bureau of Mines and University of New Mexico, Socorro and Albuquerque.

Weaver, Muriel Porter
1993 *The Aztecs, Mayas, and Their Predecessors*. 3rd ed. Academic Press, San Diego.

Webster, David, Susan Toby Evans, and William Sanders
1993 *Out of the Past*. Mayfield Publishing Company, Mountain View, CA.

Welker, Eden A.
1997 *Attributes of Aggregation at Pueblo San Marcos and Pecos Pueblo in the Northern Rio Grande of New Mexico*. Ph.D. diss., University of Colorado, Boulder.

Welling, William
1978 *Photography in America: The Formative Years 1839–1900*. Thomas Y. Crowell Company, New York.

Wendorf, Fred
1953 "Excavations at Te'ewi." In *Salvage Archaeology in the Chama Valley, New Mexico*, assembled by F. Wendorf, pp. 34–93. Monographs of the School of American Research No. 17, Santa Fe.

1954 "A Reconstruction of Rio Grande Prehistory." *American Anthropologist* 56:200–227.

Wendorf, Fred, and John P. Miller
1959 "Artifacts from High Mountain Sites in the Sangre de Cristo Range, New Mexico." *El Palacio* 66(2):37–51.

Wendorf, Fred, and Erik K. Reed
1955 "An Alternative Reconstruction of Northern Rio Grande Prehistory." *El Palacio* 62(5–6):131–173.

Wendt, James J.
2004 *Waking the Dead: New Approaches to Understanding Social Patterns in the Colorado Woodland Mortuary Context.* Master's Thesis, Colorado State University, Fort Collins.

Wetterstrom, Wilma
1986 *Food, Diet, and Population at Historic Arroyo Hondo Pueblo, New Mexico.* School of American Research Press, Santa Fe.

Whalen, Michael, and Paul Minnis
2001 *Casas Grandes and Its Hinterland: Prehistoric Regional Organization in Northwest Mexico.* University of Arizona Press, Tucson.

Whiteley, Peter M.
2004 "Social Formations in the Pueblo IV Southwest: an Ethnological View." In *Cluster Analysis*, edited by E. Charles Adams and Andrew Duff, pp. 144–155, University of Arizona Press, Tucson.

Whittlesey, Stephanie, M., ed.
1999 *Sixty Years of Mogollon Archaeology : Papers from the Ninth Mogollon Conference, Silver City, New Mexico, 1996.* SRI Press, Tucson.

Willey, Gordon R., and Jeremy A. Sabloff
1993 *A History of American Archaeology.* 3rd ed. W. H. Freeman and Company, New York.

Williams, Paul R., John Roney, and E. Schoeneberg
1996 *Cultural Resources Reconnaissance and Recording of LA 112527: La Caja del Rio Paleoindian Site.* Cultural Resources Report 96–4, Bureau of Land Management, Taos. Report on file, ARMS, Laboratory of Anthropology, Museum of New Mexico, Santa Fe.

Williams, Robert A.
1990 *The American Indian in Western Legal Thought: The Discourses of Conquest.* Oxford University Press, New York.

Williston, S. W.
1905 "On the Occurrence of an Arrow-Head with the Bones of an Extinct Bison." *International Congress of Americanists. Thirteenth Session Held in New York in 1902,* pp. 335–337.

Williston, S. W., and H. T. Martin
1900 "Some Pueblo Ruins in Scott County, Kansas." *Transactions of the Kansas State Historical Society, 1897–1900,* No. 6, pp. 124–130.

Wills, W. H.
1988 *Early Prehistoric Agriculture in the American Southwest.* School of American Research Press, Santa Fe.

1995 "Archaic Foraging and the Beginning of Food Production in the American Southwest." In *Last Hunters, First Farmers,* edited by T. Douglas Price and Anne Birgitte Gebauer, pp. 215–242, School of American Research Press, Santa Fe.

Wilmeth, Rosco
1956 *Cuyumongue Pueblo.* Master's Thesis, University of New Mexico, Albuquerque. Manuscript on file at the Laboratory of Anthropology, Santa Fe.

Wilson, Chris
1997 *The Myth of Santa Fe: Creating a Modern Regional Tradition.* University of New Mexico Press, Albuquerque.

Winters, Ron
2006 *A Class III Archaeological Survey of 26.799 Acres Near I-25 and Richards Avenue, Santa Fe County, New Mexico.* Report submitted to the Archaeological Review Committee for the City of Santa Fe. NMCRIS No. 98726. Report on file, Planning Division for the City of Santa Fe, New Mexico.

Wiseman, Regge
> 1995 "Reassessment of the Dating of the Pojoaque Grant Site (LA 835), A Key Site of the Rio Grande Developmental Period." *Of Pots and Rocks, Papers in Honor of A. Helen Warren.* Archaeological Society of New Mexico, Vol. 21, pp. 237–248, Rio Rancho.

> 1989 *The KP Site and Late Developmental Period Archaeology in the Santa Fe District.* Laboratory of Anthropology Notes No. 494, Museum of New Mexico, Santa Fe.

> 1978 *An Archaeological Survey for the Community Development Program, Santa Fe, New Mexico.* Museum of New Mexico, Laboratory of Anthropology Notes No. 197. Museum of New Mexico, Santa Fe.

Wissler, Clark
> 1914 "Material Cultures of the North American Indian." *American Anthropologist* 16:447–505.

Wormington, H. M.
> 1961 *Prehistoric Indians of the Southwest.* Denver Museum of Natural History. Denver.

> 1957 *Ancient Man in North America,* 4th ed. Denver Museum of Natural History. Denver.

Yesner, David R.
> 1994 "Seasonality and Resource 'Stress' Among Hunter-Gatherers: Archaeological Signatures." In *Key Issues In Hunter-Gatherer Research*, edited by Ernest Burch, Jr. and Linda J. Ellana, pp. 151–167, Berg Publishers, Inc., Providence, RI.

Natural environment, 1–12, 31–32, 44–47, 51, 53, 73, 78, 93, 96, 118

Navajo, 135–139

Nelson, Nels, 105, *110*, *119*, *129*, *131*

Neolithic Period (New Stone Age), 71, 79–80

New Mexico, 1912, *110*

New Stone Age, 71

Northern Rio Grande region, xvii, 51, 67, *68*, 78, 81, 92–95, 99, 108, 112, 114–115, 118, 125, 131

Numic-speaking people, 139

Office of Archaeological Studies, Museum of New Mexico, 106

Ogapoge, 20, 31, 106

O'gha po'oghe. see Ogapoge

Oñate, Juan de, 137, 143–144

O'odham, 14, 140

Orayvi (Hopi Mesas), 83

Pajarito Plateau, 20, 29, 41, 113

Palace of the Governors, xvi, xvii

Paleoindians, 31–47, 49–52

Pecos Classification scheme, 22–23

Pecos, New Mexico, 113–114, 130

Pedra Furada site (Brazil), 35

Pena Blanca sites, 75

Peopling of the Americas, 33–37

Peralta, Pedro de, 49, 144–145

Petroglyphs, 101, *103*, *121*, 126

Piedra Lumbre Phase, 138

Pindi Pueblo, 89, 91–92, 94, 96, 98–103, 107, 112, 119, 129

Pinnacle site, 94

Plant gathering, 51, 56–57, 71, 75–76, 89, 96, 137

Pleistocene Period, *30*, 40, 43, 45, 47, 50, 71–72

Pleistocene Period, Late, 31–33

Pojoaque Grant site, 80

Pottery: analysis of, 98, 103–105, 115, 118, 137–138; "Black-on-white", 105; Cibola white ware, 107; clay sources for, 5, 97–98; as commodity, 129–130; as cultural identifiers, 20, 22–23, 92, 118; decorated wares, 77, 94, 97; distribution of, 118–120; glaze "A", 115, *116*; glaze "B", 129, *130*; imported to Santa Fe, *76*, 78; Kwahe'e Black-on-white designs, 97; lead-glaze paint and, 112, 115; Mesa Verde-style, 93; Mimbres, 15–16; Navajo Dinéteh gray, 137–138; pit kilns for, 98–99; plainware, 16, 77; preservation of, 27; Red Mesa Black-on-white, 85; Santa Fe Black-on-white, *96*, 97–98, 119; study of, 94; uses of, 77–78, 87, 94; as village industry, 129–130; White Mountain red ware, 107

Prado, Juan de, 142

Preservation of artifacts, 22, 27

Projectile points: agate, 42; in Archaic Period, 55–58, 65; basalt, 57; flint, 42; illustrations of, *33*, *40*, *43*, *55*; obsidian, 41–42; stone, 31–35, 38–40, 44, 46, 55

Pueblo Bonito, 111

Pueblo revolts, 135, 139–140

Puebloans: contact with Spanish and, 142–144; droughts and, 83–84; economic equality of, 119–120; farming of, 75, 89, 95, 130, 143; interaction with non-Puebloans, 138–139; settlement shifting and, 130; village life and, 75, 79, 87, 92

Pueblos, 16, 28–29, 85, 89, 91, 99–101, 103–109, 111, 117, 141. *see also* individual names

Radiocarbon dating, 24–25, 35, 63–64, 66, 72, 87

Rio de Santa Fe. *see* Santa Fe River

Rio Grande Classic Period, 92

Rio Grande Classification scheme, 22–24

Rio Grande River, 2, 5–6, 43–44, 98

Rio Grande Valley, xix, 10, 12, 22, 53, 60, 79, 92, 94, 111, 138

Rio Nambe, 75

Rocky Mountains, 6, 12, 31, 44, 46